Stones of Contention

Africa in World History

SERIES EDITORS: DAVID ROBINSON AND JOSEPH C. MILLER

James C. McCann
Stirring the Pot: A History of African Cuisine

Peter Alegi
African Soccerscapes: How a Continent Changed the World's Game

Todd Cleveland
Stones of Contention: A History of Africa's Diamonds

Forthcoming:

Laura Lee Huttenbach
The Boy Is Gone: Memoirs of a Mau Mau General

John M. Mugane
The Story of Swahili

Charles Ambler
Mass Media and Popular Culture in Modern Africa

Stones of Contention

A History of Africa's Diamonds

Todd Cleveland

OHIO UNIVERSITY PRESS

in association with the

OHIO UNIVERSITY CENTER FOR INTERNATIONAL STUDIES

Athens

Ohio University Press, Athens, Ohio 45701
www.ohioswallow.com
© 2014 by Ohio University Center for International Studies
All rights reserved

To obtain permission to quote, reprint, or otherwise reproduce or distribute material from
Ohio University Press publications, please contact our rights and permissions department
at (740) 593–1154 or (740) 593–4536 (fax).

Printed in the United States of America
Ohio University Press books are printed on acid-free paper ⊗ ™

24 23 22 21 20 19 18 17 16 15 14   5 4 3 2 1

Books in this series are published with support from the
Ohio University National Resource Center for African Studies.

Library of Congress Cataloging-in-Publication Data
Cleveland, Todd, author.
Stones of contention : a history of Africa's diamonds / Todd Cleveland.
    pages cm. — (Africa in world history)
Includes bibliographical references and index.
ISBN 978-0-8214-2100-0 (pb : alk. paper) — ISBN 978-0-8214-4482-5 (pdf)
1. Diamond mines and mining—Africa—History. 2. Diamond industry and trade—
Africa—History. 3. Diamond industry and trade—Social aspects—Africa. 4. Diamond
mines and mining—Economic aspects—Africa. I. Title. II. Series: Africa in world history.
TN994.A35C54 2014
338.2782096—dc23
                    2014007945

To Julianna, Lucas, and Byers

CONTENTS

ILLUSTRATIONS

Figures

Maps

Table

ACKNOWLEDGMENTS

First and foremost, I would like to thank Gillian Berchowitz, David Robinson, and Joseph Miller. After initially approaching me about this book project, they subsequently provided unwavering support and displayed boundless patience throughout the extended research and writing processes. The concrete forms of their support were myriad, but as this project concludes, I will remember particularly fondly (and miss) Dave's steady provision of relevant readings and superb ideas, Gill's sage and serene guidance, and Joe's timely and innovative suggestions. The uniformly enthusiastic approach of this remarkable editorial team kept this project enjoyable at every turn. I'd also like to express my gratitude to the various staff members with whom I interacted at Ohio University Press; to a person, they were consistently helpful and highly professional. At Augustana College, I am grateful for the assistance of the Tredway Library staff, whose members handled my innumerable requests and orders for both on- and off-site materials promptly, always with a smile and often with a welcomed witticism. I would also like to thank former students Bryce Johnson, Anden Drolet, Jaron Gaier and, especially, Sarah Clement for their contributions during the process of compiling the requisite data for the story I've attempted to tell. Elsewhere, Richard Saunders was extremely helpful, and his writings and insights constituted a much-needed compass as I began to delve into Zimbabwe's rapidly shifting diamond mining landscape. Chadia Chambers-Samadi, John Pfautz, and Odino Grubessi provided important assistance as I secured images to incorporate into the text. The inclusion of passages that outline the colonial-era history of diamond mining in Angola was only possible due to the efforts of a great many people on the ground in both Angola and Portugal during my years of fieldwork in those settings. In particular, I'd like to thank Drs. Rosa Cruz e Silva, Jorge Varanda, and Nuno Porto, as well as Carl Niemann, and also my many African informants in Angola, whose comprehension of the nature and experience of diamond mining—past and present—will forever outdistance my own. I'm also very grateful to the anonymous readers, whose comments and suggestions were instrumental as I proceeded through the manuscript revision. Finally, this highly edifying and enjoyable endeavor would never have reached fruition had it not been for the relentless support of my wife, Julianna, and the inspirational energy provided by our two sons, Lucas and Byers, the latter of whom joined us in the midst of this project.

Stones of Contention

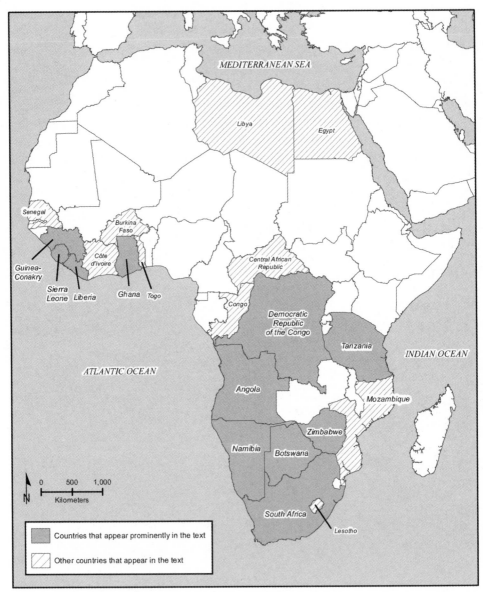

MAP 1. Africa. *Map by Brian Edward Balsley, GISP*

CHAPTER ONE

An Introduction to Africa's Diamonds

> In America, it [a diamond] is "bling bling." But out here [in Africa] it's "bling bang."
>
> —"Danny Archer," Leonardo DiCaprio's character in the 2006 film *Blood Diamond*

> Every time you purchase a piece of diamond jewelry there is a real probability that you will be contributing to the provision of schools, clinics, drinking water, or roads for a poor community in Botswana or South Africa or Namibia.
>
> —Former Botswana president Festus Mogae, 2008 winner of the Ibrahim Prize, awarded to African heads of state who deliver security, health, education, and economic development to their constituents, and who democratically transfer power to their successors

AFTER A recent talk I gave on the history of diamond production in Angola, an audience member posed the following questions: "Have you ever purchased a diamond? And, would you ever purchase an African diamond knowing what you know now?" The answer to the first question was easy. "Yes, I have purchased a diamond." Before addressing the second question, though, I paused before responding. "Actually, I haven't had the occasion to buy one since learning what I've learned." After the audience both moaned and chuckled in response to my equivocation, they prodded me to answer more decidedly. After further deliberation, I finally replied. "Yes, I suppose I would."

In the pages that follow, this book strives to enable you to formulate your own informed answers to that audience member's second question.

Most readers will come to this book with at least some knowledge of the continent's diamonds, often gleaned from different forms of popular culture. This output includes Graham Greene's famous novel *The Heart of the Matter* (1948), and, more recently, both Kanye West's Grammy-winning single, "Diamonds from Sierra Leone" (2005), and the blockbuster film *Blood Diamond* (2006).[1] Other readers will have formed their impressions via the mainstream media, which has highlighted the African origins of many of the diamonds that consumers marvel at behind glass jewelry cases the world over. All of these sources, however, link African diamonds to unbridled chaos and, often, to unimaginable violence. What has been ignored is the much wider range of human experience associated with the extraction of diamonds from Africa's soils.

For centuries, Africa's diamonds and other minerals have piqued the interest of outsiders and shaped the lives of countless African men, women, and children. This mineral wealth has subjected the continent's residents to carnage, exploitation, and widespread suffering. Yet, this wealth has also prompted Africans to pursue creative migration, livelihood, and household strategies; cooperate across potential divides; and acquire technical and managerial skills; and has even facilitated the construction of peaceful, democratic states. In other words, exactly the types of developments that you'll never encounter in newspaper headlines or on TV news broadcasts.

This book explores the major developments in the remarkable history of Africa's diamonds, from the initial international interest in the continent's mineral wealth during the first millennium A.D., down to the present day. This narrative includes the discovery of diamonds in South Africa in 1867, which ushered in an era of unprecedented greed, manifested in exploitative mining operations. Following the ensuing "scramble for Africa," during which European powers assumed control of virtually the entire continent, colonial regimes fashioned environments conducive to the commercial objectives of monopolistic diamond enterprises. These companies included, most famously, the industry giant De Beers (explored in detail in chapters 3 and 4). In the aftermath of the birth of independent Africa states, beginning at the end of the 1950s, both rapacious and more responsible regimes joined De Beers and other multinational corporations to oversee mining activity on the continent.

Beyond examinations of these commercial entities, the book also considers the stories of Africans who have been involved with the continent's diamonds over the centuries. These individuals include artisanal miners, company mine workers, and the women who support(ed) them; the "headmen" who often furnished these laborers; armed rebels; mining executives; and premiers of mineral-rich states. Although the industrial literature on diamonds tends to render these individuals anonymous, this text explores the highly varied relationships and experiences that Africans have had with the continent's diamonds. By exploring the multiplicity of the human experiences associated with the history of diamond production in Africa, I hope that you will "see" more than just a glittering accessory the next time you view a diamond in a glass jewelry case. Ultimately, the book aims to help you generate your own answers to the challenging question that the audience member posed to me.

The Global History of the Diamond

Diamonds have been around a long, long time and continue to possess an almost mythical quality. Well before their discovery in Africa, the global pursuit of these gemstones had destroyed the fortunes of innumerable individuals while enriching the lives of many others. Legends about the importance of diamonds going well back into the past abound, but most simply reflect a more recent fondness for these stones' aesthetic brilliance projected onto earlier times. Yet, we can with some certainty trace the desirability of diamonds back at least two millennia. For example, diamonds featured in a treatise in statecraft prepared during the reign of the Indian general Chandragupta, who had driven the Greeks from India in 322 B.C.E.

In fact, India had long been the epicenter of global diamond production, before yielding to Brazil, and then Africa in more recent times. For centuries, or perhaps even millennia, leading up to the exhaustion of deposits in the mid-1700s, the Indian region of Golconda had been yielding stones to adorn the local nobility and, eventually, European royalty. In fact, two of the most famous diamonds in the world today: the Hope and the Koh-i-Noor, came from the alluvial diggings around Golconda. The latter was so brilliant that it was said that whoever possessed it would rule the world. Given that the British forcibly seized the magnificent stone in the mid-eighteenth century, on their way to establishing the most significant global empire the world had ever seen, this prophecy seemingly contained an element of truth.

Europeans' love affair with diamonds had actually started much earlier. Over two millennia ago, the Greeks began facilitating the importation of precious stones from India to a receptive audience in Europe. The famous historian Herodotus (c. 484 B.C.E.–c. 425 B.C.E.) was the first of the early

Greek writers to note the displays of precious stones in the palaces and temples of Eastern kings. He mentions, for example, the signet rings of Darius and Polycrates and the emerald column in the Temple of Hercules in Tyre. Via these and other accounts, the mineral riches of both the Near and Far East became known to increasing numbers of Europeans, well beyond Greece's borders.

The citizens of ancient Rome also valued diamonds, as well as other precious stones. Few gems initially reached mainland Europe during this period, as Middle Eastern rulers and nobles ensured that any stones that arrived in their territories did not travel any further west. However, following the Roman expansion into Asia Minor in the first century B.C.E., vast quantities of gems began to reach Rome, rendering them increasingly affordable. In fact, over time, gem ownership and the custom of incorporating precious stones into daily dress had become so excessive in Rome that the latter practice was eventually restricted by law.

For all the attention lavished on gems by the citizens of ancient Greece and Rome, roughly a thousand years would pass before the diamond became the preeminent gemstone. With the conclusion of the Crusades and the concomitant establishment of extensive trading networks linking Europe and the Levant, gems originating in the East once again began to circulate in Europe. This increased commercial access to the East, combined with the growing wealth of the European nobility, led to the proliferation of (increasingly affordable) precious stone ownership on the continent.

Europeans began using gems for all manner of things, including studding picture frames, ornamenting statuary, decorating arms, as well as for personal adornment. Yet, throughout this "creative explosion" in precious stone usage, rubies, emeralds, opals, and sapphires continued to rank above diamonds, as did pearls. Why? Well, anyone who has observed a diamond in rough form, that is, uncut and unpolished and, thus, aesthetically unspectacular, can answer that question. Moreover, the diamond's legendary hardness actually limited its utility and, thus, its allure. At this time, consumers of precious stones valued a gem's color and proportion much more than its hardness. Around the 1460s, however, the diamond's position at the pinnacle of the gem hierarchy was set in motion by a Flemish lapidary (a person who cuts, polishes, or engraves precious stones) named Louis de Berguem. A rather unlikely historymaker, to be sure.

Although Indian lapidaries had long been working with diamonds, their techniques failed to reveal the stones' brilliance. Even when these artisans began to revise their methods in the 1400s, the proportioning remained so poor that much of the stone's latent brilliancy remained "unreleased." Only after de Berguem's re-cutting of the Beau Sancy diamond did the art of modern cutting begin. De Berguem demonstrated how to successfully cut facets on the face of a diamond, which became known as scientific faceting. This technique rendered the diamond a perfect reflector of light and unleashed its interior beauty and, thus, helped establish diamonds as the most coveted of all gems, which, in turn, further fueled demand.

The novel forms of aesthetic activity and appreciation that were central to the European Renaissance provided a perfect environment for the ascendance of the diamond. Two developments, in particular, thrust the diamond into its paramount position. First was the establishment of a reliable international trade network linking India's diamondiferous Golconda region directly to Europe. Diamonds were procured and transported by intrepid merchant travelers to eagerly awaiting Europeans, who were now consuming these stones in unprecedented quantities. Perhaps the most famous of these merchants was the Frenchman, Jean-Baptiste Tavernier, who, in 1668, sold the legendary Hope Diamond to the French king Louis XIV. Second was the development of the "rose cut." As European lapidaries gained experience working with ever greater numbers of stones, their elevated levels of craftsmanship enabled them to improve upon de Berguem's work—a clear case of "practice makes perfect." In turn, they further highlighted, or "revealed," the diamond's brilliance, which heightened demand for a stone whose post-cut beauty was quickly outpacing the aesthetics of rival gemstones.

The increased demand for Indian diamonds in Europe was further spurred on by the invention of the "brilliant cut," an improvement on the rose cut. This rapidly expanding market was now supporting an industry that stretched across three continents. Caravans had once transported these stones across Arabia and offloaded them to traders waiting in Aden, Aleppo, and Alexandria (the initial extent of Africa's involvement in the trade). However, ships were now increasingly employed to convey these stones to Europe, utilizing the Red Sea but otherwise largely bypassing the Middle East.[2] Upon reaching Europe, Jewish diamond merchants in places as far-flung as Lisbon, Venice and Frankfurt arranged to purchase these precious imports. Jewish involvement in the burgeoning diamond industry in Europe was logical for two main reasons. First, those Jews who served as moneylenders naturally concerned themselves with assessing, repairing, and selling gems that had been offered to them as collateral for loans. And, second, the cutting and polishing of diamonds, initially centered in Lisbon before shifting to Antwerp, was one of the few crafts in which guilds permitted Jews to participate.

Unfortunately for the European market, the supply of Indian diamonds required to meet the growing demand on the continent was unsustainable. Despite the bountifulness of the Indian mines, they were virtually exhausted by the eighteenth century. This dearth threatened to put an abrupt end to the global supply of these increasingly coveted—and affordable— stones. Yet, as if on cue, gold miners working in 1725 in the Province of Minas Gerais in Portuguese-controlled Brazil stumbled on a new source of diamonds. Virtually overnight, diamond focus shifted halfway around the world and the "rush" to Brazil was on. In response, within a decade of the discovery, the Portuguese crown had declared diamond mining in Brazil a state monopoly—a foreshadowing of future diamond developments in Africa. Meanwhile, overall Brazilian output had already exceeded India's, thereby cutting the global price of a carat by two-thirds. Yet, by the middle of the following century, carat prices were again rising because of the multitude of wealthy consumers that the Industrial Revolution was spawning; these gems were now within their financial grasp. As with India, however, supply could not keep pace with the exploding demand.

And, then, just when it seemed that the global supply of diamonds had been exhausted, along came Africa. As the dwindling Brazilian supplies were generating panic in diamond circles, a fifteen-year-old named Erasmus Jacobs made a superbly timed, if entirely unintentional, find of the aptly named Eureka Diamond in the heart of South Africa. Once again, global diamond attention immediately shifted, this time to a heretofore virtually ignored, very small corner of the world.

The History of Diamonds in Africa

From these humble beginnings, Africa rapidly came to dominate the international diamond landscape, even if relatively few Africans benefited along the way. Although the Industrial Revolution had enabled increasing numbers of people to purchase previously cost-prohibitive diamonds, the South African discovery occurred at an even more propitious moment in global history. The unearthing of these deposits corresponded with the growth of the middle classes and their amplified consumption, especially in Great Britain and the United States, just as increased availability rendered

Africa's stones ever more attainable. By the end of the Second World War, the United States had overtaken Europe as the largest consumer of African diamonds, while shortly thereafter, postwar Japan emerged as an important new market. From Jacobs's discovery of the Eureka to the subsequent creation and dominance of the industry behemoth De Beers, headquartered in South Africa, diamonds would become inextricably linked to Africa.

Although recent finds elsewhere in the world have cut into Africa's diamond supremacy, the continent continues to supply the world with over half of its total supply and the African nation of Botswana remains the global leader. These stones have historically drawn African states, populations, and individuals—even from places on the continent that have no diamond deposits, or even any proximate ones—into their orbit, while also profoundly connecting the continent to the rest of the world. Indeed, if the continent's soils did not harbor these stones, the political, social, and economic experiences of millions of Africans since Jacobs's discovery would be drastically different. And, many would argue, far better.

A Geological Overview of Africa's Diamonds

What is a diamond? Quite simply, it's carbon that has been subjected to intense heat and pressure. The products of this process are thrust toward the earth's surface from depths of more than a thousand miles, embedded within what is known as a kimberlite pipe—named after Kimberley, the city that sprung up in the midst of the South African diamond finds. In Africa, these kimberlite eruptions brought diamond deposits to the surface as recently as a million years ago. Over time, wind and rain have slowly eroded these eruptive pipes so that they now generally blend into the surrounding landscape. During this erosive process, stones are washed out of the once-protruding pipes and into the surrounding countryside, as well as into streams and rivers, which often carry them far from their original points of emergence. As such, upwards of a third of the diamonds harvested from Africa's soils have come from far-flung alluvial fields, rather than from the subterranean portions of the original kimberlite pipes.

Kimberlite is a relatively "soft" rock, which over time breaks down into a mass of secondary clay minerals that contain resistant residual materials, including diamonds. The products of this process are found in both a superficial zone of "yellow ground" and a deeper one made up of more diamondiferous "blue ground," which eventually transitions into "primary kimberlite." During the weathering process, the diamonds contained in the pipe come to rest in both the yellow and blue grounds. Although fabulous riches are often extracted from both of these layers, the mining of the blue ground is ultimately the more lucrative undertaking.

Unfortunately for prospectors and others interested in tapping the earth for diamond wealth, not every kimberlite pipe is diamondiferous. In South Africa, for example, roughly only one pipe in two hundred is worth mining, though in other places, such as Botswana, the ratio can be as high as one in fifteen. Moreover, the surface diameters of payable pipes are often only a hundred yards across. Even the Mwadvi diamond mine in Tanzania, among the largest in the world, is only a mile and a half long and a mile wide. Prospecting for lucrative deposits can, therefore, be a time-consuming project.

In this respect, the case of Dr. John Williamson, who worked in colonial Tanganyika (Tanzania), comes to mind. Inspired by his find at Mwadvi in 1953, roughly three hundred prospecting engineers subsequently spent more than three years trying to identify additional regional deposits—almost entirely unsuccessfully! In order to avoid this type of inefficiency, contemporary prospectors now focus on what are known in the industry as "indicator minerals" that suggest the presence of diamond deposits.[3] Resistant and heavy, these minerals tend to work their way into drainage systems via processes such as downslope soil creep or rainfall runoff. They then radiate outward along drainage channels, trailing off the circular, superficial footprint of the kimberlite pipe.

Diamond deposits are present throughout the continent. Although they are most abundant in Southern Africa, substantial lodes also exist in Central Africa, and to lesser degrees in Western and Eastern Africa. After the discoveries in South Africa in the 1860s, diamonds were subsequently discovered in a number of other locations on the continent, including the Congo in 1906; Namibia in 1908; Tanzania in 1910; Angola in 1912; the Central African Republic in 1913; Ghana in 1919; Sierra Leone in 1930; Guinea-Conakry in 1930; Liberia c. 1935; and Botswana in 1967, with lesser finds made in Zambia, Mali, Gabon, Lesotho, Mozambique, and Swaziland. Most recently, Zimbabwe has come online as a major diamond exporter. Both across and within these countries, diamond deposits can be located in drastically different terrain, such that a single country can feature both kimberlite and alluvial deposits, as well as an array of access conditions. In the case of Namibia, for example, many diamonds are "vacuumed" from the ocean shelf off the Atlantic coastline by workers operating behind massive walls that keep the powerful waters at bay. Although these stones constitute an extreme example, most onshore diamonds can be mined profitably even in the most remote and seemingly inaccessible locations, often with nothing more than a shovel and a sieve. This virtually guaranteed financial score is owing to the fact that bringing the product to a potential buyer does not require a vast or developed transportation infrastructure. Indeed, Hollywood constantly reminds us that a small pouch of stones can be easily moved around the world, often leaving a trail of cinematic intrigue, violence, and shadowy financial dealings in its wake.

Africa's Diamond Ascension and the Historical Importance of These Stones

Neither the role of diamonds in Africa's history nor the importance of the continent's stones in global history can be overstated. The discovery of payable deposits anywhere in the world invariably prompts an immediate response. Yet, in Africa's case, the series of actions and reactions following the discovery of the Eureka Diamond were both exceptionally decisive and continue to have momentous implications for the continent's residents. Virtually overnight, thousands of Africans, Europeans, Americans, and Australians, among others, descended on the dusty, dry, scarcely populated terrain where the South African fields were located. The trading post of Kimberley that sprung up in the midst of these discoveries quickly grew to become South Africa's second-most-populated city, behind only the long-established port of Cape Town. Going forward, this diamond-driven, demographic phenomenon would recur across the continent as countless individuals, a range of imperial states, and dozens of mining enterprises vied for the stones embedded in Africa's mineral-rich soils. Indeed, it is from the long history of contention for these coveted stones that the book draws its title.

One of the primary impetuses for the European colonization of Africa at the end of the nineteenth century was the continent's storied mineral wealth. Following the diamond discoveries near Kimberley, Great Britain moved to consolidate its control of South Africa, fighting a series of wars against indigenous populations and Dutch descendant, or "Boer," settlers. Other European powers subsequently mimicked this aggressive approach elsewhere on the continent, forcibly establishing control over previously sovereign African spaces. The particular geographical targets of these military advances were based on claims made leading up to, during, and following the 1884–85 Berlin Conference. In this fashion, the European imperial states literally mapped out the future occupation of Africa. Profound investment in and exploitation of the continent's mineral riches marked the ensuing colonial period.

As investors poured more and more capital into the continent following a succession of diamond discoveries, Africa's place in the global diamond industry rapidly ascended. As early as 1872, for example, South Africa was already producing six times the quantity of stones that Brazil had produced just a decade earlier. And with the emergence of South African–based De Beers in the 1870s, Africa was to become synonymous with diamonds. Legitimate rivals began to appear only in the middle of the twentieth century, following significant discoveries in the Soviet Union and, more recently, Canada. Yet, once these major non-African producers came online, De Beers strategically negotiated to purchase most of this new production and, thereby, maintain its legendary (near) monopoly. Meanwhile, during the colonial era in Africa, this type of supply-side manipulation of the market helped generate sorely needed funds for a number of white minority governments, including in Angola, Sierra Leone, and the Belgian Congo.

During the 1930s, as purveyors of the ultimate luxury item, the diamond industry naturally suffered due to the worldwide recession. Even De Beers was forced to cease production in a number of its mines for approximately five years in response to severely reduced global demand. However, following the outbreak of the Second World War, Africa's diamonds regained their importance, though this time primarily in a martial rather than aesthetic sense. Indeed, you may be surprised to learn that these deposits were invaluable to the Allied powers' war effort. During the peak years of the conflict, not only did Africa supply significant portions of the world's gold, manganese, copper, cobalt, and uranium, but also 98 percent of the industrial diamonds, which were newly essential for the production of military hardware. The production of "industrial" diamonds—that is, small and/or low-quality stones and, thus, not "gem quality"—was centered on the Belgian Congo, from the mines of the Forminière company. With production soaring to 10,386,000 metric tons in 1945, the Congo alone supplied over 65 percent of the Allies' industrial diamond and "bort" (low-quality industrial) needs during the war. Meanwhile, the Axis powers were forced to rely on prewar stocks and on a number of lesser sources, including French Guinea (Guinea-Conakry) in West Africa, which was controlled by France's sympathetic Vichy government, and a much smaller stream of stones smuggled out of the Congo.[4] So, did Africa's diamonds win the war for the Allies? Not quite. But, they did provide the victors with an important edge.

The Congo (DRC) continues to be a leading producer of industrials, which constitute roughly 80 percent of all mined diamonds, and are nowadays used in a variety of commercial applications. Given a diamond's unparalleled hardness, industrials are often used for cutting and grinding, including as drill bits and in various types of saws. In fact, every time you ride in a car, industrial diamonds have helped facilitate that journey, as they are used in highway construction and repair; in gas, mineral, and oil exploration; and in the production of every car made in the United States (the manufacturing process for each automobile consumes over one carat of industrial diamond).

Since their invention in the 1950s, synthetic diamonds have steadily replaced natural-forming industrials, but they perform essentially the same tasks. Today, synthetics annually account for some 98 percent of the industrial market, and the United States is both a major producer and a consumer of these stones. Synthetics are less expensive, can be produced in almost unlimited quantities, and can be customized for specific applications. Synthetic industrials also show great promise as semiconductors in the construction of microchips and as heat sinks, which are used to cool down electronics, such as laptop computers. Given all of the current and potential usages for synthetic industrials, this industry is fast rivaling the overall value of the gemstone market.

Although synthetic stones, which can cost as little as 40 cents per carat, dominate the industrial market, buyers still insist on the "real thing" when seeking diamonds for jewelry or other ornamentation. Global demand for gem-quality stones resumed soon after the Second World War ended. Facilitated by De Beers's monopolistic buying and selling schemes, extractive colonial mining companies quickly resumed pumping the wealth out of the continent's soils and back into European coffers.

As the political "winds of change" blew across Africa in the 1960s and 1970s, during which time virtually the entire continent achieved independence from its European colonial overlords, the African leaders of the newly independent states adopted various approaches to diamond revenues. In some cases, including Ghana, Sierra Leone, Angola, and the Democratic Republic of the Congo (DRC), novice statesmen aggressively moved to nationalize domestic output. Yet, these measures typically met with dismal results for a number of reasons, including a lack of technical knowledge; an inability to prohibit access to alluvial supplies; operational mismanagement and corruption; insufficient capital to replace aging or broken equipment;

and even civil conflicts. Conversely, other governments, in Botswana and Namibia, for example, proceeded down a different path by establishing successful public-private mining enterprises. It should be noted, though, that the circumstances in these two cases are somewhat unique: in Botswana, diamonds were discovered only in 1967, one year *after* political independence, and, in Namibia, independence arrived only in 1990. Furthermore, in both cases, deposits were in hard to access/easy to cordon off locations, which allowed for easier governmental control.

While African states contemplated how to manage their diamond resources following independence, both formal and informal miners continued to pry, dig, dislodge, and remove in every other conceivable way, these precious stones. By the end of the first decade of the twenty-first century, Africa had endured a series of devastating diamond-related developments, including "resource conflicts" and the emergence of "blood diamonds"—an occurrence that threatened to spark a consumer backlash reminiscent of that against the fur industry in the 1980s. Well beyond Africa's control, though, a series of global recessions had also reduced demand for both gem and industrial stones. Yet despite these formidable challenges, Africa continues to be the premier continent for diamond production, with Botswana leading the way (see table 1).

TABLE 1.
Estimated production by value of top producers (in US dollars), 2011

Botswana	3,902,115,904
Russia	2,674,713,800
Canada	2,550,875,198
South Africa	1,730,323,570
Angola	1,163,625,471
Namibia	872,567,637
Zimbabwe	476,218,677
Australia	220,720,063
Congo (DRC)	179,608,541

Source: http://geology.com/articles/gem-diamond-map/. Data source is the USGS Mineral Commodity Summaries.

Regardless of the periodic headline-grabbing discoveries of diamond deposits made far from Africa's borders, De Beers's ongoing, if slightly eroded, dominance ensures that the continent retains its preeminence in the industry. In 2004, for example, De Beers sold $5.7 billion worth of rough diamonds—or 48 percent of the world's total—and reported earnings for the year of $652 million. Via production from its own mines, as well as a series of strategic agreements and partnerships with other mining operations, De Beers currently controls roughly 45 percent of the global output of diamonds. Through its vast commercial network, which as of 2002 also newly included dozens of high-end retail stores located around the world, the enterprise and its practices affect millions of diamond-industry employees worldwide. This combination of De Beers's high-profile, global impact and its historic and well-publicized South African roots ensures that Africa's association with diamonds is continually highlighted and reinforced.

Diamonds in Africa: A Blessing or a Curse?

Much has been made about whether Africa's natural resources constitute a "blessing" or "curse" for the countries (un)lucky enough to possess them. Have Africa's diamonds been, as Leonardo DiCaprio's character in the film *Blood Diamond* declares, all about "bling bang," that is, death and destruction? Or, do these stones offer a viable means to economic development and social improvement, as suggested in the quote by Botswana's former president, Festus Mogae, which also led off this chapter? In practice, the answer is probably: both. Or, perhaps: neither. In certain settings, including Angola, Sierra Leone, and the DRC, the presence of diamonds has resulted in significant harm for resident populations. This damage has been physical, measured by the thousands of casualties and millions of people displaced by the diamond-fueled conflicts that have raged in these countries. The damage has also been economic, as large inflows of foreign capital and the attendant inflation of local currency rates—the symptoms of so-called "Dutch Disease"—have either crippled or precluded the development of other potentially promising sectors of national economies and thereby deepened resource dependency.[5] Yet in other countries, such as Namibia and Botswana, diamond deposits have generally improved the overall standards of living, failed to critically distort national economies, and, if anything, helped keep the peace rather than disrupt it.

At first glance, these contrasting examples appear reasonably clear-cut. However, a closer look is warranted. Consideration of shifting historical contexts and particular subsegments of national populations tends to muddy these otherwise seemingly clear waters. For example, with the diamond-fueled conflicts now over in both Sierra Leone and Angola, local populations are increasingly benefiting from diamond revenues, whereas in Botswana, if one were to invite commentary about the country's diamond industry from the "Bushmen," many of whom were forcibly relocated in order to facilitate formal prospecting, it's unlikely that they would share Festus Mogae's sanguine assessment. Thus even if on balance diamonds may appear to constitute either a "blessing" or "curse" for Africa and its peoples, it is probably neither prudent nor analytically useful to spend too much time trying to shoehorn the broad range of Africans' lived experiences into these types of binaries. After all, diamonds are just inanimate objects, as incapable of launching a violent rebellion as they are of establishing prudent ministerial resource management policy. In this book, I provide in-depth examinations of the individuals, enterprises, and countries involved in order to provide more insightful understandings than those attainable via the simplistic formulation *blessing or curse?*

Book Content and Chapter Outline

The book features a series of loosely chronological chapters that seek to highlight the significance of Africa's diamonds during different historical periods. To tell this story, I have drawn upon a wide range of primary source materials, oral interviews, African and international newspapers and other popular media sources, as well as the significant body of existing literature dedicated to diamonds the world over. The text attempts to weave these disparate sources together to highlight the key developments in the global history of the continent's "stones of contention" up through the present day and, whenever possible, to place Africans at the center of this narrative. This approach entails consideration of Africans situated in an assortment of historical and geographical contexts, but does not include systematic coverage of every diamond-generating venue on the continent. Rather, specific examples are drawn from a variety of settings to illustrate broader themes and trends; consequently, some sites receive more attention than others. The chapters unfold as follows:

Chapter 2 examines external notions of Africa as a treasure trove of mineral wealth in the pre-Kimberley period, as well as some of the mining endeavors in which Africans were engaged that helped fuel these impressions. For centuries, Europeans understood that the provenance of the gold that appeared on the southern shores of the Mediterranean lay somewhere in the uncharted lands beyond the Sahara. In turn, this speculative knowledge helped prompt the first interactions between Europeans and sub-Saharan Africans, as Portuguese sailors steadily made their way south along Africa's

Atlantic shores in the fifteenth century. Following the resultant cross-cultural encounters, Europeans learned a great deal about Africans' mining endeavors—alternately exciting and disappointing these interlopers depending on the existence and availability of the minerals they coveted. Yet for centuries Africans remained in firm control of their mineral resources, even when interacting with the most aggressive foreigners. This chapter explores the often divergent ways that Africans and outsiders regarded these resources and how, over time, these valuations shaped Africans' encounters with those Europeans and Asians who reached the continent's shores.

Chapter 3 considers the explosion of mining in South Africa following the Eureka discovery and the identification of significant diamond concentrations in the late 1860s in and around what became the commercial center of Kimberley. If Europeans had previously imagined Africa as a repository of precious minerals, these finds surpassed even their most optimistic estimations. Virtually overnight, these bountiful deposits precipitated a "rush" that resembled gold prospectors' assault on California two decades earlier. In spite of this influx of both foreigners and international capital and the enactment of rac(ial)ist laws, African diggers held their own for some time following the discoveries; many even fared better than their white counterparts. Yet, following new legislation that permitted the amalgamation of individual claims, astute (and well-funded) businessmen such as Barney Barnato and Cecil Rhodes began to consolidate their holdings, ultimately leading to the emergence and eminence of De Beers. Africans were soon pushed to the margins to make way for foreign capital and local white mining interests, eventually limited to manual labor positions at the very bottom of the pecking order.

Chapter 4 explores the means by which De Beers revolutionized the diamond industry and over time became internationally synonymous with these stones. Africans, perhaps ironically, suffered the most in the wake of this development. The increasingly oppressive, racist South African state implemented policies that ensured that De Beers enjoyed a steady flow of indigenous labor to its mines. Once on site, the company monitored workers by requiring that they live in restrictive housing compounds. De Beers was motivated to introduce this form of housing in order to inhibit diamond theft, control allegedly "unruly" Africans, and draw a distinction between white and black miners. In turn, compound inhabitants experienced some of the worst conditions on mines anywhere in Africa, characterized by acute overcrowding and a variety of violent, intracompound antagonisms.

Meanwhile, under the decades-long leadership of the Oppenheimer family, De Beers expanded its interests beyond South Africa, gaining exclusive control of output from South West Africa (Namibia), Angola, and the (Belgian) Congo. The company also reorganized itself into a vertical enterprise by introducing "single-channel marketing." This aggressive arrangement saw an international cartel of producers, including De Beers, funnel all rough stones through its selling arm, the Central Selling Organization. In turn, the company was able to control supply and, eventually, demand—in great part by convincing global consumers that naturally occurring diamonds are rare, when, in fact, De Beers's practice of limiting and stockpiling rough output is responsible for producing this artificial scarcity. For all of the enterprise's success, though, its meteoric ascension was not without problems. In fact, acute mismanagement and catastrophic miscalculations in the 1920s saw the famed firm absorbed by the better-managed Anglo American conglomerate. Only because Anglo opted to retain the De Beers name for this portion of its diverse business is it possible to say that "De Beers" dictated the fate of the vast majority of the world's diamonds from the 1920s to the 1990s.

Chapter 5 traces the establishment of diamond-mining operations across the continent as Africa came under European colonial rule. Unlike the "wild west" of the early Kimberley days or the violent chaos depicted in films such as *Blood Diamond,* most diamond-mining settings during the colonial period were actually highly organized and reasonably orderly affairs. Yet they also featured a host of disagreeable conditions for the African laborers who toiled on them. These employees' experiences were further shaped according to whether a mine's diamonds were located in superficial, alluvial deposits or buried deep in kimberlite pipes. The particular colonial master involved in local recruitment also played a major role in differentiating employees' experiences. African headmen also influenced matters by compelling young male followers to engage with mining operations, typically in exchange for corporate or governmental compensation. Exceptionally, in the British colony of the Gold Coast, traditional African authorities themselves retained control of diamond deposits, renting out access to foreign mining companies and thereby playing a central role in the regional development of the industry. This chapter explores the diverse diamond-mining environments that colonial states, extractive companies, and African headmen collaboratively created. I examine the series of early twentieth-century discoveries of deposits scattered across the continent and trace the subsequent developments in these settings through the conclusion of the process of African political independence, which extended from the 1950s until the 1990s.

Chapter 6 continues the examination of colonial-era diamond mines, but adjusts the angle of approach away from states, corporations, and indigenous authorities in order to consider the motivations, strategies, and experiences of African laborers. Irrespective of whether forceful measures or attractive incentives brought Africans to diamond mines, it was on the backs of these workers that mining enterprises generated prodigious profits. Africans engaged with their respective employers in different ways, with some cyclically migrating for work, often according to the agricultural season(s), and others permanently relocating to take advantage of the wage-earning opportunities that increasingly urbanized mining environments offered. In certain settings, family members accompanied adult male laborers, but in most cases these men departed alone. Once on the mines, workers endured long, taxing days before returning to typically modest housing. In response to these challenging conditions, laborers creatively shaped their plights by employing an array of strategies. More aggressive measures included diamond theft, flight, and work slowdowns and stoppages, though most workers opted for less risky undertakings such as sharing tasks, singing songs, and befriending fellow employees. Only with the end of the colonial era in the 1960s and the dissolution of the apartheid regime in South Africa in the early 1990s, would mine workers come to enjoy significantly improved conditions and wages.

Chapter 7 explores the ways that a range of Africans have utilized diamond revenues to prop up oppressive governments, to destabilize others, and, in both of these scenarios, to precipitate widespread displacement and death. Arguably, the most notorious development of this nature was the emergence of "blood" or "conflict diamonds," which helped fuel civil conflicts in Sierra Leone, Angola, and the DRC in the 1990s. In fact, it is now widely understood that even if social and political grievances may have originally precipitated these conflicts, rebel leaders eventually fought these wars (or, in the case of the DRC, *fight* them) primarily for the profits available rather than for any coherent political purpose(s). In other cases, dictators such as the DRC's Mobutu Sese Seko, and, more recently, Liberia's Charles Taylor and Zimbabwe's Robert Mugabe, have used diamond sales to purchase arms in order to brutally perpetuate their regimes and deeply enrich themselves. Although the era of "blood diamonds" is arguably over, the industry is still struggling to contain the violent legacy of these stones and striving to change consumers' perceptions about the relationship between Africa and these precious resources.

Chapter 8 offers refreshing counterexamples to those that appeared in the previous chapter via an examination of the ways that the leaders of independent African governments, namely Botswana and Namibia, have used diamond profits to build democratic states characterized by pacific foreign and domestic policies. These stable, transparent nations have distributed the revenues from their prodigious mineral wealth in a reasonably equitable manner and have also generated meaningful local employment opportunities within their mining sectors. Although their diamond industries are not completely problem-free, Botswana and Namibia, the first and sixth largest producers (by value) of stones, respectively, offer hope for African nations still struggling to effectively manage their diamond resources. Today, Botswana is classified by the UN as an "upper-middle-income country"; clearly, diamond profits are reaching the country's inhabitants, even if inequity issues continue to trouble the nation.

Finally, a concluding chapter reflects upon the material introduced over the preceding chapters in order to consider what the continent's diamond future might look like. Although there have been a number of promising recent developments in the industry, including the creation of managerial opportunities for women and the emergence of black mining executives, many Africans are still operating on the fringes of the industry, barely eking out a living. In many settings, Africans without high-level connections or significant firepower survive as artisanal miners, and thereby enjoy little in the way of personal or financial security. Traditionally ignored by both mining corporations and local governments alike, these highly vulnerable individuals are only now beginning to receive attention and support. This encouraging development, combined with the successful implementation of the Kimberley Process Certification Scheme (KPCS), which has helped stem the flow of "conflict diamonds"; the cessation of civil wars in Angola and Sierra Leone; increased employment opportunities; heightened corporate responsibility, which has included the allocation of diamond profits to fight HIV/AIDS; and the growing demand for good governance across the continent, suggests that diamonds are poised to play a positive role in shaping Africa's future.

CHAPTER TWO

Africa's Mineral Wealth

Material and Mythical

> Off their coast . . . lies an island . . . and there is in the island a lake,
> from which the young maidens of the country draw up gold-dust, by
> dipping into the mud birds' feathers smeared with pitch. If this be
> true, I know not; I but write what is said.
>
> —Herodotus, in his account of the peoples of the west coast of
> Africa, c. 500 B.C.E.

> The men of this land are ruddy in color and of good physique. . . .
> Their clothes are of very thin linen and cotton, of many colors . . . ;
> they are rich and embroidered. They all wear toques on their heads
> with piping of silk worked with gold thread. They are merchants,
> and they trade with white Moors . . . carrying gold and silver, cloves,
> pepper and ginger, rings of silver with many pearls. . . . Men of this
> land wear all these things.
>
> —Vasco da Gama, describing Mozambique Island, 1498

IMAGINE HOW enticing the prospect of accessing Africa's mineral riches
might have seemed to you after reading Herodotus's alluring depiction or
Vasco da Gama's sensational observations as the Portuguese "discovered"
Africa, some two millennia later. Although the lapse in time between these
two passages is significant, it is clear that Africa's minerals were long valued
by both insiders and outsiders. For their part, Africans had been tapping
the continent's vast mineral wealth well before Erasmus Jacobs discovered

the Eureka Diamond in 1867. The metals and alloys that African societies valued included copper, iron, bronze, lead, and tin. Yet it was Africa's gold that was primarily responsible for thrusting the continent into a series of durable engagements with the global community. Africans widely treasured this metal, using it domestically for both personal and architectural ornamentation, but they also introduced it into regional and long-distance trade networks. For example, African gold figured prominently in Trans-Saharan and Indian Ocean commerce, reaching destinations around the globe. In turn, the provenance of this precious metal helped foster external notions of Africa as a treasure trove of mineral riches. Coupled with powerful myths of the continent's magnificent mineral endowments, foreigners aggressively attempted to locate the suspected sources of this prodigious wealth. European sailors and explorers had myriad motivations to investigate Africa in da Gama's day, but the most compelling was the desire to access the continent's legendary gold deposits.

For all of the enthusiasm that these maritime merchants displayed, misguided as it may have been, persistence turned out to be their most important attribute. For centuries prior to finally "hitting the jackpot" in South Africa, European commercial missions typically ended in disappointment rather than bonanza. On Africa's Atlantic shores, for example, European merchants correctly identified the West African sources of gold that featured in the Trans-Saharan trade. And, after initiating commerce with African littoral communities, they were even able to redirect supplies of this commodity southward, to what they named—not surprisingly—the "Gold Coast." However, local African leaders retained control of the trade between the inland producers and these foreign merchants, effectively denying the Europeans direct access to the gold deposits. Further south, European explorers' and merchants' dreams of additional, substantial mineral deposits proved to be illusory. The centuries that these foreigners spent fruitlessly searching along Africa's south-central and southwestern coasts confirmed that their grandiose notions of significant mineral deposits in these areas were unfounded. Meanwhile, along Africa's eastern coast, Middle Easterners, Asians, and, eventually, Europeans were unable to penetrate deeply enough, or for any sustained period of time, into the interior to gain access to the gold mines that fed the Indian Ocean trade. Regardless, by the middle of the eighteenth century this desire to access the continent's gold was eclipsed by the insatiable demand for an even more lucrative African commodity: slaves.

This chapter examines the pre-Kimberley period and considers the ways that Africans engaged with the minerals buried in the continent's soils and the manner in which outsiders sought to exploit this wealth. Despite foreigners' relentless efforts to gain direct access to these real and imagined mineral deposits, Africans successfully safeguarded their endowments with relative ease and thereby largely dictated the terms of trade. Africans' sustained dominance is explained by their superior force; the location of most mineral deposits far into the interior, rendering them hard to access; and outsiders' acute vulnerability to an array of tropical diseases. But the outsiders never fully abandoned their dreams of deriving financial fortune from Africa's mineral wealth. Rather, these aspirations merely went dormant for a time.

Domestic Utilization of Africa's Minerals

It is impossible to pinpoint exactly when Africans began to value and mine the array of minerals with which the continent is endowed. We do know, however, that the ancient Egyptians believed that gold was a divine, indestructible metal associated with the sun and also that the skin of their gods was golden. Moreover, during the earliest periods of dynastic Egypt (beginning c. 3100 B.C.E.), only the pharaohs were permitted to use gold for personal adornment, while the chamber that held a pharaoh's sarcophagus was known as the "house of gold," owing to these leaders' propensity to include large quantities of this metal in and around their tombs. The grave robbers of later years did not, after all, go to all of the trouble that they did just to marvel at the intricacy of a sarcophagus or to catch a glimpse of a mummified body. Yet, for all of the local reverence associated with this prized metal, gold did not possess great importance as either a currency or commodity. Instead, it was used primarily for funerary and ornamental purposes, most likely due to the limited deposits located within the Egyptian kingdom. Although gold may well be the most aesthetically appreciated of the minerals that Africans have historically mined, others, such as iron, were valued mainly for their functionality. African communities smelted iron ore in order to make weapons and cooking utensils, and even employed it as currency in certain settings in Western and Central Africa. Archaeological evidence suggests that Africans were mining and working iron ore from at least 1500 B.C.E., though scholars are continually revising the dates, exact locations, and patterns of knowledge transmission related to ironworking on the continent. Although Africans did not value iron for its aesthetic qualities in the same way that they did gold and other minerals, they did greatly revere the smiths who oversaw the complex process of producing ironware. It was widely believed that these individuals' esoteric knowledge meant that they also possessed mystical powers.

If Africans, in the main, valued gold for its aesthetic appeal and iron for its utility, copper was considered both attractive and functional. Copper was utilized on the continent earlier than iron and in much greater quantities than gold. Africans appear to have embraced the metal so strongly due to its durability and malleability, but also for its unique color, luminosity, and even sonorous qualities. As such, Africans employed copper and its alloys (bronze, which is composed of copper and tin, and brass, which is made from copper and zinc) in a variety of ways. Copper was incorporated into various forms of artistic expression; it was also used as a medium of exchange when shaped into rods, as ingots in the form of crosses, and even as basins of varying size and weight. Beginning sometime before 2000 B.C.E., Africans began mining and smithing copper, bestowing on it an importance that far exceeded continental valuations of gold. In fact, when Africans began to trade gold as a commodity to outsiders, they often sought copper in exchange. Consequently, for some time Europeans believed that the continent did not feature significant copper deposits.

African Minerals as Export Commodities

Although Africans valued iron, copper, and a number of other metals and alloys, their willingness to export gold was responsible for sparking the global interest in the continent's mineral endowments. By the first millennium A.D., gold was exiting the continent via both Trans-Saharan and Indian Ocean trade networks, ultimately reaching distant locations in Europe and Asia via a series of intermediary merchants.

The north-south trade that flowed back and forth across the Sahara was barely feasible until the domestication of the camel, which occurred sometime after 100 A.D. Starting as early as the third century, gold was one of the trade goods that these beasts of burden carried north across the desert in the form of dust, bars, nuggets, and sometimes jewelry. Mines controlled by the inland West African kingdoms of Ghana and Mali initially supplied virtually all of this gold. Over time, this output was supplemented, and eventually surpassed, by the production of the Akan mines located in the forest regions of what is the contemporary state of Ghana—mines that continue to generate mineral wealth to this day. In the tenth century, al-Masudi, the peripatetic, Baghdad-born "Herodotus of the Arabs," described the form of "silent" or "dumb bartering" that these miners preferred—and also the extent to which they would go *not* to reveal the source(s) of this gold, thereby perpetuating the mysteriousness of its provenance:

> Their donkeys, ladened with grains, leather, cloth and salt, and traders arrived . . . where men lived in holes (no doubt, mines). There, the traders spread out their goods along a stream or near a thicket. Then they announced their presence by beating on a special drum. . . . The merchants went away. The shy . . . miners crept from their hiding places and laid out a measure of gold dust. They, too, departed. Sometime later the traders returned, and, if the amount of gold dust was acceptable, they took it and left. If not, they went away again and the miners came back and made a counteroffer. Each group went back and forth until an agreement was satisfactory to both sides. Through years of experience, both sides had a general idea of what exchange would be acceptable, so the system generally moved quickly and smoothly. The silent miners inspired a lot of curiosity by trading in this manner. But, even if they were captured, as sometimes they were, the . . . miners chose death over betraying the location of the mines.[1]

Whether or not al-Masudi's account was accurate, these miners' alleged "death before divulgence" approach further deepened the intrigue associated with Africa's mineral wealth. To be sure, the commitment to secrecy that these miners displayed would be considered extreme in any era. Meanwhile, almost a millennium earlier, Herodotus had described a similar form of silent, gold-centered commerce between West Africans and the Carthaginians, while also claiming that the Ethiopians located far up the Nile were so rich that they bound their prisoners in gold fetters. No less an individual than the so-called "Father of History" himself can, thus, be counted among the contributors to the powerful illusions and delusions associated with Africa's mineral wealth.

The gold that was exchanged in this rather unconventional form of commerce eventually reached the southern shores of the Mediterranean. Upon arrival on Africa's northern coast, it was either retained and used, for example, to mint local currency, or was shipped across the sea to Europe. In exchange, Berber and Arab merchants transported salt, copper, and, to a lesser extent, food southward. Although the journeys across the Sahara were arduous and the prices of goods going in both directions quite high, demand was unremitting, and many of the items that survived the trip south, including different styles of cloth, became favorites within African elite circles. In order to protect the gold mines—the engine that drove this cross-desert luxury trade—the kingdoms that emerged on the northern edge of the West African savannah, such as Mali, Ghana, and Songhay, featured large armies that effectively blocked attempts by North Africans to gain direct access to the deposits. Thus, just as sub-Saharan Africans successfully fended off foreigners' efforts to make direct contact with the producers of coveted minerals elsewhere on the continent, so too did these West African states prevent their intracontinental neighbors to the north from wresting control of valuable gold deposits.

Along the East African coast, gold also played an important role in local commerce, as well as in long-distance, transoceanic trade. In this region, the Swahili city-states that had sprung up along the Indian Ocean coast from present-day Somalia to Mozambique resembled the termini located on either side of the Sahara due to their geographical and commercial importance.[2] And, similar to the way that Saharan traders linked the populations lying to the north and south of the desert, merchants operating out of these coastal centers acted as the commercial bridge between the mineral wealth emanating from the African interior and the buyers who came from as far as East Asia.

Just as Muslim writers were familiar with the trade in West African gold, they also knew of the existence of gold on Africa's eastern coast. And, as we saw earlier, they didn't hesitate to craft, and perhaps embellish, depictions of it. These accounts date as far back as to the time of al-Masudi (871–957), who mentioned in his writings that the source of this precious export was located in the region that is now Zimbabwe. Some centuries later, in 1225, Zhao Rukua, the superintendent of customs at the Chinese port of Quanzhou, also mentioned the presence of gold on the Swahili Coast in his work *The Description of the Barbarians,* an account of the countries where Chinese merchants traded and the goods that the populations of these nations offered. In fact, the production of this volume may very well have coincided with the emergence of gold as a significant commodity in the Indian Ocean trade, initially along the coast of present-day Somalia. By the fifteenth century, following the ascendancy of the city-state of Kilwa and its control of Sofala, the Swahili Coast polity through which this mineral was exported, gold had become the chief source of wealth of the southern portion of the East African coast.

As al-Masudi had correctly noted, the African goldfields that fed this expansive, transoceanic network were located in present-day Zimbabwe. These mines were managed by a succession of regional states, one of which was known as "Great Zimbabwe" (c. 1100–1450), whose kings allegedly lived surrounded by locally mined gold and copper ornaments and ate off of plates imported from Persia and China. Positioned at the head of the Sabi River valley, this kingdom was ideally situated for exploiting the long-distance trade between the goldfields of the plateau to its west and the (Indian) oceanic coast to the east. Not coincidentally, Great Zimbabwe's ascendance corresponded with the rise of the coastal city-state of Kilwa. The inland kingdom supplied the coast with the gold and ivory that, from roughly 1300 to 1450, made Kilwa the richest in the array of these coastal polities. Duties imposed by the leader of Great Zimbabwe upon goods traveling overland to the coast also constituted a major source of wealth for the kingdom. So too did the tribute that regional, ethnic Shona chiefdoms offered in the form of ivory, gold, and food. Craftsmen resident at the capital of Great Zimbabwe worked this gold into fine jewelry, both for local, royal consumption and for trade with coastal communities, often in exchange for iron, cloth, or beads. Swahili merchants would typically then introduce this gold into the wider Indian Ocean trade. Eventually, Monomotapa (the Kingdom of Mutapa) replaced Great Zimbabwe, but this succession only bolstered the flow of gold to the coast. Unlike the rulers of Great Zimbabwe, who imported from further west the gold that they sent onward to the coast, Mutapa's regents could rely on readily available, alluvial gold from the streams of the Mazoe region of the plateau.

Undoubtedly, the most sensational broadcast of Africa's mineral wealth was the pilgrimage of Mansa Musa, the ruler of the Mali Empire (c. 1230–1600), to Mecca in 1324–25. En route to the Arabian Peninsula, he and his massive entourage arrived in Cairo, in a procession of five hundred slaves, each carrying a six-pound staff of gold; one hundred camels, each carrying three hundred pounds of gold; and another one hundred carrying food, clothing, and other supplies. Just imagine the impact that this spectacle must have had! Moreover, Mansa Musa spent so abundantly in Egypt and gave away so many gifts of gold that the value in Cairo of this precious metal fell and failed to recover for some time thereafter. Over the ensuing decades, and then centuries, Mali's fame continued to spread—no doubt as a consequence of Mansa Musa's profligate trip. Indeed, as early as the fourteenth century, European geographers and cartographers began to grant the kingdom particular attention, regularly featuring it on maps. For example, in the Catalan map produced by Abraham Crepques in 1375, the king of Mali is shown seated on a throne in the center of West Africa holding a rather sizable nugget of gold in his right hand (see figure 1).[3]

For all of the attention that Africa's minerals were generating, the continent's diamonds played no part in this global fervor. This seeming implausibility can be quite easily explained: Africans bestowed no value on these stones, and foreigners were completely unaware that the continent was endowed with diamond deposits. Hence this immense mineral wealth remained embedded, untapped. As stated in the previous chapter, anyone who has seen a rough, uncut diamond can comprehend the lack of interest in these stones. Even centuries later, as rumors began to abound within European communities resident on the continent that this or that African society utilized diamonds to adorn their homes, or employed them to weigh down their hunting sticks, or just revered them for their hardness and indestructibility, no evidence exists that suggests Africans had developed any aesthetic appreciation or functional utilization for these stones. In fact, it appears that whenever one of these claims circulated, Europeans were responsible for generating them, perhaps out of incredulity that Africans seemingly had no interest in a mineral that these outsiders treasured so greatly.

External Imaginations of Africa's Mineral Wealth

European curiosity regarding Africa's mineral wealth mounted considerably over time. But access to these minerals would require more than mere desire or intrigue. Prior to the fifteenth century, despite Europeans' comprehension that the gold that reached the Mediterranean originated somewhere south of the great Saharan expanse, they possessed neither the military nor the technical means (nor perhaps the necessary appetite) to impose themselves much beyond the northern African coastal regions. Only after the Portuguese developed the navigational technology necessary for oceanic journeys and the military technology necessary to ensure that they could return home safely, did the prospect of foreigners reaching Africa's gold mines become a possibility and, eventually, a reality.

Fueling Europeans' unrelenting desire to reach these lands to the south was a series of long-standing, powerful myths that colored their imaginations of Africa's mineral wealth. In many respects, the illusions that these

FIGURE 1. Abraham Crepques's map, c. 1375. *Bibliothèque nationale de France.*

myths helped engender were merely the latest examples in the long history of gold-generated fantasies, from Jason and the Golden Fleece to Coronado's Seven Cities of Cíbola. In this case, however, Catalan, Italian, and Jewish merchant communities operating in North Africa were supplying firsthand accounts of Africa's significant mineral exports, which lent these myths an aura of authenticity. These traders also suggested that the African gold that was reaching Europe constituted just a minute fraction of what would be available if the sources of these mineral commodities could be located. These European merchants believed that the gold for which they were trading derived from the mythical "Island of Gold," a recurring site in the history of external imaginations of West African mineral wealth. In fact, many European maps of the period featured the "River of Gold," which was probably the Senegal River. According to the myth, the "mouth of the river was large and deep enough for even the biggest ship," and although the actual gold fields lay far upstream, by the early fourteenth century the allure had propelled a Catalan merchant to attempt to reach this legendary source. Indeed, the many unsuccessful efforts to find this deposit, which was most likely composed of the gold-producing regions of Bambuk (on the upper Senegal) and Bure (on the upper Niger), preoccupied both Muslim and Christian rulers alike for hundreds of years. As one scholar has soberly commented, this enduring obsession ultimately "cost kings their thrones, peoples their freedom, and thousands their lives."[4]

Arab and European written accounts further stimulated these ill-advised quests. Authors regularly referred to the elusive, mythical commercial centers of the gold trade in the West African interior as the "Lands of Gold," of which the aforementioned "Island of Gold" was often an integral component. The initial provocateur was probably the Arab writer, al-Fazari, who first referred to a "Land of Gold" (most likely the incipient kingdom of Ghana) sometime prior to 800 A.D. Numerous Arab authors would subsequently echo him, though none, as far as is known, ever actually traveled to the region. A number of learned Arab and European writers also surmised—mostly incorrectly—that the major West African trading centers for gold were situated near the sources of this precious metal. Speculation of this nature, coupled with geological ignorance, led the Persian geographer Ibn Khurdadhbih to assert in the ninth century that in the kingdom of Ghana's capital city gold "grew in the sand like carrots" and was gathered each morning at sunrise! Displaying similar license, three centuries later the Arab geographer and historian al-Bakri described the kingdom of Ghana's court as follows: "The king . . . sits in a pavilion around which stand his horses caparisoned in cloth of gold; behind him stand ten pages holding shields and gold-mounted swords; and on his right hand are the sons of princes of his empire, splendidly clad and with gold plaited into their hair. . . . The gate of the chamber is guarded by dogs of an excellent breed, who never leave the king's seat; they wear collars of gold and silver."[5] Although these sorts of literary speculation were obviously fanciful, the Portuguese and other Europeans would later discover that this West African land of "golden carrots and gold-collared canines" was, in fact, quite tangibly bountiful.

Legendary accounts of Africa's mineral wealth were not limited to West Africa. Further south, the Zimbabwean output was so profuse that many Europeans were convinced that its origins must be the biblical land of Ophir, from which the illustrious Queen of Sheba allegedly procured the copious gold that she traded with King Solomon of Israel. This durable myth, fed by the actual gold that these interior states were furnishing for the coastal trade, over time compelled countless foreigners to brave the African hinterland in search of the famed source.

Perhaps the most provocative of the many myths that circulated was that of Prester John. This fabled Christian priest-king allegedly oversaw an immensely wealthy kingdom, which propelled innumerable journeys seeking his/its location. Although early notions of Prester John's kingdom placed it in Asia, Europeans later believed his realm lay in Africa, in great part due to the Abyssinian King Wadem Ar'ad's decision in 1306 to dispatch an embassy to the Papal Court at Avignon. Its arrival in Europe seemingly corroborated the Prester John myth and prompted the Holy See to send legates to Abyssinia (Ethiopia) to seek an alliance with the king, who was now perceived to be the elusive monarch. Subsequently, African and European envoys were sent with some regularity between Ethiopia and Rome. In this respect, Africans were fueling outsiders' delusions, even if unintentionally. Down through the centuries, Prester John fantasies persisted, periodically reinvigorated by fantastical European accounts, including the following by the Italian poet Ludovico Ariosto in 1516:

> The castle in which the Ethiopian sovereign resided was in an opulence far in excess of its strength: the chains on the drawbridges and gates, every hinge and bolt from top to bottom, indeed everything for which we use iron, here was made of gold. Even though this finest metal was in such abundance, it was not disdained. The great loggias of the royal palace consisted of arcades in limpid crystal. Rubies, emeralds, sapphires, and topaz, spaced out proportionately, provided a glittering frieze of red and white, green, blue, and yellow beneath the fine ceilings.[6]

In the wake of Mansa Musa's trek, there were even some who believed that the Malian ruler was, in fact, the legendary Prester John. Regardless of the particular "speculation du jour," though, Europeans' perpetuation of the Prester John myth continued to shape their interactions with and beliefs toward Africa long after the legend should have been dismissed and taken its rightful place in history, somewhere near the final resting spot of Jason and his Golden Fleece.

Actively Seeking Africa's Treasures

Despite Europeans' commitment to gain unmediated access to Africa's mineral resources, neither Portugal nor any of its immediate imperial imitators were able to capture areas of significant mineral wealth. Indeed, for centuries following their initial encounters, Africans successfully prevented Europeans from gaining access to the continent's mineral deposits. Only following the Kimberley diamond finds, the subsequent discovery of gold on the South African Rand, and the contemporaneous onset of formal European colonization, would foreigners enjoy direct access to Africa's mineral endowments. Having waited patiently for these opportunities, these covetous outsiders wasted no time in exploiting the riches about which they had been dreaming, literally, for centuries.

In addition to the allure of Africa's mineral wealth, a number of other motivations drove the initial European ships southward. Primary among these impetuses was the search for a sea route to Asia and, in particular, India, so as to circumnavigate the hostile Ottoman Empire, which had expanded from western Asia into southeastern Europe. Merchants were also energized by the possibility of establishing new markets for a range of European goods and then returning home to sell exotic wares from distant lands. An aspiration to spread Christianity to new domains also played a role, as did the desire to replenish dwindling monetary reserves and to se- cure the various metals used in specie. Yet, of all the factors that encouraged the European navigation of the southern Atlantic, the prospect of a short route to the West African goldfields was arguably the most influential. While the immense profits that could be generated if this objective could be met undoubtedly played an instigative role, so too did Europeans' desire to disengage commercially from Muslim North Africa and thereby reduce their reliance on a people who held antagonistic religious beliefs. Bypass- ing the middleman is, of course, a time-honored business strategy, but it's even more appealing when you truly dislike him. Ultimately, Europeans believed that by gaining direct access to the West African goldfields they could finance further exploration, which would eventually reveal a sea route to India.

By the early fifteenth century, Portuguese sailors began to reach points south of the Sahara. Along the West African coast they began interacting and trading with, for example, the rulers of the Senegambia region, offering salt, cloth, and especially horses in exchange for slaves and limited quantities of gold. They also brought back to Lisbon alluring stories about the con- tinent, including the practice of silent barter that al-Masudi had described some centuries earlier. The demonstrable availability of gold, in turn, whet- ted the appetites of metropolitan Portuguese and helped render commercial voyages less speculative and more assuredly profitable. The greater likeli- hood of financial success generated significant interest within Portuguese noble and merchant circles, and also among Castilians and Italians, includ- ing one Christopher Columbus, prior to his "sailing the ocean blue."

Just as this initial commercial activity on the Atlantic shores of the West African coast began to develop, a discovery further south that would transform Europe's relations with sub-Saharan Africa and, ultimately, with the rest of the world, almost completely obscured it. In the early 1470s, Portuguese merchants sailing along the southern coast of West Africa discovered that they could obtain large quantities of gold from local traders, prompting the birth of the regional moniker: the "Gold Coast." Predictably, news regarding this new commerce spread rapidly and drove other European nations to attempt to gain access to this lucrative trade.

The Gold Coast: The Origins of Africa's Mineral Exodus

Upon finally reaching the shores of the Gold Coast and, thus, a "back door" to the mineral deposits that featured in this region's hinterlands, the Portuguese were both excited and disappointed. The realization that they had finally reached their destination, as confirmed by the gold both on display and on offer, heightened their enthusiasm. Yet they were also frustrated by an inability to generate much local interest in the trade goods they were plying in exchange. As a result of centuries of trade with communities to the north, local African elites had developed tastes for items that the Portuguese were not offering, such as Muslim-style textiles and clothing. Consequently, the Europeans found that they could trade their own goods only when they were combined with more desirable North African and, later, Indian items. And, even then, they were forced to offer their African buyers prices that were competitive with those that the experienced Saharan caravan merchants were offering. In short, Africans remained firmly in control of the terms of the trade.

Despite the limited appeal of the European wares, Portuguese merchants were able to generate interest in at least some of the items they were offering, including copper and brass utensils, woolen and cotton cloth, and even carpets. As word of these exchanges spread into the African interior, regional gold producers and merchants began to redirect to the Gold Coast portions of the output that would have traditionally gone north, across the Sahara.

In order to further encourage this welcomed development, the Portuguese realized that they would have to devise more commercially creative measures. To this end, the most enterprising merchants calculated that instead of transporting goods all the way from Europe to Africa they could instead buy and then resell commodities that were already available locally, namely slaves. Indeed, in order to satisfy these new consumers' demand for gold (coupled with the persistent demand for gold on the Mediterranean coast), African producers were forced to secure ever-greater numbers of slaves to work in the mines—a long-standing regional utilization of captive labor. The marriage of these African and Portuguese commercial objectives resulted in European merchants buying Africans on offer at certain points along the West African coast, and then reselling these human commodities elsewhere along the same coast. Soon, a vicious commercial cycle emerged in which African masters required additional slaves to mine increasing quantities of gold that they, in turn, often exchanged for more slaves. Portugal's Christian merchants, who had started buying slaves, at least in part, "for the good of their souls," now found themselves selling the "redeemed" men to "heathen" mineowners as the most expedient means of capturing a share in the West African gold market. As has so often happened throughout history, the pursuit of riches once again trumped any moral concerns. After later introducing cowrie shells and luxury cloths derived from the Indian Ocean trade, Europeans were eventually able to capture roughly half of the overall regional gold production, drawing much of it away from the trans-Saharan trade.

Elmina: Fortifying Access to Africa's Minerals

In order to consolidate control of this emerging commerce, in 1481 Portugal's King Dom João II declared the gold trade a royal monopoly and ordered the construction of a fortified settlement in the center of the Gold Coast, which came to be called São Jorge da Mina, or Elmina (figure 2). Elmina was constructed as a *feitoria*, or (trading) "factory," poised to defend and safeguard Lisbon's regional commercial interests, rather than to serve as a foothold on the African continent from which to launch invasions into the interior. Indeed, Elmina's cannons pointed outward, toward the sea, aimed at potentially hostile ships dispatched by Portugal's European rivals instead of inland toward prospective African armies. In contrast to what was to happen when the Castilians discovered gold in the New World a decade later, the Portuguese interacted and traded relatively peacefully with local African communities. Absent in this context was a systematic attempt to conquer or enslave the indigenous population. That subordinative model of human interaction in Africa came only later.

Lisbon's measured approach, combined with the Portuguese Crown's campaign of misinformation, secrecy, and obfuscation regarding this source of mineral wealth, proved to be financially prudent. It wasn't until the last

FIGURE 2. Elmina Castle. *Photograph by Todd Cleveland*

years of the fifteenth century that Portugal's European rivals would challenge its monopoly on the local trade in gold. Meanwhile, in the decades that followed Elmina's construction, the Portuguese were able to convince Africans to sell gold and gold dust to them at the fort rather than to send these items in the other direction, across the desert to North Africa. In a rather short time, this commerce transformed a humble fishing village on the West African coast into a major, global supplier of bullion. With exports of more than a half ton of gold annually, the trade integrated the region into an expanding Atlantic commercial system. Ultimately, it was the gold trade, rather than the transatlantic slave traffic, that prompted the proliferation of European fortifications along the West African coast in the 1500s and 1600s, many of which continue to this day to serve as legacies of this early pattern of Euro-African commerce.

Ever Southward . . .

Despite, or perhaps because of, the lucrative trade in gold and slaves into which the Portuguese and coastal Africans had entered, the Europeans engaged in further maritime forays, proceeding ever southward via a series of successive expeditions. Although the commercial success in West

Africa unquestionably spurred them on, many of the original, nonmineral impetuses outlined above continued to apply. Perhaps the most notable event in the Portuguese procession southward was their arrival on the coast of modern-day Angola, which Lisbon would eventually claim during the nineteenth-century "Scramble for Africa."

Early encounters with Africans in Angola led the Portuguese to believe that abundant mineral deposits were present. Their speculation was not predicated on any ostentatious display of precious metals by the indigenous population, but rather the realization that they had stumbled on a powerful political entity: the Kongo kingdom (c. 1400–1914). This polity stretched across present-day Angola, Congo-Brazzaville, and the DRC. Yet, despite its expanse and significant regional power, beyond small quantities of copper and iron, little in the way of precious minerals was available for exchange. Yet the Portuguese remained convinced that African silver and gold mines existed in the region. Lisbon was aware that the Spaniards had encountered bountiful mines in South and Central America (in particular, the Peruvian mines of Potosi in the 1580s) and, thus, Portuguese cosmologists predicted the presence of rich veins of silver at the same latitude in Africa. This conviction precipitated a tragifarcical "silver rush" in the territory. Adventurers from all walks of life sailed for Angola, where for decades they inched their way up the Kwanza River, many perishing in the process, in order to reach the chimerical mountains of silver that had featured in a report by an early Jesuit explorer.[7] This same kind of delusionary thinking would dominate Europe's approach to Africa for centuries to come.

Around the Cape of Good Hope

Although the Portuguese enjoyed largely peaceful relations with the Kongolese rulers, as they rounded the Cape of Good Hope, they jettisoned any semblance of cordiality that might have remained onboard. Along Africa's southeastern coast, the Portuguese encountered communities largely uninterested in commercial engagement; in response, the Iberians unleashed the full firepower of their cannons. Committed to gaining access to additional mineral deposits, the Portuguese attempted to achieve their commercial objectives by violently imposing themselves in the region. In the process, household names, such as Vasco da Gama, acted as little more than "state-registered pirates," employing the artillery at their disposal to bombard ports along the southern Indian Ocean coast in an attempt to disrupt, and consequently dictate, local trade.[8] The Portuguese were just as ruthless and relentless further up the Swahili coast, sacking a series of city-states in an attempt to compel the local rulers to submit to their commercial demands. Their hostility toward the Muslim identity of many of the coastal inhabitants certainly played a role in this aggression. Yet for all of the destruction that the Portuguese sowed, they did little to disrupt the flow of African gold to India, as well as to other points in the Middle East and Asia, that traveled along the well-established Indian Ocean trade networks.

Centuries prior to the appearance of the Portuguese along this coast, ethnic Shirazi had arrived from the Middle East (most likely Persia), established the island city-state of Kilwa, and broken the hold on the gold trade that the Muslim merchants of Mogadishu had formerly enjoyed. The creation of Kilwa as a commercial center was strategically practical, as it was located at the furthest point south that ships could reach in a single season. From Kilwa, local merchants ventured south to found a commercial post at Sofala, on the proximate coast of present-day Mozambique. "Golden Sofala" became the terminus for gold that emanated from the Zimbabwe plateau and was transported down through the Limpopo valley, thereby redirecting the flow of this precious metal away from points further north. By at least 1200 A.D., these Shirazi merchants had supplanted their rivals from Mogadishu and were commanding the gold trade of southeastern Africa.

Not content with carrying out artillery bombardments from their ships in order to realize their commercial objectives, the Portuguese journeyed inland in order reach the regional source of gold: the famed mines of Monomotapa. Europeans had initially been inspired to reach this fabled site after consuming a series of Arab accounts. Tales of their own perpetuated and further fueled these illusions, typically by rekindling the myth of Ophir and King Solomon's mines. For example, João dos Santos, a missionary working in the area in the late 1500s, wrote of the stone settlements found in the region:

> The natives of these lands . . . assert that they have a tradition from their ancestors and that the (stone) houses (here) were anciently a factory of the Queen of Sheba, and that from this place a great quantity of gold was brought to her, it being conveyed down the rivers . . . to the Indian Ocean. . . . Others say that these are the ruins of the factory of Solomon, where he had his factors who procured a great quantity of gold from these

lands conveying it down the same rivers to the Indian Ocean. They say further that the gold of Ophir which was brought to Solomon was from a place called Fura or Afura, and that there is little difference between Afura and Ophir, which name has been corrupted by the changes in time in the ages between that period and the present.[9]

Propelled by such accounts, the Portuguese built fortresses at Sofala and Mozambique Island and tried repeatedly to reach the sources of the gold on the Zambezi plateau. Due in great part to Swahili merchants' simple diversion of this trade to the coastal port of Angoche, though, these endeavors proved unsuccessful. Beginning in the 1530s and continuing over the ensuing decades, Portuguese soldiers and sailors moved up the Zambezi River, assaulting the series of Muslim trading centers that they encountered. On finally reaching their inland target, the Portuguese had been prepared to pay tribute to the Monomotapa king for permission to trade within his territory. Dissatisfied with the small amount of gold that was on offer, they instead sought direct access to the local gold mines. For all of their determination and firepower, though, their incursions never seriously threatened the main gold-bearing region that lay further to the west. Although the Portuguese had been willing to leave their ships and trek into the interior in an attempt to secure direct access to the continent's mineral wealth, Africans again stymied their commercial designs.

For all of the frustration it experienced, Portugal never abandoned its efforts in this area. For centuries, the country's rulers remained captivated by a mineral-driven fantasy that disregarded economic prudence, or even reality, in an attempt to revive the golden years of the empire—Sofala as Ophir had become an integral part of Lisbon's plan for its eastern realm. In practice, Sofala was often perceived not as it was, but as the Portuguese envisioned it: a gateway to fabled lands of gold and glory. It existed not merely as a place, but as a state of mind.[10] Much the same could be said for Europeans' imaginative approach to the rest of the continent.

Africa's Mineral Wealth: Durable Popular Appeal

Tangible commercial success, combined with powerful, durable misperceptions and myths, continued to drive outsiders to Africa's shores in search of mineral treasure long after the initial Portuguese encounters and the subsequent arrival of more powerful European nations. The notion of and attendant quests for an "African Eldorado" persisted for hundreds of years, but would have to wait for fruition until the subjugation of the continent at the end of the 1800s. Only after a series of epidemiological, technological, and military advances were European armies able to finally pry open the door to the African interior and realize unobstructed access to the continent's mineral wealth.

At about this same time, the European "discovery" of the massive ruins of Great Zimbabwe reinvigorated the myth of Ophir. Although biblical accounts of King Solomon's wealth had motivated the Portuguese to penetrate the Zambezia plain centuries earlier, the European "rediscovery" of the Zimbabwean ruins and mining sites in the nineteenth century seemed to finally confirm the enduring notions. To the Victorian mind, the impressive stone workings resembled nothing less than Solomon's legendary temple.

Although this (mis)perception was amateur archaeology at its very worst, the resultant delusional fervor spawned dozens of books claiming that the riddle of Ophir had at last been solved. Following both the Kimberley and Great Zimbabwe "discoveries," external writers once again raced to depict Africa as an untapped treasure trove, flush with mineral endowments that were simply waiting their heroic (European) discoverer. In 1885, for example, H. Rider Haggard's famous novel *King Solomon's Mines* was published. The book featured diamond mines, rather than the biblical gold mines, and was set not in Zimbabwe but in South Africa, where Haggard had spent time in the colonial service. On into the twentieth century, innumerable authors, including perhaps most notably Wilbur Smith, have continued to echo Haggard's romantic approach to Africa's mysterious, often-mythical mineral treasures.

The film industry has also attempted to capitalize on popular notions of Africa as a land of "mystical" mineral endowments. The diamond has powerfully come to life on the silver screen, just as it has on the pages of books, and this trend shows no sign of abating. From *Star of the South* (1911), the first feature film made in South Africa, to the box-office hit *Blood Diamond* (2006), the film industry has portrayed diamonds as symbols of romance and adventure, assuming a role that fiction writers had earlier pioneered. Given the general public's deeply entrenched appetite for Africa as a place of undiscovered treasure and latent wealth, which both authors and screenwriters alike have helped cultivate and reinforce, Hollywood's involvement is unlikely to subside. Meanwhile, ongoing, sensational mineral discoveries in Africa continue to provide fodder for the creators and purveyors of mass entertainment, reaching audiences eager to believe in the continent's seemingly inexhaustible mineral endowments—a conviction that outsiders have long held.

FOR CENTURIES prior to the Kimberley discoveries, Africans had been both utilizing and exporting the continent's minerals. The highly speculative, or at least limited, nature of Europeans' knowledge of the sources of these coveted metals precipitated the generation of a multitude of outlandish legends. Notwithstanding the geographic inaccuracies and geological falsities that these tales fostered, their grandiosity helped prompt the first interactions between Europeans and sub-Saharan Africans. Soon after the Portuguese began generating revenue for Lisbon, crews and ships from other European nations traced the Iberians' nautical footsteps, experiencing some success but also fruitlessly chasing the same myths and misperceptions. Financial disappointments rarely discouraged European fortune seekers for long, though, and the ongoing circulation of dubious accounts of untouched, colossal treasures continued to spur quests to unlock Africa's mineral wealth. Into the seventeenth and eighteenth centuries, for example, British and French explorer-merchants maintained a belief that Timbuktu was situated in the heart of the West African goldfields, prompting repeated attempts to reach that legendary city. Yet Africans were able to protect their mineral wealth with little trouble due to an array of factors, including their military prowess, the inland location of the deposits, and an assortment of local diseases that rendered the continent "the white man's grave." Only in the nineteenth century would Africa finally succumb to the external hunger for direct access to its mineral wealth.

CHAPTER THREE

From Illusion to Reality

The Kimberley Discoveries, the Diamond "Rush," and the "Wild West" in Africa

> Gentlemen, this is the rock upon which the future of South Africa will be built.
>
> > —Richard Southey, the Colonial Secretary of Cape Town, addressing the South African Parliament in 1869 while standing over the 85-carat "Star of South Africa," the second major diamond discovered in the colony

> As this influx from the dark continent met and mingled with the rush from the outside world in the diamond-mines . . . how greatly vivid, unique, and stirring were the kaleidoscopic shifts of this strange concourse! Europe, Asia, Africa, and America had boiled over into a hotch-potch, splashed on a diamond bed in the heart of South Africa.
>
> > —Gardner F. Williams, longtime De Beers manager, writing in 1902 about the initial "rush" to the diamond mines

ALTHOUGH MOST readers will have at least some level of familiarity with the California Gold Rush of the 1840s and '50s, the history of the global convergence upon South Africa following the discovery of the Eureka Diamond is certainly less well known. In practice, these two "rushes" were strikingly similar and were, in fact, strongly connected. In both settings, a motley group of fortune seekers, profiteers, speculators, and criminals gathered. And, in both scenarios, previously largely neglected spaces were transformed into thriving, frenetic commercial centers pulsating with money—San Francisco and Kimberley, respectively. Moreover, many individuals who had either struck it rich or at least tried their luck in California could be found two decades later seeking their fortunes in the heart of South Africa.

But foreigners were not the only ones "rushing" to the mines in and around Kimberley. Thousands of Africans also descended upon the digging sites, similarly hoping for a piece of the mineral action. Although many of these African "rushers" came from nearby communities, over time increasingly distant societies also began hemorrhaging members to the mines. And just as the California Gold Rush forever shaped America's development, the profound upheaval and chain of events that followed the discovery of the Eureka Diamond would be felt not only in South Africa but also in places far removed.

This chapter considers the explosion of mining in South Africa following the discovery of diamond concentrations in and around Kimberley in the late 1860s. If Europeans had previously imagined Africa as a repository of precious minerals, these finds surpassed even their wildest dreams. At long last, illusion had become reality. Virtually overnight, central South Africa became the epicenter of the global mineral landscape—a type of African "Wild West"—unrecognizable to anyone who had traversed this area prior to Erasmus Jacobs's discovery of the Eureka.

Despite the influx of foreigners and international capital, African diggers were initially able to own and work claims. Going forward, however, heightened competition with white diggers both generated and deepened racial tension. This antagonism eventually prompted legislation that enabled entrepreneurial businessmen such as Barney Barnato and Cecil Rhodes to amalgamate claims and thereby consolidate control of the deposits, which, in turn, ultimately led to the eminence of the famed De Beers enterprise. Collectively, these commercial developments, both intentionally and inadvertently, marginalized Africans involved in the diamond industry, reducing them to an ever-expanding migratory labor force.

Setting the Stage: The Resident Populations on the Diamond Fields

The South African terrain to which the treasure hunters rushed was certainly remote, but it was not entirely unpopulated. Local residents included the Griqua, a Europeanized African community whose origins can be traced to miscegenation between the original Dutch settlers in the Cape Colony and the resident indigenous populations, and the Boers, an Africanized European (Dutch) community. The Griqua had a slightly longer history in the region, though given their racially mixed ancestry they, too, were relative newcomers. In the following section, I outline the processes by which these two communities came to inhabit this space—a place that had been largely neglected until the Eureka changed, well, everything.

In the decades leading up to the diamond discoveries, African societies throughout the southern portion of the continent had been facing formidable challenges to their very survival. In the first half of the century, the upheaval known as the *mfecane* (c. 1815–40) saw Africans in the region violently thrust upon one another; the resulting waves of refugees unsettled much of the subcontinent. Following the eventual conclusion of this unrest, redwater fever and lung sickness decimated cattle holdings across the region on into the 1850s and '60s. And, to make matters worse, widespread drought in the early 1860s further reduced cattle populations and limited crop output. The Griqua arguably experienced this environmental calamity most acutely, as their water table dropped, local streams and springs dried up, and the fields that they had once cultivated dried out. Game levels also declined, as Africans were acquiring ever-greater numbers of firearms through trade with white merchants and were consequently decimating animal populations faster than the fauna could recover. Indeed, by the time of the first diamond discoveries, hunters had killed off most of the large game south of the Molopo River.

Meanwhile, the Dutch descendants—Boers, or "Afrikaaners"—were streaming into the region and exacerbating the already dire situation for the Griqua. In the 1830s, large numbers of Afrikaaner farmers from the Cape Colony loaded their possessions into wagons and plodded northward. The reasons for the exodus of these "voortrekkers" included bitterness toward British overrule and sense of propriety in the Cape Colony, population pressures, and increasingly restrictive laws on slavery. As these farmers and their families trekked northward, they eventually arrived at the junction of the Orange and Vaal Rivers, where many of them opted to establish farms. Unbeknown to them, they were settling atop the richest diamond deposits in the world. Eventually, these migrant farmers founded two republics in the vicinity: the Transvaal (or South African Republic), north of the Vaal River, and the Orange Free State, just to the east of the (future) diamond fields.

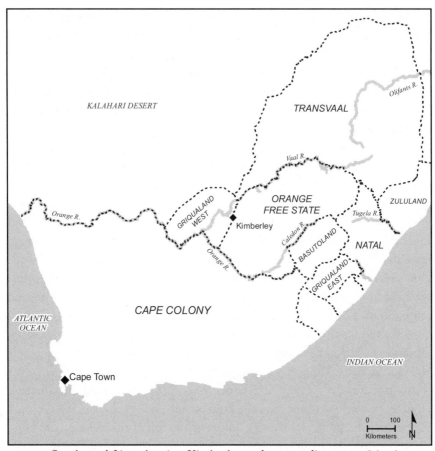

MAP 2. Southern Africa, showing Kimberley and surrounding areas. *Map by Brian Edward Balsley, GISP*

In settling in the region, Boer trekkers displaced certain Griqua communities, often violently. Even when the Afrikaaners didn't directly impinge on Griqua residents, though, these white settlers were hunters and pastoralists, in competition with their local rivals for the same things: game, cattle, and land. Predictably, contention for these resources grew more intense over time. Thus, well before the discovery of diamonds, the combination of overhunting and ecological decline forced Africans to seek new ways to restructure their economic, social, and political relations. From the 1840s on, as white settlement and merchant capitalism spread further into the interior of the subcontinent, increasing numbers of African males identified novel ways to raise the funds necessary to purchase cattle and guns and also to pay *lobola*, or bridewealth, in order to secure a wife and leave their fathers' compounds. In order to generate sufficient revenue, members of some African societies, including the Pedi and Tswana, sold products obtained from local fauna, including ivory, hides, and feathers. However, over time, overhunting and drought limited their ability to secure and trade such items. Beginning in the 1840s, large numbers of Africans migrated south, often for several months at a time, to sell their labor. Thus, on the eve of the discovery of the diamond fields, an uneasy tension between Boer and Griqua existed in the heart of South Africa, while a number of other African communities were already sending off their young men to labor for white employers—a foreshadowing of events to come.

The Global Rush to South Africa

In practice, the "rush" is better understood as a process rather than a single event. Following Jacobs's discovery in 1867, fortune seekers from around the globe initially descended on what became known as the "river diggings." And although interest in these deposits endured for some time thereafter, attention quickly turned to the more lucrative "dry diggings" at "New Rush." These "dry" deposits eventually far outpaced the riverine sites in terms of carats produced, and it was around these sites that De Beers ultimately emerged. Prior to that far-reaching development, though, white diggers of all nationalities busied themselves working individual claims in both the "wet" and "dry" sites, sometimes successfully, oftentimes not. Regardless of their individual fortunes, the growing presence of these white migrants quickly transformed what had been an arid, dusty, largely forgotten place into a burgeoning urban area and eventually, via the efforts of some of the more entrepreneurial members of this rather unsavory crowd, the global epicenter of the diamond industry.

More immediately, shortly after the diamond deposits were discovered and fortune hunters began to descend on the region, state-level wrangling over the minerals buried in the regional soils and riverbeds commenced. The Orange Free State acted first, asserting legal domain over the "diamond rivers." The Transvaal followed closely behind, proclaiming ownership of the entire north bank of the Vaal River until its intersection with the Hartz River. Meanwhile, at least until early 1870, local African chiefs had been able to successfully restrict white prospectors' access to the diggings on the northern bank of the Vaal. In July of that year, only a modest number, approximately eight hundred whites, were congregated at Klipdrift (later renamed Barkly West).

However, it wouldn't have been a "rush," if there wasn't a massive influx of people. Sure enough, by October, tents and shanties that stretched along over eighty miles of the banks of the Vaal served as the temporary homes for some five thousand white diggers, packed virtually on top of one another, while *ten times* that many were present by the following year. By the end of 1871, local chiefs had lost all control of the river diggings to both the teeming "rushers" and, more ominously, to Great Britain, which had intervened to annex a considerable portion of the area.

If varying yields from the river diggings dictated the fortunes of the thousands of white speculators and diggers that they attracted, the opening up of the nearby dry diggings, clustered around what would become the city of Kimberley, forever changed the course of Africa's modern history. Indeed, the initial diamond rush might well have done little more than empty a handful of rivers in central South Africa of their diamonds and then subsequently fade into history like so many other short-lived, mineral-inspired rushes. However, the discovery of bountiful deposits away from the rivers not only prompted many of the initial treasure hunters to abruptly decamp for the nearby dry sites but also attracted many thousands more to the area who had previously been sitting on the sidelines. One local observer unflatteringly described this new wave of migrants as follows:

> Rabbis, rebels, rogues and roués from Russia and the Riviera, transports from Tasmania, convicts from Caledonia, ex-prisoners from Portland, brigands from Bulgaria, and the choicest pickings of the dirtiest street-corners in all Europe . . . came here to escape grinding poverty or in many cases punishment of their crimes. . . . Unfrocked clergymen with the air of saints and souls of sinners. . . . It was a horde that increased and multiplied, and would have made a fine haul for the Devil.[1]

Another eyewitness commented on the reckless impulsiveness that this motley assortment of diggers exhibited: "They tore down their tents and abandoned the Vaal [River]. The camps were forsaken in a week. . . . The Boer farmers [near the dry diggings] watched in despair as diggers trampled the vegetation, cut down trees and stole cattle. A cloud of dust, visible for miles, hung above the diggings."[2] From just these two accounts, it's easy to imagine how wretched this group of treasure seekers truly was!

In practice, a blatant disregard for private property of any type characterized the rush. An account from 1869 by an English digger named Alderson provides insights into the destructive indifference of the community of diggers, which often operated more like a mob; the ways that local landowners futilely tried to retain control; and even the simmering tension between the long-standing descendant communities of the original Dutch settlers in the colony (Boers) and the more recently arrived British. According to the Englishman:

> We heard that a farmer named Van Wyk was giving out ground to Boers on his farm, and that they were . . . finding diamonds. . . . We accordingly trekked over with our carts and oxen. . . . Then we were told by two [Orange] Free Staters of English descent that Van Wyk would not allow anyone but a Dutchman to work on his farm. The next rumor that reached us was that in a furrow which stretched across the north end of the present mine, 92 diamonds had been found. Van Wyk came up to us . . . to warn us against attempting to dig on his farm and gave us just one hour in which to . . . clear off. Whilst we were pondering over the position . . . two Free Staters advised us to leave, otherwise we should be fired at from the homestead. I, however, gathered up my pick and pegs, calling out "Who follows me?". . . and I made for the kopje [a small, granite hill], expecting to be fired on at any moment. No such thing happened. I had advanced about 50 yards . . . then the remainder of our party came. On arriving at the top of the kopje I pegged out the first 30 ft. by 30 claim that was ever pegged, previous claims having been 20 ft. by 20. The others pegged the same areas. There were about 200 Dutchmen below the kopje, who seeing that no shots were flying round, rushed up with wild screams and marked out claims also. Thereupon Van Wyk . . . appeared. Van Wyk asked us all to stop work as he was willing to come to terms. He was immediately carried shoulder high to a wagon, and from that point of vantage he announced that he was by no means averse to Englishmen, and that we might all work on his place on payment of 15/- [15 shillings] per month per claim. I acted as the spokesman for the others; I told him I had been the first to rush the mine, and that I considered he would be well paid at 7/6 [7 shillings 6 pence] per claim. The Dutchmen unanimously supported the suggestions, and eventually the

> farmer agreed. We paid down our money. . . . They constituted
> to all intents and purposes leases in perpetuity.[3]

Other times, landowners were not so fortunate and either fled as diggers overran their farms or hastily sold off their properties, electing to receive at least some compensation before forever parting with their soon-to-be-ravaged land. Most famously, the De Beer brothers exchanged their namesake farm—which possessed promising diamond deposits and would eventually serve as the landmark site for the eponymous enterprise—to a group of investors, which included an aspiring industrialist named Cecil Rhodes, for only £6,000 (roughly a mere $650,000 today). It's safe to say that this transaction delivered one of the greatest windfalls in the history of mining!

Eventually, the dry diggings came to be composed of four mines: Kimberley (initially known as "Colesburg Kopje" or "New Rush"), De Beers, Dutoitspan (originally owned by the aforementioned Van Wyk), and Bultfontein. The sites varied dramatically in terms of both their overall output and the quality of their respective yields. For example, the Kimberley mine (figure 3),[4] with 470 original claims, featured the highest average number of carats found in each load extracted, followed by the De Beers mine. Dutoitspan, which initially contained twice as many claims as De Beers (1,441 to 622), was the largest of the four mines, and although its diamonds fetched the highest average price per carat, it never matched Kimberley's yields. Finally, Bultfontein, which contained 1,067 claims, was known as the "poor man's kopje," while its most barren sections even earned the dispiriting nickname: "the graveyard."

Epistolary Accounts of the Physical and Emotional Nature of the "Rush"

To reconstruct the experiences of the white "rushers" on the diamond mines, we are fortunate that a rich cache of letters has survived. This correspondence typically consisted of diggers' or prospectors' firsthand accounts of the chaos, sent to wives and other relatives. Via these letters, it's easy to see how the rush indelibly affected these individuals, vaulting some fortunate souls into elation following lucrative finds, while banishing to the depths of fiscal insolvency those whose luck failed them. For example, the financial unpredictability of this venture prompted an English fortune seeker named John Thompson Dugmore to write to his wife in September 1870 that "The whole (digging experience) is a lottery in the strictest sense of the

FIGURE 3. Kimberley Mine, 1872, showing an end view of the excavations. From Gardner F. Williams, *The Diamond Mines of South Africa: Some Account of Their Rise and Development* (London: Macmillan, 1902), 196

word."[5] Beyond reflecting the alternating optimism and despair inherent in any get-rich-quick endeavor, these letters also played important roles in convincing ever more "rushers" to descend on Kimberley. A June 1870 letter from Mary Barber, a South African resident of European descent, to a friend illuminates the initial hope, excitement, infectiousness, and even "jolliness" that characterized this episode of "diamond fever":

> Mr. Barber and Freddy together with several other members of the family started for the diamond fields ten days ago . . . and many others in this neighborhood are preparing to go. It was not the newspaper reports which set our people "agoing" it was the private letters from the diamond fields from relations of ours, letters of which there can be no doubt of their truth, which caused them to go. . . . I never saw anyone so excited as Freddy was about diamonds, his sheep farming prospects were very good, but he at once let one of his larger flocks and another Hal will look after. . . . His angora goats too he let, and his favorite . . . gun he sold for a share in a diamond company . . . started about a month ago. . . . In fact the whole party went off in high spirits; very many other parties are preparing to go. . . . I must say I should like to go. . . . How jolly it would be.[6]

Passages such as the following from an 1872 letter written by J. X. Merriman (who would later go on to become a South African parliamentarian and eventually the prime minister of the Cape Colony) conveyed exactly the type of optimism that drove Mary Barber's "Freddy" to abandon his livestock in the pursuit of diamonds: "I promised to try to give you some kind of account of this place but nothing is more difficult. It is, you must confess, something strange to see any place in South Africa where everyone seems at once busy and prosperous, where everyone makes more or less money and the sound of bankruptcy . . . is unknown. I am as much pleased and surprised with this place (the dry diggings) as I was disgusted with the river diggings. . . . The honest Dutchman is quite in the minority and is freely blackguarded even by black fellows."[7] Naturally, not all of the correspondence emanating from the mines was so sanguine. The regional destitution and topographical starkness were often as discouraging for the authors/miners as was the absence of any good fortune digging for diamonds. For example, one of the first letters that the aforementioned Englishman, John Dugmore, sent back home to his wife indicated that "the appearance was one of the most dreary and barren you could imagine, my spirits fell to zero at the very appearance. Not a vestige of grass and the few bushes almost all leafless and scarce but a gravel free from stones with the exception of a bed of sand so deep that the oxen could barely tow the wagon through. . . . There are hundreds of people here working hard from day-to-day and from mouth-to-mouth without the least success." Whether or not these letters compelled some individuals to flock to the mines and others to give them a wide berth, they do offer a colorful glimpse into the early days of South Africa's "Wild West."

The "African Rush"

If the white diggers and speculators who flocked to the diggings originated from far-flung places, a much more proximate "regional rush" of black Africans unfolded in parallel. Arguably more important than the arrival of foreigners, without this regional influx the diamond industry would have failed to develop so rapidly. In October 1880, for example, the local *Daily Independent* declared: "Native labour is the life of the Diamond Fields, and just as in proportion as the supply and demand of this commodity varies, so in a great measure is the prosperity of the community gauged." In general, African communities situated closest to the diggings provisioned the mining operations, whereas societies further removed supplied migrant labor, though exceptions to this generalization certainly existed. The first Africans to engage were the Griqua—prompted by perceived opportunity or resigned destitution, or both. These local residents initially roamed the diamondiferous area looking for plainly visible or easily accessible stones, until all of these gems had been removed. Subsequently, as people in further-removed African communities of, for example, Pedi, Sotho, Zulu, Thlapong, and Tsonga became aware of the remunerative opportunities on the mines, they descended on the diggings to purchase and work their own claims. Or, as happened much more commonly as time passed, they went to work for white claim holders and, eventually, the emergent, white-run diamond enterprises.

African claim holders initially operated on a par with their white counterparts, but as competition between blacks and whites over access to plots and labor increased, African participants soon felt the harsh effects of racism. Racial prejudice, manifested in both informal practices and official policies, eventually relegated African claim holders to the less-productive riverine sites before ultimately preventing them from owning any claims at all. This legal preclusion reduced Africans to migrant laborers and/or extra-legal participants in the diamond trade, involved in creative, yet increasingly criminalized, activities. Over time, and especially after confronted with rapidly deteriorating living conditions in the wake of the European colonial conquests, legions of Africans migrated to the mines from throughout the subcontinent. These individuals typically trekked for long stretches simply to reach the mines and then remained there for months, or even years, before returning home, if they did at all.

Africans' Temporary Autonomy

Africans' decline in the emerging South African diamond industry was precipitous, with roughly only a decade elapsing between the existence of black claim holders and their complete disappearance. Although they descended on the mines as independent diggers in significantly smaller numbers than white fortune seekers and, once there, met with only limited success, these Africans still drew the racist ire of the expanding white community. Yet in the heady, early days of the rush, this racially dictated fate was far from the minds of Africans as they actively chased the revenue-generating opportunities that were materializing on the mines.

In the initial period of the river diggings, black claim owners tried their luck alongside whites. In 1872, for example, in addition to a handful of white claim owners, there were over 45 African claim holders active in the Dutoitspan and Bultfontein mines. These diggers typically slept where they labored in temporary, makeshift accommodations that usually consisted of nothing more than a tent. In practice, no occupational challenge was too disagreeable when the pursuit of a diamond was at stake. By the early 1870s, however, white diggers had already begun to abandon these digging sites, including "the graveyard." As such, by 1874, 120 out of the roughly 140 claim holders on these largely exhausted mines were black.

Owing to the limited yields at Dutoitspan and the particularly unproductive Bultfontein mine, some African claim holders augmented their income via other employment, including as masons, carpenters, and drivers. Many of these early entrepreneurial sorts were Christian and as a result of their interaction with missionaries had developed an independent spirit that inspired them to relocate, away from the control of traditional authorities. They also possessed the types of skills on which they could fall back if their digging endeavors proved fruitless, or simply inadequate. For example, John Komali, an African Christian from Natal, arrived in Kimberley in 1873 and proceeded to work a claim he purchased at Dutoitspan, but he also hired himself out to both dig and oversee operations for various white claim holders in the more bountiful Kimberley mine. These resourceful, often educated individuals even generated a positive impression among some white observers. For example, in 1876, a local missionary wrote: "Not all blacks on the Diamond Fields are servants. There are many quite well educated diggers or merchants. These are mostly from the [Cape] Colony and they are mostly those who tend to remain and build up a nucleus of permanency to which newcomers adhere."[8]

Respect across racial lines was, however, quite rare. Despite the very limited success that Africans had in generating diamonds from their own holdings, they were unable to avoid the racial antagonism that white diggers were increasingly directing at them. Downtrodden white miners, who were resentful that blacks owned claims and that at least some of them (though certainly not many) were succeeding, fabricated and spread rumors that nonwhite claim holders were more successful. According to J. W. Matthews, writing in 1887, "A great deal of animosity toward the natives existed during this period [the 1870s] . . . (and it) originated from many white men not possessed of claims being jealous of their black brethren digging at Du Toit's Pan and Bultfontein."[9] At other times, outright racism rather than racially driven jealously motivated whites, especially those who fundamentally objected to Africans' right to own claims. For example, an editorial from the mid-1870s that appeared in the *Diamond Field*, the white diggers' newspaper, proclaimed, "Ruin, financial ruin for the whites, more ruin for the natives, these are the results of the attempt to elevate in one day the servant to an equality with his master. Class legislation, restrictive laws and the holding in check of the native races, till by education they are fit to be our equals, is the only policy that finds favor here." As tensions simmered, arbitrary abuse toward blacks increased. Violence and extralegal "justice" were now layered upon the existing chaos—intrinsic features of any "Wild West" scenario. Eventually, the situation exploded.

During the calamitous "Black Flag Rebellion" of 1875, frustrated white diggers demanded, among other things, that blacks be stripped of any claims and be denied the right to own them in the future. Alarmed and frightened, African claim owners and diggers at Dutoitspan and Bultfontein sent a petition to the lieutenant-governor of the Cape Colony that articulated their concerns and stated that if the white miners' "unjust and unreasonable demands" were met, that this concession would generate "poverty and ruin upon your Petitioners." A tangible hostility now permeated the Kimberley air.

Even though Africans formally retained their right to possess claims for some time thereafter, the persistent racism that they endured soon rendered (prospective) financial success a thing of the past. Extremely, and exceedingly, rare were individuals like Africa Kinde, who had amassed a substantial sum of money via his claims (he had over £4,600 deposited in Standard Bank in 1881) before selling them off and successfully investing in farmland and cattle. The last African to hold a claim at Dutoitspan was the Reverend Gway Tyamzashe, a Congregational minister, in 1883.[10] Subsequently, with the diamond focus having long since gravitated to Kimberley and the dry diggings, blacks held claims in only the nearly barren river sites. Following the Black Flag Rebellion, Africans survived almost exclusively as wage laborers, either for white diggers or, increasingly, for the emerging diamond enterprises. In the relatively short time that had elapsed since the discovery of the Eureka, it had become abundantly clear that Africa's diamonds were, quite simply, not for Africans.

Unskilled, Migrant African Labor

The discoveries at Kimberley greatly accelerated the existing regional practice of migrating to seek wage labor. As early as 1872, for example, between

15,000 and 35,000 Africans were residing in Kimberley, making it the second largest population center in South Africa (behind only Cape Town). Moreover, each year during the early 1870s, a remarkable 50,000 to 80,000 Africans arrived in and departed from the "diamond city." During the first decade of mining, many of these migrants came only to earn enough money to purchase a firearm prior to returning to their homelands. As such, between 1872 and 1877, when the British banned Africans from purchasing firearms, approximately 150,000 single-barreled guns came into the Cape Colony, of which roughly half were transshipped to Kimberley, while another 3,000 arrived on the diamond fields via Natal.[11] By 1869, Africans from ever-further distances had begun descending on the diggings seeking work from both white and black claim holders. They quickly came to constitute the heart of the labor force. Yet because they were virtually all unskilled, they endured extremely challenging conditions and were undercompensated for their efforts. Only during the periodic labor shortages that occurred during the first decade of mining were migrant laborers able to secure improved wages. Over time, though, this strategy became increasingly infeasible due to the consolidative reduction in the overall number of employers, the introduction of labor compounds and the ever-tightening regulation and regimentation of the industry.

For at least two decades prior to the discovery of the Eureka, Africans, including Pedi, Tsonga, and (South) Sotho, from the central and northern parts of modern-day South Africa had been migrating southward for work. Their target destinations included a variety of wage labor posts in Natal and the Cape Colony, farm labor and public works projects in the Cape, and, to a lesser extent, agricultural work on farms in the Orange Free State. A number of military and ecological factors had precipitated and shaped these migratory practices, including regional conflict, especially during the tumultuous *mfecane,* but also related to the increasingly aggressive Boer presence in the interior; diminished productive capacity, stemming from large-scale losses of cattle due to disease and reduced crop yields due to drought; and a decline in the profitability of hunting, as groups had to travel further and further north to reap ivory. These migrant laborers typically remained on the job for between four and eight months—not coincidentally, roughly the amount of time it took them to earn enough to purchase a rifle.

For many of these migrants, the diamond discoveries at Kimberley were a welcome development. To begin with, Kimberley was a much shorter walk than, for example, the eastern Cape. Wages were also higher—at least 50 percent more than those on offer in the Cape and double what was paid out on farms—and thus laborers required less time to save enough for a firearm. However, as the heretofore voluntary nature of this undertaking began to abate, even these appealing features began to recede in importance.

Sensing the economic opportunities available on the mines and desperate to defend their peoples from attack, regional paramount and subchiefs began directing their male subjects to the mines in order to procure guns. These African headmen attempted to cast this endeavor as a political duty, though many subjects undermined this proposed arrangement by permanently relocating to the mines, never returning home with the anticipated firearms. For those subjects who did comply, though, chiefs collected a tribute or tax in the form of wages, guns, or (stolen) diamonds, though they also occasionally negotiated for improved wages and/or working conditions on behalf of their labor contingents. As such, we can place these African authorities somewhere between "exploitative" and "advocative" on a scale that measures overall human interaction. Chiefs could also withdraw their subjects when threats materialized on the home front, which gutted the African labor force on the mines and, thereby, crippled production. For example, in 1876, the Pedi paramount chief, Sekhukhune, summoned his men back from the diamond fields as part of a successful riposte to Boer hostility. Following the departure of roughly six thousand workers/ defenders from May to July of that year, the overall African labor force on the mines was cut in half. Four years later, the outbreak of the Gun War in Basutoland provoked a similar exodus of some four thousand Sotho laborers. Their departure brought the mines to a standstill and prompted mineowners to look further north for workers in order to reduce their dependence on "unreliable local labor."[12] During this early period of mining, migrant labor, though increasingly important, was neither vital to African societies nor was it forcibly imposed on them by mining capital. Rather, it grew out of existing social relationships within rural economies whose participants were now strategically responding to the new opportunities on the mines.

For these migrants who, over time, trekked to the mines from ever-further distances, a world unlike any they had previously experienced awaited them. In the 1870s, white labor touts (recruiters) offering employment on the mines often intercepted Africans as they approached Kimberley. An

FIGURE 4. Africans seeking work on the mines. From Gardner F. Williams, *The Diamond Mines of South Africa: Some Account of Their Rise and Development* (London: Macmillan, 1902), 188

account from this decade from a white observer describes what the weary migrants may have looked like as they encountered the recruiters (figure 4):

> Some stalked proudly over the veld in the full plumage of the Zulu veteran, with flowing ox-tail girdles, armlets, and anklets, decked with waving feathers and gleaming ear-rings and bracelets. Others . . . in greasy red shakos, faded blouses, and other cast-off equipments of soldiers and hunters. So the parade ran down to the barest loin cloth or utter nakedness, through leopard skin wraps, dirty karosses, ragged breeches, tattered shirts, and every other meager covering of the native hunter or shepherd. Some of this drift to the mines tramped more than 1,000 miles over mountain ridges and sun-scorched veld, swimming through rivers, scrambling down steep ravines, and plunging deep in mud and desert sand, to reach their goal, as many did, gaunt skeletons of men, with bleeding feet, and bodies scratched and sore and tottering with weariness and hunger.[13]

If the touts failed to sign them up, the migrants found work on their own, often after consulting with others from their home areas regarding the best wages and working conditions available. Fortunately, we are afforded some insight into this process courtesy of Z. K. Matthews, a well-educated son of a mine worker: "My father used to tell us of the time he worked as a laborer in the diamond mine and this lore was a constant topic when relatives, come to Kimberley to work in one of the mines, would stop with us for a while. . . . The talk then would be about the different mines, the merits of this or that labor boss, how this one was rough, that one easier, and this one a hard driver, that one a little fairer in his dealings with the men."[14] Only in rare circumstances did a glut of African labor exist on the mines, thereby forcing desperate migrants to accept less attractive wages and working conditions. In even rarer cases, a labor surplus could preclude employment altogether for some migrants due to the inability of the industry to absorb them.

During the first half of the 1870s, migrant workers typically committed to only one- or two-month contracts to retain their flexibility in the labor market. These workers often took advantage of the competitive demand for African labor by regularly swapping one employer for another. By adopting this strategy, they were able to quintuple their average wages between 1871 and 1875—much to the chagrin of claim holders, whose wage bills could constitute over 85 percent of their average operating costs and over 50 percent of their combined working and living expenses. African laborers were indispensable to the growth of the mines, though, and both parties seemed to recognize this fact. Despite the resultant animosity directed at them by many white residents, the long-serving De Beers manager, Gardner F. Williams, offered a favorable assessment of African talent and industry: "Those who have thought Africans lazy, indolent, beer-drinking beings, should visit the diamond mines . . . and they will get a new impression of the working capacity of these despised black men. The natives working in the diamond mines, if they are old hands in the service, are uniformly active and industrious men, while natives fresh from the kraals are soon taught their duties, which they learn to perform with nearly as much skill as most European miners."[15] Quite simply, white claim holders needed this form of inexpensive labor, else they would have had to divert themselves from key tasks, including pumping away any obstructive water, differentiating diamonds from similar-looking stones on sorting tables and procuring supplies and equipment. As such, during this period, each white claim holder on the river diggings employed roughly five African laborers, while those based on the dry diggings were utilizing, on average, twenty or more. Indigenous labor had become the backbone of the growing industry.

During this early stage of the industry's development, the length of time that African migrants remained on the mines generally corresponded with the distance they had traveled to reach the diamond fields, for example, three to six months for those who had traveled at least five hundred miles, four to eight for those coming from further afield, and correspondingly less for those whose homelands were closer.[16] Africans also regularly withdrew their labor, returning home according to agricultural cycles, to respond to a headman's summons, or, most commonly, after sufficient funds had been earned to purchase a rifle. For example, ethnic Pedi, who made up the majority of wage laborers in the 1870s, typically departed for home roughly six months after their arrival. These early migrants were clearly not divorced from the rural economy and not (yet) dependent on the mines for their livelihood.

Over time, however, this migratory labor force did become semipermanent, giving rise to a budding proletariat. By the end of the 1870s, for example, the diamond fields featured a resident African population of roughly 9,000, though many more workers continued to migrate to and from the mines each year. Eventually, the emergence of consolidated diamond enterprises would both stabilize and constrain this burgeoning community of African laborers, forcing them into mining compounds, standardizing their wages, and generally dictating the terms of their labor engagement. Although African workers consequently lost much of their labor freedom and flexibility, improved living and working conditions typically accompanied these developments. At the same time, these companies' relentless quest to harvest more diamonds increasingly drove operations further and further underground, and thereby generated increased occupational risks.

Deepening Racial Discrimination and the Eventual Transition to a "More Orderly West"

Although the Black Flag Rebellion of 1875 constituted the most sensational challenge to regional opportunities and protections for Africans, their situation was already deteriorating prior to the uprising. Combining to restrict the range of permissible activities for Africans in and around the mines were disgruntled and increasingly hostile white diggers; emerging companies eager to harness indigenous labor; the conclusion of the tenure of Richard Southey, the sympathetic lieutenant-governor of the Cape; and laws that targeted Africans due to their alleged widespread involvement in diamond theft and illegal buying and selling (popularly known by the loosely acronymic term "IDB"). Eventually, these pressures forced Africans into "locations," whereby they became a reliable labor pool. In sum, racial discrimination against blacks was exhibited, justified, and ultimately codified. Africans were consequently left with few remunerative possibilities, other than employment with one of the companies that had come to dominate the mining landscape by the end of the 1870s. This process of heightened control stabilized the region, setting the stage for a long period of Pax De Beers, during which the mining behemoth came to manage virtually every aspect of life on the diamond fields.

Although each of the developments that restricted Africans' endeavors in Kimberley was racially motivated, the Black Flag "rebels" arguably posed the greatest threat. British troops were eventually required to subdue these disaffected white miners, but even though they won some of their demands, they remained dissatisfied and increasingly directed their ire at the black community. At issue was their insistence that the Cape Colony's "master-servant" ordinance be applied locally. In its absence, these white diggers roamed the streets of Kimberley harassing blacks, "vigilante style," in an attempt to teach them "the proper subordination and deference required of servile races in colonial societies."[17] White claim holders resented the black claim holders, who were naturally engaged in competition with them. African laborers who accepted wages that were far below the rates that desperate white miners were seeking, as well as those Africans who stole diamonds from their white employers' claims, also fueled the racial hostility. Ultimately, though, discontented white diggers' deepest concerns lay with the companies that were increasingly buying up individual claims on the more bountiful mines and driving small operators out of business. By persecuting Africans, they were simply (re)directing their frustrations toward a more immediate, more vulnerable target.

Even those Africans who weren't directly involved in mining saw their economic prospects dim because of a cloud of racially motivated sentiments and developments. Boer farmers gradually squeezed out members of nearby African communities who had been provisioning the mines. The emerging mining enterprises also contributed to these Africans' demise by arranging for more distant, yet less expensive, goods for their operations. African chiefs and headmen also experienced a similar decline in their fortunes. In the years following the initial diamond discoveries, these regional leaders had successfully limited white rushers' access to diamondiferous areas under their control and benefited from the wages that migrant workers repatriated, often in the form of firearms and fees. However, as time passed, these headmen similarly found themselves on the wrong side of the racial divide. With so much wealth latent in the Kimberley soil, these once-proud leaders were eventually reduced to mere labor suppliers or were swept aside altogether by the powerful forces at play.

The Disempowerment of an African Chief: The Story of Nicolaas Waterboer

No case better exemplifies the shifting power dynamics, social disruption, and marginalization of African leaders in the region than that of Nicolaas Waterboer, a Griqua chief. Just prior to the Eureka discovery, in 1866, Waterboer had been comfortable enough with the regional state of affairs to agree to cede a portion of the land he oversaw, near where the Vaal feeds into the Orange River, to the developer of a prospective white settlement project. Although Waterboer did harbor concerns about the border region between the lands he controlled, known as Griqualand, and the neighboring Orange Free State, local matters were otherwise generally quiet. By 1872, however, Waterboer's lands had been confiscated and soon afterward he found himself arrested and imprisoned, eventually fading into historical obscurity.

Long before these tragic developments reached fruition, as with just about everyone else in the region, Waterboer had been attempting to capitalize on the new mineral discoveries. As early as 1868, his subjects were actively hunting for diamonds, confirming that the chief recognized how he might secure a portion of this newfound wealth. Claiming absolute entitlement, Waterboer insisted that his Griqua followers turn over any mineral findings to him so that he could arrange for their sale. But Waterboer's subjects increasingly began selling their finds to others to maximize their own profits. For example, in October of 1868, the local civil commissioner, W. B. Chalmers, commented, "I have just seen another diamond, brought in by a Griqua . . . purchased from him by one of the shopkeepers here. . . . Now that the Griquas are making a regular search for them [diamonds] they are turning up sharp. . . . But they are very sly with them, and keep them very secret, for fear of Waterboer claiming them."[18] The buyers of these stones were foreigners, who had seemingly materialized in the region overnight.

Increasingly disregarded by his subjects, Waterboer steadily began to realize that he could not effectively exploit the mineral wealth that his territory featured. Consequently, by the end of 1868, he had signed a deed of concession for all "diamonds, metals, and minerals . . . found in his dominions" to a private mining concern. The concession was to last thirty years and the headman was slated to receive one-fifteenth of the gross revenue from the sale of any diamonds harvested. Lest Waterboer appear to have been solely concerned about his personal wealth, the agreement also prohibited the concessionaires from selling intoxicating beverages to his followers.

The concessionary agreement effectively marked the onset of a long period of economic marginalization for Waterboer's people. In early 1869, for example, before the concessionary company even began operations, a Griqua herdsman derogatorily referred to as "Swartboy" (literally, "black boy") found an 83.5-carat diamond, later coined "The Star of South Africa." Swartboy proceeded to sell it, receiving ample livestock in return, rather than turn it over to Waterboer. Yet the concessionary company now had legal rights to the stone and eventually sued for it. Thus, in just two short years following the discovery of the Eureka Diamond, indigenous residents of Griqualand had lost the right to pick up a stone on which they might literally be standing, legally claim it as their own, and then sell it. There were to be no more "Swartboys."

With the diamond rush now in full swing, Waterboer feared a hostile takeover of his territory by the Orange Free State and, therefore, requested British protection for Griqualand. Great Britain, eager to consolidate access to the diamond wealth for the Crown and concerned that the Free Staters might close the highly lucrative trading route to the north, annexed not only the area around the diamond fields but also a considerable portion of Waterboer's land, giving birth to the colony of Griqualand West in October 1871. By the end of that year, a key portion of the richest diamond-bearing territory in the world had been added to the long list of British colonial possessions. Even among this extensive catalog of territories, this one shone "particularly brightly." Shortly thereafter, in 1876, Waterboer was imprisoned after attempting to free some of his subjects from a prison work gang whom he believed had been wrongfully detained and badly treated. His political enfeeblement was complete following his subsequent retirement to distant Griqualand East. Once there, he allegedly survived as a handyman, swept into historical irrelevance by the tremendous forces that Jacobs's seemingly innocent discovery had unleashed.

Enforcing the Law: The Pass System and IDB

Waterboer's rapid decline in fortune illustrates the powerful confluence of international and local, political and economic forces in and around

Kimberley. Yet African mine workers were not nearly as concerned with abstract influences on regional developments as they were with much more immediate, daily challenges, such as the pass system. Instituted in 1872, but initially only laxly enforced, the pass scheme obliged Africans to register upon arriving on the diamond fields. Through the imposition of registration fees, this system was devised to generate revenue. But it also generated cheap labor, as incoming migrants who failed to register were imprisoned and subsequently offered up as convict labor. Not all Africans, though, were subject to the pass system. Exempted were those migrants whom local officials subjectively categorized as "civilized." These fortunate few were educated, often Christian, and displayed "Western" manners, as opposed to "tribal" styles and habits. A commissioner's report from 1876 reveals the divergent treatment that "civilized" and "uncivilized" Africans might receive: "There are many natives, half-castes, and others from the Colony, who are honest, intelligent and respectable men and these must of course be treated in every way similar to the whites, but the great mass of the laboring colored population consists of raw Kaffirs [a disparaging term for black Africans], who come from the interior with every element of barbarism, and no touch of civilization among them. . . . They must be treated as children incapable of governing themselves."[19] Predictably, in this increasingly racist context, the vast majority of migrants were deemed "uncivilized." The mid-1870s also marks the point at which authorities began taking enforcement of the pass system more seriously: pass law arrests jumped from 95 in 1875 to 971 the following year. Police regularly required Africans to produce their passes while in town and often raided areas that featured significant black populations. Although it was impossible to apprehend all offenders owing to the large numbers of Africans present, the unpredictability of these aggressive police tactics created a climate of fear and insecurity. South Africa's "Wild West" finally had its metaphorical sheriff and team of deputies attempting to impose order, though this particular brand of justice was racially tinted.

For all of the energy that was spent enacting and enforcing the pass system, illegal diamond buying and selling (IDB) was of even greater concern for local officials. Despite rampant white involvement in buying, selling, and stealing illicit stones, enforcement policies and practices squarely targeted Africans. Over time, authorities presumed every black resident was involved in IDB in some fashion or another. In practice, the suspicion and racial hostility that eventually precipitated the spate of legal and policing measures intended to curb IDB were evident from the commencement of mining. As early as 1872, for example, white diggers were arguing that Africans should not be allowed to own claims because, as owners, they were legally entitled to sell diamonds. This right could, it was argued, enable Africans to fence diamonds that their black "brothers" (suggesting a racial unity that certainly did not exist at this point, if ever) had stolen, or allegedly would steal, from white claim owners. Although Africans were undoubtedly participating in the outflow of illicit stones in 1872—and well beyond that date—these allegations were clearly racially motivated.

The changing means by which IDB diamonds left Kimberley were well known. Prior to 1875, it was common for a purchaser of stolen diamonds to buy straight from individual mine laborers without the intervention of intermediaries. Going forward, African workers began selling stolen stones, often at rates well below market value, to diamond "touts," who would frequent canteens, compounds, locations, and jails. The stones would subsequently travel up a chain of buyers and sellers, the links of which were most discernible in the early stages, before eventually fading to obscurity. An alternative, and even more devious, system featured the deliberate placement of dishonest African employees in the mines whose sole object was to steal diamonds and bring them to their "real master." It should be noted that regardless of the particular ploy involved, IDB almost always required cooperation across racial lines.

From the 1880s on, the government instituted increasingly aggressive measures to curtail IDB in Kimberley. By this time, the practice had become so regionally prevalent that it was jokingly referred to in both formal and informal settings as "*the* prevailing industry." In response, a Special Court was established in 1880 to handle diamond theft cases. The presiding Special Magistrate could dole out penalties of up to fifteen years imprisonment, fines of £1,000, banishment from Griqualand West and, for black offenders, flogging as well. Two years later, the sweeping Diamond Trade Act upheld an 1880 initiative that introduced trial without jury for IDB defendants. The act also granted law enforcement officers broad search and seizure powers, created an investigative department for IDB activities, and required blacks, if so ordered, to work naked and submit to body searches.

Collectively, these measures turned any presumption of "innocence until proven guilty" on its head, especially as it pertained to Africans in Kimberley. By this time, authorities were taking this form of criminal activity so seriously that when an African curiously known as "Bloody Fool" killed his wife with a crowbar, "the murder was considered secondary to his alleged IDB offense"![20] Each and every African—"civilized," or not—was now presumed to be participating in this parallel, shadow industry. According to the committee that founded Kimberley's IDB investigative force in the 1880s, "Many natives register themselves to Companies for three to six months, simply for the sake of the pass. Having obtained this, they desert, and are allowed to wander under its protection, and, in a majority of cases, to act as middlemen between the white illicit buyer and the raw native."[21] Overlooked by this committee was the fact that rival employers regularly encouraged these "raw" workers to desert in exchange for more favorable conditions and higher wages on offer at *their* operations.

Although Africans were clearly the targets of this series of IDB countermeasures, whites in and around Kimberley were not entirely spared the attentions of the local authorities. For example, the judges presiding over the Special Court periodically invoked the stereotype of the naïve, otherwise honest, African laborer who had been corrupted only after interacting with unscrupulous whites. These Africans were apparently, so the argument went, unable to resist temptation and thus had to be protected by (concerned) whites from themselves. During one trial, for example, a certain Judge Laurence posed the following rhetorical question from the bench: "Do we as a community do all that we might do for the Natives whom we attract here in such large numbers and for whose moral as well as material well-being I think we ought to hold ourselves in some measure responsible?"[22] Most whites, however, merely feigned concern or even contrition following these types of abstract admonishments, while staying safely away from at least the front lines of the illicit diamond trade. White participants in IDB—allegedly including the famous Barnato brothers, who would later become some of the wealthiest and most respected industrialists on the mines—typically purchased stones only after they were well removed from their illicit origins. Local shop owners also benefited from the illegal traffic that these stones generated, even if they weren't actively buying stones. This type of indirect engagement with IDB prompted W. H. Rennie, a Standard Bank inspector in the early years of mining in Kimberley, to comment: "Illicit diamond buying, although being very ruinous to the . . . industry, is remarkably profitable to the storekeepers. It is very rife at present and many hundreds of hands are believed to be engaged in it . . . all of them live in 'good style,' at any rate in an 'expensive style.'"[23] Needless to say, at this time there were no Africans in Kimberley living in either a "good" or an "expensive" style.

Locations and Taxes: Dual Indignities

Foreshadowing the impending adoption of housing in compounds on the mines, local administrators extended the "location" system (which required Africans to reside in specially designated areas) to Kimberley following considerable disquiet in the area, including a revolt in Griqualand West in 1878. This regional unrest convinced these officials, or perhaps simply gave them the pretense that they had been seeking, to herd Africans onto specially demarcated "locations." These areas deliberately featured little or no fertile soil, thereby compelling location residents to seek wage labor on the mines.

The British colonial administration had first proposed the regional implementation of the location system in 1876. Following a subsequent land survey undertaken to demarcate the prospective locations, approximately one-tenth of Griqualand West was earmarked for Africans, while the rest was reserved for whites. Forebodingly, the racist apartheid system that would come into being some decades later in South Africa drew much of its sociogeographical inspiration from these early forms of segregation and discrimination. Each of the proposed locations was intentionally designed to be too small to be self-sufficient and, thus, was intended to serve as a labor reserve for the mining operations, as well as for white farmers newly entering the area, keen to sell their output in and to Kimberley. However, it wasn't until after the 1878 Griqualand Rebellion, a brief, unsuccessful revolt, that the location system could be implemented in Kimberley's agricultural hinterland. Prompted by whites' fears of black uprisings in Griqualand, and beyond, in 1879 the British colonial government extended the Cape Location Acts to Griqualand West. Meanwhile, in Kimberley proper, the Town Council insisted that these measures also be applied to mining operations within the municipality. The formal "localization" of Africans now replaced the de facto segregation that had heretofore characterized Kimberley's human geography.[24] Z. K. Matthews's account of life in "Location Number 2" from the early 1900s reveals how difficult and degrading these sites came to be for Africans:

> The threat of a visit from Bird [the white Location Superintendent] was a real threat. . . . Many a time . . . we knew of the coming of Bird by the blowing of whistles and the sound of running feet in the street outside at dawn. . . . These sounds meant that a pass raid was on. . . . On such mornings one of these

policemen would knock at our door and shout loudly: "Any one here without a pass?" The policemen were Africans but they were rude and brutal. More than once, while we huddled in a corner behind our mother, they took away one of the relatives who would be staying with us before going to work in the diamond mines, and who would not yet have secured the pass that every African needed in order to legalize his presence in the town. . . . Whenever there was a pass raid, panic ran through our house-hold. . . . [Other times] in order to check the passes of the men as they set out for work, the police would take up posts at the main exit streets of the Location before dawn. From our house we could see the knot of uniformed men, and men running past our door in the opposite direction to get away . . . arresting many of them to take them away . . . into the frightening world of the white men. . . . Public toilets were at distant intervals in the streets. There was no system of sewage or garbage disposal, only a great heap in an open space where everyone threw their waste. It grew huge and foul with the passing years.[25]

While the location system pushed Africans onto the mines, a hut tax instituted in 1879 in recently vanquished Griqualand exacerbated existing economic difficulties and, thereby, drove additional residents to participate in the industry as wage laborers. Just a year later, the inspector of locations noted that from Griqualand West "the greater part of the natives proceed to work in Kimberley for three to six months at a time . . . leaving their wives and children to take care of their stock, etc."[26] Thus, just as local headmen, such as Waterboer, had experienced a humiliating loss of control, migrant mine workers came to suffer a comparable degradation. With locations, taxes, and jails now each firmly in place, the stage was set for the emergence of, and eventual domination by, consolidated mining enterprises—a development that would further subjugate African labor.

THE HISTORY of the first decade of diamond mining in South Africa was characterized by unbridled optimism, a massive influx of both regional and more distant labor, racial tension and the attendant erosion of Africans' rights, and the gradual regulation and stabilization of the industry. Although newly enacted legislation helped provide structure to this "Wild West" environment, a handful of white, typically foreign, commercial visionaries were largely responsible for ushering in the next era of diamond mining in the region. While individual black and white diggers contended for access, labor, and profits, these farsighted entrepreneurs were aggressively increasing their control over the mining operations in and around Kimberley. No longer would the industry be composed of a multitude of small-scale claim owners lacking the capital to invest in the requisite equipment to burrow further and further into the earth to extract diamonds. Rather, it would now come to rest in the hands of a few powerful firms that would dictate how labor was recruited and utilized, how the stones would be mined, processed, and sold and, ultimately, how South Africa, and then the continent, and eventually the entire global diamond industry, would evolve. The following chapter examines these developments, which were every bit as dramatic, formative, and far-reaching as the events associated with the first decade of mining had been.

CHAPTER FOUR

Consolidation and Control

The Birth and Growth of the Cartel

> When I am in Kimberley, I often go and sit on the edge of the . . .
> De Beers Mine and I reckon up the value of the diamonds . . . and
> the power conferred by them. Every foot . . . means so much power.
>
> —Cecil Rhodes, De Beers founder, 1891

> It is more than I can bear to think my husband—once a claim
> holder—should have to submit to such indignity . . . (invasive
> searching). . . . The ill effects it would have on our children to see
> their father . . . placed on a level with the natives, who, as a rule, do
> not consider stealing to be a sin. . . . Why place a white man on a
> level with a black?
>
> —From the July 16, 1880, edition of *The Daily Independent*
> (Kimberley) in regards to the proposed searching ordinance

THESE FORMULATIONS tell much of the story of what happens next.
One comes from the power-hungry founder of De Beers, the other from
an exasperated wife of a mine worker. Together, they capture the two main
developments in the rapidly unfolding history of Africa's diamonds: the
consolidation of power within the industry by a handful of elite mining
companies, on one side, and the marginalization of just about everyone else
involved, on the other. Although the wife certainly doesn't come off as an
overly sympathetic figure, Rhodes and his fellow industrialists cared little
about the plight of individual white laborers, and even less about African
workers. Diamonds and the considerable revenues they generated were

now all that mattered. For all the transformation that had occurred in the heart of South Africa over the course of the first decade of mining, these even more revolutionary developments would come to define the next stage in this emerging history.

While both white and black miners were toiling on scattered claims with varying degrees of success, a number of visionary businessmen, including Cecil Rhodes, were steadily increasing their control over the mining industry. In 1876, the existing ten-claim limit was revoked, prying open the gates of the "mineral revolution" to investment capital and thereby paving the way for mine consolidation. Individuals such as Rhodes and Barney Barnato capitalized on the opportunities that the newly liberalized structure presented, aggressively amassing claims and eliminating competition. Capital-poor, white claim owners and semiautonomous African laborers quickly became features of a seemingly distant past, as the industry came to be dominated by a handful of well-funded joint-stock companies—and, eventually, just one: De Beers. This process of consolidation shaped how African labor was procured and managed, how the precious stones were excavated, processed, and marketed and, ultimately, how the global diamond industry would develop.

This chapter traces the key developments in this process, including the conditions and events that facilitated the ascension of De Beers; the increasingly dangerous nature of mining as it moved underground; the further erosion of Africans' legal rights and the attendant, heightened supply and control of laborers, both during the work day and, via the introduction of compounds, "after the whistle blew." The final topic considered is the development of the industry on into the twentieth century, with a focus on De Beers's eventual envelopment of global production as the company transitioned from a regional enterprise into the central, controlling entity of the international diamond cartel. Throughout this process, Africans played vital roles in removing diamonds from the continent's soils—from Sierra Leone, to Tanzania, to South Africa—but because of persistent racism and monopoly capitalism, only a handful of foreign industrialists were able to successfully harness this colossal mineral wealth. The barefaced looting of the continent's diamonds was now well and truly under way.

The Emergence of De Beers: Consolidation and Stabilization

Long before De Beers came to dominate the global diamond industry, the enterprise's very existence depended on a series of propitious circumstances and events, some well-timed entrepreneurism, and aggressive, visionary leadership—in other words, some luck but also a great deal of ability. The initial phase of this process of corporate development lasted approximately twenty years, from the 1867 discovery of the Eureka Diamond until De Beers eventually monopolized the output of the Kimberley mine in 1889. This period saw the regional consolidation of British rule, which compelled an increasing number of Africans, from an ever-expanding geographic area, to seek wage labor on the diamond mines. Meanwhile, the move underground required expensive equipment and significant investment capital. In this scenario, a man needed to have ambition, calculation, vision, and, ultimately, financial backing, in order to succeed. Cecil Rhodes and Barney Barnato were two such men.

Setting the Foundation: An Ideal Set of Circumstances

The new remunerative opportunities in the heart of South Africa "pulled" countless Africans to the mines, while a series of regional events "pushed" many others to Kimberley. Yet coercive measures were also required to ensure that these inflows were not interrupted. Enter the British army, followed by its European counterparts. By the middle of the 1870s, a growing sentiment among both private employers and state officials reasoned that additional areas on the continent should come under British control so as to compel even more Africans into wage labor and, thereby, solve the "native labor problem." For the array of nineteenth-century European imperial powers, including Great Britain, force so often appeared to be the most expedient, effective, and thus attractive course of action. In keeping with this approach, by the end of the decade the British had annexed the Transvaal and fought successful wars against the Xhosa (1877–78), the Pedi (1877–79), and the Zulu (1879); the latter two nations had previously been the most powerful in the subcontinent. With the expansion of British hegemony, these once powerful African states were largely reduced to labor pools.

Following the conclusion of the Berlin Conference in 1884–85, the British continued to forcefully expand and solidify their control in Southern Africa, with the Germans and Portuguese actively "pacifying" the remaining regional populations. Meanwhile, in and around Kimberley, the burgeoning diamond industry had completely consumed all local game, as well any wood utilizable for either timber or charcoal. Collectively, these regional developments drove members of formally independent African communities into the eagerly awaiting arms of mining employers. The mines could now rely on a series of subjugated, geographically diverse labor streams. The "native labor problem" had, at last, been solved.

In order to move forward with the planned exploitation, corporations were needed that could supply the necessary capital to consolidate the scattered claims on the lucrative "dry diggings" sites, profit from economies of scale and employ throngs of workers. Just a short time earlier, Kimberley's "Wild West" environment had appeared unlikely to spawn such large mining enterprises. In 1871, for example, the year that Rhodes arrived from England, thousands of diggers—many of whom didn't even know what a diamond looked like—were working individual claims assisted only by relatives and/or perhaps a handful of African employees. Ironically, the De Beers mine opened the same year that Rhodes arrived. Following the sale of the farm, the original owners of the land, the De Beer brothers, disappear into history, leaving behind only their name and acreage that would, over the forty-three years it was in production, yield some 14.5 million carats worth more than £600 million.

Long before this development, though, the incipient industry remained, like the De Beers's farm, promising, but little more than that. *Diamond Field*, a local newspaper, described this situation in 1872, declaring: "The average digger is getting impoverished, the lately successful one is barely paying expenses, while only the few happy possessors of exceptionally rich claims are coining money." Due to this uncertainty, wool, wheat, wine, hides, copper, and ostrich feathers continued to dominate the Cape economy, whereas investment in mining remained limited. In fact, not until 1880 did diamonds surpass wool in terms of export revenues. By that time, South Africa was generating over three million carats a year, far outpacing Brazil, the previous world leader.

By the 1880s, the deep(er) location of the diamonds necessitated significant amounts of capital to harvest profitably. The principal mines had become massive, deep, open pits requiring costly equipment to haul the soils upward and pump out any obstructive water. In response, capital-rich, joint-stock companies were formed to both provide the requisite funding and manage production. In turn, individual claim holders were squeezed out or relegated to much less bountiful sites. With these "pesky," small-scale competitors out of the way, deep-pocketed industrialists commenced a process of consolidation that would not stop until only a single company remained.

The Magnates

From the early chaos that characterized Kimberley, two individuals emerged to dominate the industry: Barney Barnato and Cecil Rhodes. Commercial success, though, was all that these dueling magnates had in common. Barnato was originally a stage performer who had once starred in his own magic act, playing the role of "The Wizard"—hardly the sort to strike fear in the hearts of his mining competitors. Conversely, Rhodes would go on to become prime minister of the Cape Colony, spearhead British imperial expansion in Southern Africa, have two colonies named after him (Southern and Northern Rhodesia—the modern states of Zimbabwe and Zambia, respectively), and, as part of his last will and testament, establish the prestigious Rhodes Scholarship program. Gardner Williams confirmed that the two colorful characters could not have been less alike. "The little, chunky, bullet-headed, near-sighted Hebrew [Barnato] taking a hand in current sport or traffic, and the tall thoughtful young overseer [Rhodes], sitting moodily on a bucket, deaf to the chatter and rattle around him, and fixing his blue eyes intently on his work or some fabric of his brain, were as unlike as two men could possibly be."[1] Yet their personal ambitions were identical: to amass as much wealth as possible by controlling as much of the South African diamond industry as possible. In the pursuit of this objective, these visionary industrialists were equally as ruthless.

By the time he was just thirty-five years old, Rhodes controlled 90 percent of the world's diamond production. Yet for all of his eventual success, Rhodes began his career in Kimberley rather humbly, renting pumps to diggers to clear away water that blocked access to the soil underneath. Beginning in the 1880s, he began using these earnings to acquire and consolidate claims, eventually securing funding from the venerable Rothschild family to finance more significant purchases. Via these procurements, Rhodes sought to achieve monopolistic control of the local output, which would, in turn, enable him to address the problem of steadily sinking carat prices due to overproduction. Finally, in 1889, he bought out Barnato's rival enterprise for £5,338,650, signing what was, at that time, the largest check ever written. For the check writer himself, the field was now clear of competitors. By controlling the entire output of South Africa's diamond mines, Rhodes could now throttle supply and, if necessary, expand it.

The Evolution of Mining

Well before Rhodes maneuvered De Beers into its commanding position in the industry, mining companies of all sizes operating in Kimberley had been forced to address the immediate problem of how to extract the submerged wealth. As the yields from the richer mines in the dry diggings continued to mount, the potential revenues contained in these diamondiferous soils seemed infinite. The problem, though, which was not inconsiderable, was that these profits were buried deeper and deeper in the ground. Yet the individuals who owned these choice claims, including Barnato and Rhodes, were in an ideal position. They could pay higher wages, hire more workers, mechanize their operations and, thus, reach deeper and deeper points, outperforming—literally outdigging—their competition. The transition to subterranean settings saw manual procedures gradually give way to increasingly mechanized approaches, while operations also became highly organized. This shift to underground mining also delivered new challenges for African laborers, who outnumbered white employees eight to one in "the belly of the earth."

Ever Deeper: The Shifting Mining Process

By the mid- to late 1870s, well-funded operators were beginning to mechanize the highest-yielding mines using steam power, a practice that accelerated significantly into the 1880s. Following the amalgamation of claims, these consolidated mines were increasingly composed of large, deep, open pits rather than clusters of small diggings. As such, they required machinery to both haul the soils to the surface and, just as importantly, pump out floodwater, which could hinder further excavation and also endanger workers. Hundreds of feet down and encircled by the containing walls, or "reef," Africans were employed to remove the earth using an array of tools, including hammers and different types of drills. According to Gardner Williams, "The native workers become very skillful in . . . methods of drilling, and do quite as much work as white men would do under similar conditions."[2] Once the soil was removed, it was initially carted into tubs and subsequently placed in a haulage system, which had been introduced at the Kimberley mine in the mid-1870s. This procedure brought the soil to the surface, at which point workers moved it to sites where it was broken into pieces. Pulverization was initially performed manually, but from the mid-1870s on, large, rotary "washing" machines produced chunks sufficiently small to examine for diamonds. As a by-product of this process, mounds of picked over, discarded soil, known as tailings, became a telltale feature of Kimberley. Despondent residents often re-combed these piles, searching for stones of any size or quality to enable them to secure their next meal. This type of scavenging signaled the deepening marginalization and impoverishment of so many involved in the (otherwise booming) industry.

In 1882, the increasingly aggressive mining companies first attempted underground mining. However, they quickly abandoned this approach because of recurring rock falls, and subsequently suspended it for roughly another two years. In the meantime, horses, mules, and oxen remained operational mainstays at the principal mining enterprises, which included Kimberley Central, Standard Company, the French Company, Victoria Mining Company, Barnato Brothers, and De Beers. The year 1884, however, marked the beginning of the end for open-pit mining, which steadily gave way to underground operations in which vertical shafts were sunk in order to access the depths. This operational development dramatically shaped the mining experience for African laborers, who now endured round-the-clock production and even more precarious and potentially lethal conditions, including underground accidents and a host of respiratory ailments. The move underground was also accompanied by the introduction of more powerful machinery into the hauling and washing processes, though many of the removal methods at the rock face—blasting, (hand)drilling, loading, and tramming—remained the same. Thus African laborers continued to play a central role despite the rapid series of operational and procedural modifications to the mining process.

Accounts from the Field: Writing about "The Abyss"

Just as the many extant letters from the initial "rush" to Kimberley help deepen our understanding of that period, similar accounts from observers during the consolidation phase provide superb insights into the series of briskly unfolding regional developments. By the mid-1880s, for example, Kimberley had become the first South African town lit by electricity; it was also now being served by the Cape Town railway. Letters from the period provide revealing observations about these innovations, as well as the shifting labor process on the mines. For example, an account from 1877 by William Morton offers an illuminative description of mining operations as they stood at the end of that decade, as well as commentary regarding the immensity of the Kimberley mine:

> Before and beneath us lies an abyss—a mighty oval-shaped cauldron, open full to the skies. We look over its edge, down a sheer descent of 200 feet . . . and across from side to side a thousand

feet, or a fifth of a mile. One stands bewildered and a little dazed at the volume of the view, if I may so express it. . . . There are hills higher than the pyramids, but we look upon them unmoved. We are used to the wonders of nature, but we have not seen a creation of human hands of this magnitude. . . . Ten thousand men are working below and around us—five thousand down in the pit and five thousand around its edge. Far below, little black pigmy men—so they seem in the distance—are moving about, but not singly or at random, for closer observation shows that they are working in groups, each group upon a certain well-defined square patch of solid earth, at which they are picking and delving, or walking to and fro over it, carrying little buckets of loosened soil.[3]

A letter from J. X. Merriman to his wife from 1885, almost a decade after Morton's correspondence, provides an updated account of local mining operations and, in particular, the considerable technological progress that had been made since the early days of the industry:

I have just come up from the bowels of the earth in the De Beers Mine. This is a huge pit about 300 feet deep—a yawning chasm: on the edge of this is a wooden kind of trestle 20 feet high over which wires are strained which reach down at a very steep angle some 180 feet into the edge of the crater. Up and down these wires the tubs—huge iron buckets each holding about a ton—are hauled by an engine. We clamber onto the top of the trestle and crawl into the tub, a bell rings and we glide down the wires, suspended in mid-air—thankful to reach the landing-place, from which we transfer ourselves to a sort of cage which goes down into the bowels of the earth another 200 feet, when we come to a great cave where in the dim light of candles miners are working and natives stripped to the skin are filling trucks with the precious . . . rock which contains the diamonds. These trucks run on little tramways under the shaft and are hauled up by the cage, and then emptied into the tub and hauled along the wires. In fact we came down exactly the way a load . . . goes up. After a good look round, I was not sorry to regain the upper air and find myself at the bottom of the trestle on terra firma again. But it was very interesting and is the only example of underground working which has yet succeeded.[4]

Finally, an account by William Crookes from 1908 about his visit to Kimberley five years earlier, provides additional testimony regarding both the increased complexity of the mining process and the ongoing centrality and vitality of African labor:

> In 1903, the Kimberley mine had reached a depth of 2,599 feet. Tunnels are driven from the various shafts at different levels, about 120 feet apart, to cross the mine from west to east. These tunnels are connected by two other tunnels running north and south. The scene belowground in the labyrinth of galleries is be-wildering in its complexity, and very unlike the popular notion of a diamond mine. All below is dirt, mud, grime; half-naked men dark as mahogany, lithe as athletes, dripping with perspiration, are seen in every direction, hammering, picking, shoveling, wheeling the trucks to and fro, keeping up a weird chant which rises in force and rhythm when a greater task calls for excessive muscular strain. The whole scene is more suggestive of a coal mine than of a diamond mine . . . all this mighty organization— this strenuous expenditure of energy, this costly machinery, this ceaseless toil of skilled and black labor.[5]

New Dangers Below

African laborers daily faced the prospect of occupational injury, disease, or even death—both above and below ground—in great part because of racially based corporate negligence and indifference. Prior to the move underground, for example, the reef regularly collapsed, which both crippled surface operations and injured, often severely, those African employees who worked them. Even after the transition to underground mining, fitfully from 1884 to 1888 and, thereafter, almost completely at both the Kimberley and De Beers mines, a sizable number of Africans continued to work on the surface and thus remained vulnerable to collapses. Moreover, both surface and underground workers were victimized by careless treatment of the explosives that were utilized to loosen deposits. For example, a dynamite accident in the De Beers mine in January 1884 killed three African laborers. Despite mine inspectors' concerns regarding companies' "abuse of dynamite," no investigation was ever conducted. Going forward, although the full-scale move underground may have caused the unpredictable reef to fade as a concern for mine workers, this operational shift generated an array of new threats. In 1888, for example, a fire in a De Beers mine shaft killed more than 200 employees (including 178 Africans) owing to poor ventilation and the absence of any escape routes. Again, the emerging diamond enterprise eluded prosecution.

Laborers who were lucky enough to avoid these threats to life and limb still risked contracting any one of an assortment of potentially lethal diseases. In fact, among African mine workers, it was one of these afflictions, pneumonia, which was the primary cause of death—not occupational accidents. Surpassing poor sanitation as the root of the major causes of death by the late 1880s, pneumonia was prevalent among those workers who spent long hours in inadequately ventilated mines. As part of a broader labor welfare initiative, in 1893 De Beers finally responded by reducing the number of working hours for its underground employees: three eight-hour shifts replaced the alternating thirteen-hour "night" and "day" shifts. But, the reduction in exposure did little to drive down affliction and mortality rates, in great part because medical facilities for African laborers remained poor or even nonexistent at this time. Instead, most employers preferred to procure new workers rather than pay for their existing ones to receive medical treatment.

African mine workers were also subject to corporal abuse, a form of pain and suffering from which white employees were exempted. For as long as Africans had been present on the mines, white overseers had been doling out physical abuse to motivate workers, to deter or punish diamond theft or, at times, simply arbitrarily. In January 1872, the *Diamond Field* newspaper included a report on a fatality stemming from physical abuse. Apparently, a white digger, "feeling indignant and disgusted at the laziness exhibited by his . . . (African) labourer, proceeded to kick him on the part set aside for such favours. . . . To his astonishment, from the rag which forms the only article of dress the Zulus luxuriate in, out rolled a sixty carat diamond. The digger at once made a prisoner of the black scoundrel, and tied him by the neck . . . to a pole, while he went to call for assistance. When he returned, the native was found lying dead at the bottom of the claim."[6] Later that year, another local paper, the *Diamond News,* ran an article titled "A New Way of Punishing Natives," in which a digger removed a black worker's teeth and lacerated his lips and gums using a pair of carpenter's pincers on account of the latter's alleged pilferage of a diamond. Although these cases may have been extreme examples, during these initial decades of mining, corporal abuse was unquestionably part and parcel of the daily experience for African laborers.

Only gradually did these employment hazards recede for African mine workers. Combining to reduce fatalities from industrial accidents were increased regulation and heightened managerial concern, as well as lessons (lethally) learned. Of course, work-site perils didn't disappear entirely. As mining depths began to exceed 1,000 feet, mud rushes constituted a new danger, which increasingly struck De Beers's underground galleries. For example, in May 1898, a rush occurred at the 1,120-foot level, which barely spared the lives of a large number of African workers. According to Gardner Williams:

> On this occasion "Jim" . . . was almost buried alive with his gang of 15 men. The rush shut this working party up in a narrow passage on this level for more than 64 hours. When the men were rescued at length from their stifling quarters, where they were imprisoned for more than two and a half days, without a morsel of food to eat or a drop of water to drink, all were greatly exhausted, as might be supposed. But in spite of his sufferings, the brave leader, Jim, went back at once into the mine to grope back over the mud in search of one of his gang whom he supposed was missing, and he would not return to the surface until he learned beyond doubt that all had been rescued.[7]

Thankfully for both management and underground labor forces, these types of calamities decreased over time, while the overall safety records of the mines improved—greatly reducing the need for employee heroics, such as those that Jim had displayed. Yet even if Africans were less likely to perish or incur injuries, the daily labor process remained as demanding as ever. Moreover, the profits derived from these efforts continued to flow disproportionately to the owners of the mines—the individuals who experienced the very lowest levels of physical risk.

The Expanding Supply of African Labor

Undaunted by the challenging conditions on the mines and faced with a host of rural pressures, African migrant laborers from throughout the subcontinent continued to pour into Kimberley. Once there, they were forced to engage with the emerging diamond enterprises on increasingly unfavorable terms. Pushed out of rural areas due to tightening racist legislation, hostile white encroachment, and a shrinking number of livelihood options, these African migrant flows rarely waned. Once hired, these employees constituted a dependable, durable labor force. Enjoying this vital influx of labor and keen to end the turnover that had characterized African workforces during the first decade and a half of mining, the fledgling mining companies sought to heighten their control over both the supply and cost of African labor. In 1885 and 1886, for example, the largest operations began hiring only formally recruited laborers, that is, those who were furnished by either rural chiefs or established labor agents. Many of these recruits worked longer contracts (six to twelve months, as opposed to the traditional three to six) and accepted wages that amounted to only half of what had formerly been paid out. Following amalgamation, fewer and fewer potential employers existed, and, therefore, African migrants were increasingly obliged to accept these unfavorable terms. In the early twentieth century, one De Beers manager went so far as to blithely explain that "the natives have been compelled by starvation to seek work." Apparently, Africans' motivations for seeking wage labor were of little concern to company officials at these emerging enterprises.

The Cheapest Workforce: Convict Labor

Although flows of desperate migrants streaming into Kimberley constituted an ideal labor supply, the utilization of convicts for mine work was even more appealing. Due to onerous legislation, summary trials, and a wide range of criminalized activity, Kimberley's jail featured, by far, the largest inmate population in the Cape Colony. With a daily average of 658 occupants, it held seven times more inmates than Cape Town's jail. From 1884, the year in which De Beers initially negotiated with the state to use convict labor, until the discontinuance of this practice in 1932, this arrangement served both the company and the government extremely well.

The mining enterprise received these inmates' labor via the De Beers Company Branch Convict Station, which both relieved the state of its responsibilities to house and feed them and also granted it a small sum in exchange for the provision of each individual. A report on the practice from 1890 estimated that this scheme was earning the Cape government roughly £1,000 per year. As such, in 1905, for example, the state increased the population at the De Beers Convict Station by an additional 1,200 inmates, two-thirds of whom had been sentenced for stock theft elsewhere in the colony. Although the old adage that "crime doesn't pay" certainly held for these convicts, for the state, criminal activity had never been so profitable.

The system also worked quite well for De Beers, as the company subjected thousands of these workers to longer shifts—sunrise to sunset—all without pay. Moreover, Gardner Williams explained: "We can depend on convict labour and it is always at hand. They cannot get away like ordinary labourers. We can also prevent theft better than with free boys. If the latter attempt to escape you cannot shoot them, whereas . . . Government officials can shoot a convict if he attempts to escape."[8] Although contemporary readers may well find Williams's callous rationalization disturbing, it certainly reflected the prevailing sentiments within the industry at the time he expressed it. Meanwhile, even for transgressions less extreme than flight, including perceived idleness or acquiring "forbidden articles" (e.g., tobacco), convicts could still expect to be whipped. In practice, these inmate laborers were punished twice as often as were convicts anywhere else in the Cape. They also occasionally found themselves placed in a set of stocks—a rather anachronistic penal device, and the only set permitted in the colony—for three hours a day, two to three days at a time. Due to local authorities' deep indifference toward these "criminals," these unfortunate individuals were denied even the most basic rights the moment they entered this punitive system.

The Ultimate Form of Labor Control: The Compound System

While African mine workers endured myriad forms of both informal and institutionalized racism, occupational prejudice came into sharpest relief in the mid-1880s with the implementation of the compound housing system. In practice, labor control had always been a goal for mining employers, but as the diggings became increasingly industrialized and systematic, mine owners desperately needed a fully reliable workforce. The changing nature of the mining process, in turn, prompted adjustments in the ways that companies organized and managed their African laborers, both above and below ground.

"Closed compounds" first appeared on the corporate mines of Kimberley Central and the French Company in 1885, followed shortly thereafter by De Beers, and by 1889 housed all 10,000 African employees (figure 5). Following the consolidation of the mines and the move underground, the latter of which more than doubled production costs, the new corporate operations

FIGURE 5. De Beers compound, 1880s. From Gardner F. Williams, *The Diamond Mines of South Africa: Some Account of Their Rise and Development* (London: Macmillan, 1902), 415

required a dependable, regimented labor force, which the compounds guaranteed. This accommodations system virtually imprisoned African employees for the duration of their contracts, permitting movement only between two highly secured spaces: the mine and the compound. Furthermore, in the name of combating diamond theft, African workers were subjected to invasive strip searches as they moved between spaces within this closed system. Although white employees were also actively involved in IDB, they were able to avoid these humiliating measures through rigorous protestations, such as the sentiments expressed by the distraught wife that appeared at the onset of this chapter. The diamond companies' capitulation further reinforced the racial divide within the industry. From the 1880s forward, whites served almost exclusively as managers or supervisors, whereas blacks were excluded from these types of positions for many decades to come.

The compounds themselves, though highly touted by the mining companies, were acutely overcrowded spaces, housing thousands of men in large, open barracks. These conditions fostered agitation and regular, violent manifestations of this tension—often along ethnic lines. Yet, as a labor control tool, the compound system was undeniably effective, and thus a number of mining operations elsewhere on the continent adopted elements of this housing strategy, or even the entire approach, wholesale. Again, developments in the heart of South Africa in the late nineteenth century were to have both enduring and widespread ramifications.

A Prison by Any Other Name

The fact that the closed compound was modeled on the De Beers Convict Station tells us all that we really need to know: these accommodations were little more than repackaged prisons. With Africans concentrated in fewer, if larger, compounds over time, overcrowding exacerbated already challenging conditions. In addition to fostering both tension and morbidity, this housing system also facilitated the spread of disease. Although incoming recruits who were patently ill were either denied employment or quarantined, the compounds' drafty and cool conditions resulted in innumerable illnesses, many fatal, for those men approved for mine service. For example, in 1884, Dennis Doyle, Kimberley's sanitary inspector, estimated that an alarming 1 in 15 Africans living in the compounds in the latter part of the previous year was sick, whereas among night-soil collectors, the *otherwise* unhealthiest job in Kimberley, the figure was 1 in 199. The deadliest afflictions were pulmonary in nature, including bronchitis, pneumonia, tuberculosis, and pleurisy. In the compounds, as in the mines, pneumonia was the most lethal, accounting for as much as 75 percent of African mortality, including outbreaks in 1892 and 1893 and a severe occurrence in 1897. This disease was also primarily responsible for a death rate for Africans in Kimberley of 41 per 1,000 in 1891 and 55 per 1,000 in 1892, which was 50 percent higher than the municipality's rate for whites and double that of urban black communities elsewhere in the Cape Colony.[9] In 1900, a resident physician, Dr. Stoney, opined that this disease "will continue to be our most serious cause of death . . . so long as overcrowding in the compounds continues."[10] These conditions were so appalling that J. X. Merriman had earlier (in 1886) written to his wife that "some compounds we saw are . . . a disgrace to humanity. No wonder the poor brutes steal—and no wonder that a curse seems to rest on the industry. If you treat human beings like brutes they must and will behave as such."[11]

Although for many years De Beers's management paid little attention to concerns such as Stoney's and criticism such as Merriman's, by 1903 the severe health and social problems in the compounds had prompted the company to upgrade these spaces. In turn, these improvements roughly halved mortality rates during the ensuing decade. Moreover, these belated "sites of social welfare" soon came to be considered "model," with other mining operations from both within South Africa and further abroad regularly sending managerial staff to tour them. An account by William Crookes from 1906 provides some insight, albeit inflected with racist terms, into Africans' lives in these modified spaces:

> One Sunday . . . my wife and I walked unattended about the compound, almost the only whites present among 1,700 natives. At one part a Kaffir was making a pair of trousers with a . . . sewing-machine, in which he had invested his savings. Next to him, a "boy" was reading from the Testament in his own language to an attentive audience. In a corner, a party were engaged in cooking a savory mess in an iron pot; and, further on, the orchestra was tuning up, and Zulus were putting the finishing-touches to their toilet of feathers and beads. One group was intently watching a . . . game. It is played by two sides, with stones and grooves and hollows in the ground, and appears to be of most absorbing interest.[12]

So as to provide constructive outlets for workers' frustrations, De Beers ensured that churches and missionaries were consistent features in its compounds, with Bibles furnished in a number of local languages. These clergy, however, also actively promoted hard work, temperance, punctuality, and deference to authority as the earthly route to salvation. Their ability to map out this behavioral path to the "Promised Land" rendered these company-friendly men of the cloth better positioned to motivate reverent members of the African labor force than even the most persuasive mine managers. Furthermore, the missionaries suggested that those workers who had died or been injured on the job were receiving their just punishments from "the Almighty" due to their "obvious," though unidentified, sins. Given these sentiments, it's not surprising that the following passage appeared in a 1906 copy of *Outlook,* the famous Christian mission organ: "The De Beers Company have set an example of just and reasonable treatment of their Native employees, which might with advantage be followed at other South African labour centres. What has been done at Kimberley could be done elsewhere and it is unfortunate that in other great labour centres the employers do not take the same view of their responsibilities."[13] In the eyes of at least some within the church, it seems as if the diamond enterprise had become something of a "higher power."

De Beers also offered post-shift recreational activities so that workers could physically "blow off steam." These outlets included a swimming pool in its West End Compound, as well as open spaces for activities of all sorts, which were most pronounced on Sundays, workers' day off. Compound residents also engaged in a range of other recreational endeavors, including drinking beer (spirits were forbidden, as were playing cards and all books except Bibles and hymnals), smoking *dagga* (a similarly calming, though less potent form of marijuana also used to treat a variety of ailments), singing and drumming, often along ethnic lines. Still others augmented their wages by serving as tailors and barbers and, before De Beers began supplying rations in 1896, as cooks. Predicated on these "freedoms" that workers enjoyed, in 1888 Gardner Williams boasted that "our natives are better housed and . . . fed than the uncompounded natives, and are better paid than miners in many . . . European countries," though he failed to identify any of these allegedly penny-pinching nations to the north.[14]

For all of the structural improvements De Beers made, and constructive outlets it provided, the compounds remained virtual jails. According to Z. K. Matthews, writing about this form of housing in the early twentieth century, "My father, at the time I was born, was serving a term in a Kimberley mine, which meant that he remained within the compound for at least six months, never emerging until his term was over. Once a month he could come to the gate to see relatives, but at a distance across a fence, as in a prison."[15] Only in the mid-1970s—almost a century after compounds were initially introduced—would De Beers finally open up its workers' accommodations, thereby enabling its African laborers to come and go: the ultimate freedom.

African Labor Strategies and Unrest

African diamond miners daily negotiated an array of challenging working and living conditions, and, from 1883, degrading searches in the name of IDB suppression, but they did not endure this fate passively. Although militant unionism was absent, labor strikes, slowdowns, refusals to work and smuggling (typically taking diamonds out and bringing "Cape brandy" and other contraband in) continued apace. In the early years of underground mining, some Africans even assaulted white overseers after dimming the lights, often in retaliation for physical, at times even fatal, abuse at the hands of these bosses. Other times, African workers employed much less confrontational strategies, for example by pooling wages to purchase food, sharing cooking duties, or voicing complaints in the hopes that company officials would address their concerns. De Beers tolerated minor transgressions of its policies, though it reacted harshly to any activities that threatened its control and, therefore, its revenues. Irrespective of the divergent levels of risk associated with these various activities, Africans consistently and creatively sought to improve their working conditions.

Africans' strategic action most fraught with risk was, ironically, inaction—a refusal to work. In response to this endeavor, whether it took the form of a widespread, formal strike or entailed a much smaller number of individuals, mining companies invariably countered with force, though they also occasionally made small concessions. As could be expected, the grievances that sparked these instances of labor dissent were typically associated with wages, occupational safety, or some other aspect of the overall working and living conditions. On January 17, 1885, for example, as the French Company moved one hundred of its African workers into a compound, black employees protested and the alleged "ringleaders" were "quickly placed beyond the enclosure." Going forward, African mine workers launched a formal strike—possibly the first by laborers of any sort in South Africa's history—on April 5, 1887, over the use of the speculum, an instrument used for detecting diamonds concealed in the rectum. If ever a labor protest required neither explanation nor justification, surely this was the one.

Over the ensuing decades, workers continued to periodically engage in strikes, all of which were violently suppressed, with "dissident" participants punished and banned from reemployment. In a case from the 1890s, for example, a group of roughly twenty laborers refused to work in an underground location they deemed highly unsafe. Consequently, Charles Riordan, the head guard of the West End compound, flogged the members of this team and confined them to a detention cell for five days before ultimately dismissing them. A week later, "the scars and wounds were still raw and about four inches in length."[16]

At times, African laborers also articulated their concerns instead of resorting to more extreme measures. In one such case at De Beers prior to the turn of the twentieth century, more than fifty African employees insisted that, among other things, the company cease conducting invasive searches. In particular, they objected to the enterprise's practice of locking up Africans whose contracts were concluding for a period of days with fingerless, leather gloves chained to their hands, and examining their stool for swallowed diamonds. Even the speculum may have been less objectionable.

The Kimberley Native Affairs inspector agreed with these workers that this anti-IDB measure was "humiliating," yet there is no evidence of any redress.[17] White employees were, of course, exempted from this degrading set of procedures.

Challenges, Successes, and Dominance: De Beers into the Twentieth Century

The twentieth century witnessed one of the most remarkable monopolizations of an industry in the history of international commerce. From its origins as a single-source producer, De Beers steadily expanded its operations, first regionally and then globally. The enterprise's administrators relentlessly sought to capture the output of emerging mines elsewhere on the continent and, ultimately, abroad. The company then funneled these stones through a single selling channel that it had, itself, earlier introduced. This transition to a vertical enterprise enabled De Beers to enjoy a virtual monopoly on both production and marketing and, thus, to dictate supply. Firmly in control of supply, the company was also able to manipulate demand through a series of highly effective advertising campaigns that both opened up new markets and expanded existing ones. At the heart of De Beers's global marketing was the suggestion that these gemstones are extremely scarce, although diamonds are, in fact, not rare at all. De Beers created this artificial scarcity simply by limiting the number of stones that reached the market, and keeping this trade secret safely to themselves. As De Beers's long-standing director Sir David Harris once warned: "For goodness' sake, keep out of the newspapers and Parliament the quantity of diamonds that can be produced."[18]

For all of its storied corporate accomplishments, the success of the De Beers company was neither inevitable nor devoid of challenges. Well before the enterprise could expand its operations, it needed copious African laborers to service its landmark mines in South Africa. Going forward, the company would also encounter a series of formidable domestic and external challenges associated with its meteoric ascension—some foreseeable, others unanticipated. In fact, De Beers was, itself, taken over in the 1920s by the Anglo American Corporation, which was piloted at that time by its founder, the astute, calculating, and determined Sir Ernest Oppenheimer. Had Oppenheimer not opted to leave this acquisition largely intact and retain the esteemed De Beers name, the story of this fabled diamond company would be significantly shorter.

The Supply of African Labor

Over time, De Beers phased out many of the degrading practices described earlier in the chapter and phased in a range of employee benefits. It consequently became a desirable destination for African workers, at least relative to other opportunities for work and remuneration, and helped the company achieve stability in this vital aspect of its operations. Yet as with the company's eventual industry dominance, an initial uncertainty characterized the supply of sufficient numbers of African workers.

The South African, or (Second) Boer War (1899–1902), which pitted the British against the Boers and included mineral rights and access to the contested deposits among its multiple causes, created a severe labor shortage for the mines and prompted De Beers to hire costly recruiters, launch its own employment bureau, and offer improved wages for drillers. Only gradually would the supply of African labor return to its preconflict rates.

In the early twentieth century, the sources of indigenous labor remained consistent, with ethnic Tswana, Sotho, Xhosa, Tsonga, and Zulu well represented on the mines. Although static for some decades, the monthly wages on offer, at between £3 and £5, were more than twice the rate necessary to attract these regional, unskilled laborers, even as the development of South Africa's gold-mining industry on the Rand spawned competition for these migrants' services. In justifying the lack of upward movement in AfricanΔ laborers' wages, De Beers's assistant general manager, I. R. Grimmer, explained the predominant view of a "target" worker: "The native comes here with the idea of making a certain amount of money. For instance, he does not look at it in quite the same way as a white man. He would not take into consideration the number of hours he has to work in the week, but he would calculate how much money he would get at the end of the week, and he would make up his mind that he would take a certain amount of money home, and would feed himself accordingly."[19] Although Grimmer's declarations are certainly questionable, Africans did keep coming, despite the flat wages.

By the early twentieth century, the annual recruitment and registration of workers at Kimberley had reached approximately 85,000, though the industry was still experiencing high turnover. In 1904, Williams commented that the market for labor remained "peculiar, owing to the fact that as soon as the rains come, a large percentage of the natives wish to return home to plough their lands."[20] Harvest time prompted a similar exodus. Clearly, many Africans remained economically linked to their home areas, comprising a sizable, partially autonomous segment of the broader workforce.

In the 1930s, De Beers, like so many other corporations worldwide, suffered during the Great Depression. The company responded to the drastically reduced global demand for diamonds by slashing production, which meant laying off thousands of African employees. While white staff members were largely able to weather the financial storm due to corporate paternalism, apprenticeship opportunities, and the possibility of securing employment on the gold mines (due to simultaneously ascending gold prices), most black Africans found themselves without work.

Only following the Second World War, did the diamond industry rebound and once again require large numbers of African laborers. These employees were rewarded with salaries that were among the highest for black workers anywhere in South Africa, and twice what an African gold miner earned. De Beers also phased in pension and insurance plans, thereby ensuring a steady flow of labor to the mines and the regular, voluntary renewal of contracts. In fact, many African laborers remained with the company their entire professional lives. Even into retirement, they relied on pensions paid out at 60 percent of their most recent average earnings, leaving them with higher incomes than most working black South Africans.

Irrespective of these employment benefits, from 1949 to 1994 the already challenging nature of this occupation was exacerbated due to apartheid, the system of racial segregation that shrouded South Africa. Throughout this period, black workers continued to perform the most dangerous tasks on the mines but earned only roughly a third of what white De Beers employees made. In many respects, retreating to the bowels of the earth was only slightly more disagreeable than negotiating the oppressive environment on the surface.

Corporate Challenges along the Way to the Top, and Once There

In addition to endeavoring to secure a dependable supply of African labor, De Beers faced a host of other challenges, both domestic and foreign. Although the strategic actions that the company took in response to developments within South Africa were instrumental to its success, De Beers's aggressive (re)actions toward proceedings beyond the country's borders were just as crucial to maintaining its industry domination. Over the course of the company's reign, it exercised virtual monopolistic control via several strategies, including convincing—often with considerable pressure—producers to join its single-channel selling scheme; flooding the market with stones that resembled the output of producers who were reluctant to join the cartel; and stockpiling rough stones in order to limit their supply, and thereby manipulate the per-carat price of a diamond. De Beers's approach was so aggressive that it ran afoul of American antitrust laws aimed at preventing monopoly; from 1948 to 2012, the company was banned from directly engaging in commerce in the United States, nor could its executives travel there on business. Yet, De Beers wouldn't be the household name that it is had it not adopted the ruthless business tactics that prompted these punitive measures and coupled them with brilliant marketing strategies to both manufacture demand and manipulate taste. The enterprise's monopolistic practices notwithstanding, De Beers's dominance was regularly threatened, most often by new deposits unearthed in South Africa, elsewhere on the continent or, eventually, further afield. For De Beers, each new find rendered diamonds less rare and potentially jeopardized the company's monopoly.

In fact, during Ernest Oppenheimer's directorship (ending with his death in 1957), De Beers never deliberately discovered a diamond deposit. Quite simply, there was no point in investing in prospecting since the company was not interested in identifying new sources of stones, only to be obliged to absorb the output from any new deposits in order to maintain the "scarcity" that it had so carefully engineered. As Rhodes had once presciently declared: "Our only risk is the sudden discovery of new mines, which human nature will work recklessly to the detriment of us all."[21] Of course, for Rhodes, the terms "our" and "us" referred to De Beers and, to a lesser extent, other industry entities; conversely, for the diamond-buying public, the excavation of new deposits wouldn't be detrimental at all—quite the opposite, in fact. Eventually, major, transformative discoveries were made, namely in Russia, Australia, and Canada. Although De Beers had remarkably maintained its near monopoly for decades, over time a growing number of competitors, from Africa and beyond, opted not to join the cartel. Eventually, their disinclination prompted De Beers to abandon the long-standing business model that had served the company so very well.

Threats from Within: Early Domestic Dangers

Perhaps no threat was more serious to the company's survival in its early years of operations than the siege of Kimberley, during the opening rounds of the South African War (1899–1902). At the onset of the Boers' four-month onslaught, Rhodes boldly moved into the city in order to pressure the British to focus on breaking the blockade, rather than on more strategic military objectives. Beyond simply requesting help, though, the assertive leader of De Beers took an active role in the struggle by placing the company's resources at the disposal of the defenders. He also ordered the manufacture of shells, an armored train, and a gun, fittingly named "Long Cecil," in De Beers's workshops.[22]

In 1902, just weeks prior to the end of the conflict, the talismanic founder of De Beers died, leaving behind an enterprise that controlled a remarkable 90 percent of the world's diamond production. Yet a challenge that materialized that same year would shake the very foundations of Rhodes's company. Henry Ward, the owner of Cullinan (or Premier) Mine, which had just come on line in South Africa, refused to join the De Beers cartel, opting instead to sell to Bernard and Ernest Oppenheimer—a pair of independent diamond dealers whose names in the industry would not soon be forgotten. Although an assortment of smaller mines, including alluvial operations both within and beyond South Africa, continued to operate outside the cartel, a competitor of this magnitude hadn't existed since Barney Barnato. Cullinan's production soon matched De Beers's entire output, while also generating in 1905, at 3,106 carats, the largest gem-quality stone ever discovered: the Cullinan Diamond. Despite protracted negotiations over Cullinan's output, only during the First World War was De Beers finally able to assume control of the mine.

Rhodes's Dream Dashed: Regional Trouble, a Costly Decision, and Eventual Absorption

Even as the Cullinan crisis was unfolding, De Beers was busy contending with an even more serious development—one which eventually led to its absorption by Anglo American. This challenge, unlike the one from Cullinan, came from beyond South Africa's borders, in the adjacent German colony of South West Africa (Namibia). In 1908, promising alluvial deposits had been discovered in that territory. However, having just endured a global depression, De Beers was loath to invest in the companies that had been formed to mine these new discoveries. Although De Beers had made remarkably few mistakes during its ascendancy, this decision was particularly costly, as these deposits proved to be extremely bountiful. With De Beers taking a pass, it was the enterprise's eventual acquirer, Anglo American, that would negotiate the purchase of these lucrative mines. Under the direction of its founder, Ernest Oppenheimer, who had transitioned from independent dealer to mining executive, Anglo also succeeded in securing exclusive contracts in the 1920s to purchase the output from mining operations elsewhere on the continent. These locations included the Belgian Congo (a key source for industrial-grade diamonds) and Angola, as well as recently opened mines within South Africa (at Lichtenberg and Namaqualand). In turn, this series of procurement arrangements further dented De Beers's already teetering monopoly. Collectively, these tactical moves paved the way for Anglo to become the majority stakeholder in De Beers and to build a new, more geographically expansive monopoly on the foundations of the original one, while retaining the De Beers name. Although this titular retention was testament to Rhodes's earlier, extraordinary success, the De Beers's founder was surely writhing in his final resting place, knowing that the corporate giant that he had conceived and reared from its infancy no longer called the shots in the global diamond industry.

New Initiatives and New Challenges: The Ernest Oppenheimer Era

Rarely idle, Ernest Oppenheimer understood well that maintaining a monopoly requires relentless effort, adaptation, and ingenuity. In 1930, De Beers launched a series of revolutionary marketing initiatives under the umbrella of the Central Selling Organization (CSO). This entity replaced the London Syndicate of merchants and buyers, to which De Beers had been exclusively selling since 1889. Under the new scheme, all rough diamonds were funneled through a single channel that extended from the initial purchase of newly unearthed stones to the sale of these gems to dealers at "sights." It also provided minimum sales and price guarantees to the array of companies involved. Notwithstanding this extremely successful, vertical initiative, the Great Depression rendered the 1930s an extremely challenging decade for the enterprise. De Beers cut production and closed all of its premier mines in South Africa and Namibia, while it was forced to stockpile the output it was contractually obligated to purchase from operations elsewhere. During this trying period, only Anglo American's financial might and the novel demand for industrial diamonds, which were vital to the construction of the mounting global war machines, kept De Beers afloat.

Emerging from the end of the Depression and the ensuing Second World War, De Beers was determined to reenergize sales. To this end, its ongoing invention of the rarity and value of diamonds was complemented by a brilliant marketing campaign that convinced consumers worldwide that these stones were essential symbols of esteem and success. Indeed, the popular desire to own a diamond can roughly be traced back to a slogan that most readers will instantly recognize: "A Diamond Is Forever." What these four seemingly simple words convey(ed) is actually a highly loaded message, while their remarkable endurance isn't merely a case of good fortune. In practice, the durable slogan is intended to render diamonds fundamental to any formal expressions of romance and, ultimately, love; to suggest that diamonds never lose their value; and to convince purchasers that the stones should never be resold (else the price *would* plummet, though De Beers opted not to divulge this important detail). Men had to be convinced diamonds were the only acceptable expression of their love, women needed to insist upon them, even if only passively, and once purchased, these stones were to be retained . . . forever. In 1947, the New York advertising agency N. W. Ayer & Son coined the slogan for De Beers, which had earlier inquired of Ayer if "the use of propaganda" might help boost American sales. The diamond enterprise quickly adopted this bit of "propaganda" as its official motto. Its creator was Frances Gerety, a copywriter, who struggled under the glass ceiling and would only decades later receive the public credit she was due. By 1979, this extraordinarily effective marketing had helped the industry leader expand its US sales to more than $2.1 billion, compared with only $23 million in 1939—an increase of nearly a hundredfold. Thus it's small wonder that in 2000, *Advertising Age* magazine named "A Diamond Is Forever" the best advertising slogan of the twentieth century.

Perhaps even more remarkable than De Beers's success in cultivating demand in the American market was its success in postwar Japan. No tradition of purchasing engagement rings existed in the Asian nation, unlike in the United States. In fact, Japanese conjugal customs featured scant romance, courtship, or seduction, as most marriages were arranged and were consummated simply by sharing a drink of rice wine from the same bowl. To overcome these formidable obstacles, the advertising agency that De Beers hired to tap this market, J. Walter Thompson, launched a campaign in 1967 that strongly associated diamonds with modern Western values, fashions, and customs. In short, these stones were to symbolize an important transition into modern life. And, based on sales, it seems that many Japanese were eager to make this transition. Within five years, over 25 percent of all women received a diamond engagement ring, up from less than 5 percent prior to the launch of the campaign. By 1978, half of all married

Japanese women wore a diamond. In little more than a decade, diamonds had become an integral component of the engagement process, and Japan had consequently become the second largest market (behind only the United States) for diamond engagement rings.[23] Not only had De Beers's marketing been able to generate consumer demand where none had previously existed, it had also, in the process, transformed long-standing, deeply embedded cultural traditions. Seemingly, only a diamond is *truly* forever.

In conjunction with De Beers's global marketing initiatives, Oppenheimer skillfully positioned the company to bring new sources of rough diamonds, including the Gold Coast (Ghana) and Sierra Leone, into the single channel. The discovery of significant deposits in the British colony of Tanganyika (Tanzania), however, proved to be an entirely different matter. The massive Mwadui kimberlite pipe was first discovered by Dr. John Williamson, a Canadian geologist, in March 1940, and by 1942 he had incorporated Williamson Diamonds Ltd. Sensing the enormity of this discovery, De Beers attempted to bring this new stream into the CSO, while also trying to buy the mine outright. It's important to note that, for De Beers, the maintenance of its monopoly was far more important than the money it might have to outlay to purchase these deposits. Regardless, both Williamson and the colonial authorities, eager to maintain control of these resources, were not to be pressured, or at least not immediately. Only in 1947 did these parties agree to enter the De Beers fold, thereby ensuring that this output was sold exclusively through the CSO, at agreed-upon prices.

The contentious nature of this relationship did not, however, simply end with the adoption of this agreement. Indeed, although the Tanganyikan mines had produced 195,000 carats in 1949, by 1951 none of this output was being sold. Following a price dispute with De Beers, Williamson had, instead, opted to stockpile the diamonds. Although the discontented owner was not contractually permitted to sell his output to any other prospective buyer(s), he maintained that he was, in fact, not obligated to sell any stones at all. The brash Canadian was clearly not reading from the well-established industry script. Even more troubling for De Beers were Williamson's other initiatives, which included open flirtation with Jolis and Harry Winston, American diamond dealers who were attempting to gain control of this production; threats to release his formidable stockpile of diamonds out onto the market, which would have lowered the global per-carat price and which did lower De Beers's share price; and, finally, the fact that the contract with the Tanganyikan operation was set to expire in 1951. However, the governments in Dar es Salaam and London, both of whom were feeling the pain of lost revenues, finally intervened. These administrations pressured the parties to sign a new agreement in 1952, and another in 1956, each of which was increasingly favorable for Williamson. Only in 1958, with the death of the "rogue" Canadian, did De Beers finally purchase the mine outright, before ultimately selling an equal stake in it to the colonial state. Despite the considerable delay, frustration, and lost revenue that the company had endured, De Beers was ultimately successful in ensuring that this production stayed within the cartel's single channel.

Unlikely Partners: The Politics of Monopoly

Even before De Beers fully resolved the predicament in Tanganyika, the discovery of diamonds in the Soviet Union in 1954 had delivered yet another major challenge. Many foreign observers, including the Soviets, considered De Beers, which was derisively referred to as "South Africa, Inc.," inseparable from the country's racist regime. Although Ernest Oppenheimer's son, and corporate successor, Harry, had been a consistent voice against apartheid, the company was largely unable to dispel these external notions. Given the Soviet Union's exaltation of workers' rights and its courting of nationalist movements throughout Africa, it seemed an unlikely partner for De Beers. Yet as with other finds, it was imperative for De Beers to bring the USSR's output into the CSO. In fact, in this case it was vital for the company, as the Siberian stones were high-grade, even if extremely small in size, and instantly constituted up to 20 percent of the world's gem-quality diamonds. For their part, the Soviets understood that an agreement would ultimately be in their best interests, as well. Shielded by the opacity that the diamond industry has traditionally offered its participants, the two parties ultimately struck a deal, in secret. And as testament to De Beers's marketing genius and manipulativeness, the company successfully devised the "eternity ring," which featured up to twenty-five of these tiny Russian stones. Meanwhile, for Moscow, the initial contract provided an estimated $25 million per year to route its diamonds through the cartel, though the agreement was periodically revised in the Soviets' favor. Once again, a producer concluded that as disagreeable as the single channel and its overseer might be, the massive, guaranteed revenues offered were simply too good to forgo. As has happened so often throughout history, even the most ideologically stringent are willing to disregard their own rhetoric when the price is right.

In rare cases, De Beers's financial propositions were actually rebuffed. In the heady, early days of postcolonial Africa, decisions to shun the diamond behemoth were made largely on ideological grounds. For some African leaders, as long as the apartheid regime remained in place, doing business with "South Africa, Inc." was simply unpalatable. Yet, in every case (with the exception of Ghana), De Beers was able to establish and maintain, often covertly, relationships with the governments of newly independent, diamond-producing states. By creating innocuously named subsidiary companies, such as the "Diamond Development Corporation" and "Mining and Technical Services Ltd.," registered in places like Switzerland, Luxembourg, Liechtenstein, and the Bahamas, De Beers engineered the cover that these African governments required in order to maintain their ties with the industry giant.[24] Even a deal with the devil can be arranged, so long as no one knows about it.

Conversely, when greed, rather than ideology, drove producers' uncooperativeness, De Beers wasted little time with covert overtures. This scenario played out in Zaire (the DRC) during the dictatorial reign of the ruthless and rapacious Mobutu Sese Seko, who had seized power shortly after the country's independence from Belgium in 1960. De Beers had been active in the Congo since the 1920s, working closely with the two colonial mining giants, Forminière and the Société Minière de Bakwanga (MIBA), and had long enjoyed a virtual monopoly on Congolese output. However, starting in the 1970s, Mobutu strove to gain control over the diamond industry in the same manner that he had appropriated for personal enrichment the nation's copper and cobalt industries. In 1973, he nationalized MIBA, including the portion that De Beers owned. And in 1981 Mobutu ended De Beers's purchasing monopoly of MIBA's production.

Damage to the cartel remained only hypothetical during this eight-year stretch, as De Beers continued to purchase all of MIBA's output (which had shrunk from 13.4 million carats in 1973 to only 8.7 million in 1979). However, following Mobutu's more aggressive move in 1981, De Beers hit back, ferociously. The company instantly flooded the market with massive quantities of industrial-grade diamonds similar to the ones produced in the Congo, immediately driving down the price of these stones by roughly 40 percent. The enterprise also established buying houses in the neighboring cities of Brazzaville (in the Republic of the Congo) and Bujumbura (in Burundi), traditional destinations for gem-quality stones smuggled out of the Congo. The industry giant was on a retaliatory rampage. Beaten and humbled, Mobutu reengaged with De Beers, though on much less favorable terms, with Oppenheimer suggesting that the Zairian case serve as an example to others who might be contemplating similar moves. No one immediately volunteered.

If Mobutu's actions had caused some level of concern within De Beers, arguably the greatest threat that the company faced during its durable reign was much more local in nature. With Nelson Mandela's release from prison in 1990 and the first open elections set for 1994 collectively signaling the end of the apartheid era, corporations across South Africa faced great uncertainty. Having endured decades of violence, Mandela's African National Congress (ANC) party had accused the nation's mining companies of "representing tremendous wealth in the midst of unspeakable poverty" and insisted that "the nationalization of the mines and banks . . . is the policy of the ANC and a change or modification of our views . . . is inconceivable."[25]

Sensing the danger, Anglo American representatives had earlier met in Zambia with the ANC's exiled leaders to try to soften the movement's stance and determine how the entities might productively work together in a post-apartheid South Africa. In fact, this secret gathering was not as improbable as it might initially appear. Harry Oppenheimer, who served as Anglo chairman from the mid-1950s to the mid-1980s and was also a South African parliamentarian, had long used these seats of power to criticize the apartheid system. Perhaps as a result of both Oppenheimer's personal politics and the meetings in Zambia, Mandela's ANC ultimately pursued a much less radical path than it might have on assuming power of the "New South Africa," leaving intact privately held mining operations. Alternatively, it instituted an economic empowerment program by which South African firms—including De Beers—were required to reserve jobs for "historically disadvantaged" groups, sell off portions of their assets and place Africans in higher-level positions within their organizations. Shortly thereafter, President Mandela publicly praised Harry Oppenheimer's significant contributions to the nation.

A New Chapter, a New Model

Following the ANC's change of heart, De Beers administrators could breathe a collective sigh of relief. By this time, however, South African diamonds made up only about 14 percent of the world's rough production, and even the company's vast array of mines elsewhere was collectively generating only about 45 percent of overall global output. In response to these discouraging trends, the company, now under the direction of Harry Oppenheimer's son, Nicky, made sweeping changes to De Beers's operational model. In the 1990s, it had become increasingly evident that the enterprise's supply-controlled approach was no longer viable, especially with the emergence of major Canadian and Australian mines whose owners were unwilling to participate in the cartel, but also owing to shifting consumer tastes and concerns. In response, De Beers conducted a strategic review of its operations and subsequently adopted a demand-driven business model. It also implemented new marketing strategies, as both a wholesaler and, for the first time in 2002, a retailer. Meanwhile, in 2001, De Beers had reprivatized, buying up all of its shares in order to reassume control of the company, causing it to disappear from the South African and London stock exchanges. Finally, in 2012, the Oppenheimer family famously disengaged from the venerable mining giant by selling its 40 percent share to Anglo American, thereby marking the end of a remarkable era.[26] Even though De Beers emerged from this series of radical developments with a greatly reduced market share, it is widely believed that it is now an even more profitable company than it once was.

By buying up new mines, convincing other operators to participate in the CSO, and severely punishing those producers who attempted to stray from the single channel, De Beers enjoyed a remarkable run. However, the proliferation of alluvial mining operations in Africa, from which it was impossible to purchase each and every stone pulled from a stream or riverbed, and prodigious finds in other parts of the world irreparably shattered De Beers's monopoly and eventually prompted the major, strategic changes in the company's approach to business operations outlined above. Today, lucrative, ongoing contractual agreements with a number of African producers continue to undergird the more streamlined version of De Beers that emerged from these setbacks. Although the bold move into retail would likely have been unthinkable to Rhodes and other early company executives, those same administrators would have been proud of the tradition of innovation and adaptation that their corporate successors have upheld.

OUT OF the initial chaos of Kimberley emerged one of the most storied companies in the history of global business and commerce. Whereas it had taken India some two thousand years to produce twenty million carats and Brazil roughly two centuries, South Africa achieved this milestone in just fifteen years. In great part due to De Beers, the South African mines shattered the historical perspective of diamond production.[27] For all of Cecil Rhodes's entrepreneurial vision and the Oppenheimers' business acumen, though, the company continued to depend on African laborers to shovel, cart, wash, and sort the earth in which these precious stones were embedded. While these vital workers were being coercively harnessed for South African production as early as the 1880s, African laborers throughout the continent endured similar fates following the contemporaneous onset of European imperial rule and the subsequent consolidation of colonial projects. Exploitative mining operations were key components of these broader historical processes. The following chapter examines the series of racially oppressive structures that the various colonial regimes contrived and that the diamond-mining companies readily reinforced.

CHAPTER FIVE

Creating "New Kimberleys" Elsewhere in Africa

The Government of Angola will support, morally and materially, the Diamond Company of Angola (Diamang) and will take the necessary measures to, in the interest of the colony, assure the company of the free and easy exercise of its industry.

> —Article II of the 1921 landmark state-company agreement that facilitated Diamang's commercial success in the Portuguese colony of Angola

Akwatia was properly planned from the beginning and the result is what we see today—the Bournville of the Gold Coast.

> —J. R. Dickinson, Gold Coast Labor Department director, comparing the British colony's diamond mining center to the Cadbury Company's "model village" in England, 1939

FROM NOVEMBER 1884 to February 1885, representatives from an array of European countries, including England, France, Portugal, Germany, Spain, and Italy, assembled in Berlin to carve up Africa into a series of colonial domains. Conspicuously absent were any African leaders, nor were any invited. Among the many political, social, and economic motivations for this conclave was the mineral wealth of the continent. The Kimberley mines, as well as subsequent discoveries of gold deposits in South Africa, were at the center of this latest round of "mineral fever." Spurred on by these lucrative discoveries, these imperial states were eager to experience "mineral revolutions" of their own within the borders of their newly claimed African territories. And with the steady discovery of new diamond deposits across the continent, many of these hopes were realized. To facilitate the generation of this mineral wealth, the colonial regimes actively courted mining capital, the vast majority of which was associated either partially or fully with De Beers/Anglo American. The colonial powers also instituted manipulative labor schemes and applied a host of pressures on rural Africans to push them onto the mines. The first quote that appears above, a declaration made by Angola's colonial government, is indicative of the staunch commitment to mining ventures that prompted these types of harsh measures. The social and economic structures that the new colonial states devised mimicked South Africa's exploitative environment, even as these regimes identified a multitude of supposedly model communities, or "African Bournvilles," within their respective territories. With the expansion of mining during the colonial era, members of African communities across the continent suddenly became essential entities in extractive operations that denuded the continent of a significant portion of its mineral wealth and appropriated vital manpower. In the decades that followed the departure of the European delegates from the Berlin Congress, the imperial powers created a host of exploitative, new "Kimberleys," none of which resembled the model village of Bournville, a world away to the north.

Each of these newly established mining environments featured challenging living and working conditions, as well as insufficient compensation for African laborers—hardly the stuff of a model village. The individual sites differed according to the location of the diamonds, which resided either in superficial alluvial deposits or deep in "the belly of earth" in kimberlite pipes, and according to the particular colonial master. African headmen also played a role in workers' experiences by pushing them to engage with mining companies, typically in exchange for some type of corporate or governmental compensation. Consistent with the Griqua chief, Waterboer, whose plight was considered in chapter 3, these headmen probably deserve equal amounts of empathy and criticism in any assessment of their actions. Only in the British Gold Coast colony did African authorities do more than just supply laborers: in that setting, traditional rulers retained control of diamondiferous soils. By renting access to foreign mining companies, these indigenous leaders played a central role in the development of the industry in West Africa.

This chapter explores a range of the exploitative environments that colonial states, mining companies, and various African headmen combined to forge. The examination begins with the series of early twentieth-century discoveries of diamond deposits and continues through the heady process of African political independence, which extended from the 1950s all the way until the early 1990s.

Facilitating Flows: From Rural Locations to Mining Locations

Africans' journeys to colonial-era mines differed according to a number of factors, including the proximity of the deposits and the particular colonial context, but generally became less arduous with each ensuing decade owing to upgrades in transportation. In certain settings, sizable populations already existed adjacent to, or literally on top of, diamond deposits. For these communities, this geographical happenstance was often a mixed blessing: they quickly became "wed" to the mines, experiencing all of the ups and downs that these "marriages" delivered. At other times, laborers were further removed from the mines, necessitating long(er)-distance relocations, via foot, truck, or train. Colonial states facilitated labor migration in various ways, including by instituting forced labor schemes; establishing "labor boards" that recruited and then relocated voluntary workers; and constructing roads and/or laying track, which reduced the time it took prospective laborers to reach mine sites and begin working. Mining companies also shaped recruits' migratory experiences and patterns by, for example, arranging for mechanized transport or offering incentives for accompanying wives and children. Finally, African traditional authorities often encouraged their young male subjects to venture out from their home villages to seek work on the mines. Over the course of the colonial period, this powerful combination of pressures and allurements prompted millions of Africans to relocate to one of the continent's myriad diamond mining sites.

The Colonial State as Labor Recruiter

Colonial states pushed indigenous residents to the mines by imposing taxes payable exclusively in colonial currencies and by implementing labor schemes that obligated Africans to work in order to earn the wages necessary to satisfy these levies. These measures were, in practice, ruthlessly effective and rendered colonial governments handmaidens to the array of diamond-mining companies active on the continent. Yet these measures were anything but simple expressions of statal goodwill. In return, colonial administrations derived significant revenues from mining enterprises in the form of corporate taxes, profit-sharing arrangements, concessionary rents, and formal loans—a mutually profitable collaboration, to be sure.

Colonial states also played key roles in the physical relocation of recruits to the mines. Perhaps the most egregious case of governmental involvement in procuring African labor comes from Angola, a former Portuguese colony. As the quotation that led off this chapter suggests, in 1921 the colonial state granted Diamang, the monopolistic diamond enterprise, exclusive access to African labor in its operational area. In return, the company surrendered roughly half its profits and granted a series of loans to the state featuring very favorable repayment terms. Meanwhile, for the roughly 40 percent of Diamang's African labor force that was forcibly contracted, the trip to the mines began when African police in the state's employ arrived in villages to gather a predetermined number of workers. These enforcers would then march the conscripts to administrative posts, from which they would set out for Diamang's mines. This process could take months and span hundreds of miles. Only in 1947 did Diamang phase in truck transport. And, only in the early 1960s would Portugal finally dismantle these types of forced labor schemes in its colonial empire in Africa.

Further up the West African coast, the colonial government in French Guinea struggled in its efforts to help staff the diamond mines following their establishment in 1937. Although the French were every bit as aggressive as the Portuguese had been, the inability to populate the Guinean mines was attributable to their remoteness, the sparse proximate population, and the allure of gold panning, which had expanded rapidly during the 1930s. To redress this shortage, the colonial regime instituted a forced labor system, similar to the one in place in Angola, known as *prestation,* which compelled adult males to work unless they could buy their way out of this obligation. Yet even after this labor scheme was introduced, the factors outlined above, as well as strong competition from agricultural employers, continued to hamper recruitment for the diamond operations. As a result, Guinean mines typically ran at only two-thirds capacity.

Into the 1940s, *prestateurs* continued to make up roughly two-thirds of the workforce of SOGUINEX, the dominant mining enterprise. Owing to the company's reliance on these laborers, the abandonment of the scheme in 1946 resulted in the debilitating loss of almost half of the overall workforce. In response, the enterprise began offering yearly bonuses, paid leave, rewards for sustained service, improved accommodations, and subsidized food for its indigenous employees. However, by this time, few Africans were listening. Formidable commercial competition for potential local recruits remained, forcing the diamond company to try to identify alternative sources of labor further afield, an endeavor that met with only partial success.

In other colonial settings, governments typically took a much less active role in securing laborers for diamond enterprises. Yet even a reduced level of involvement produced virtually the same result: reluctant, if resigned, African laborers who generally satisfied mining companies' staffing requirements. In South West Africa (Namibia), for example, male laborers were initially recruited by the Southern Recruiting Organisation and from 1943 until the early 1970s by the South West African Native Labour Association. Under the recruitment schemes of these organizations, the government served as a type of placement agency through which employers of all sorts obtained African workers. However, these recruiting entities ensured that the labor needs of diamond and other mining interests were satisfied first, privileging them over, for example, agricultural employers. In short, mining trumped food production. As a result of this prioritization, South West Africa's lucrative mining industries were guaranteed an ample supply of the strongest and healthiest laborers.

Creating a Healthy Environment: Screening Recruits to Maximize Profits

In every colonial diamond-mining setting, African workers typically underwent some form of medical evaluation either at the point of recruitment or once they reached the mines, or both. Mining company medical personnel typically inspected recruits en masse and individually, assessing arrivals for obvious contagious diseases and frailty, both of which could compromise productivity. Many operations, including in Angola, the Belgian Congo, and South Africa, employed the pseudoscientific Pignet index, which generated a number that supposedly measured a recruit's ability to meet the daily demands of mine labor.[1] When labor shortages existed, however, mine managers regularly ordered medical staff to ignore Pignet numbers and send along any recruit who was not carrying an infectious disease. In these situations, frailty could be overlooked, since, unlike disease, it did not directly threaten the health of the white mining staff. This type of imperfect, and often demeaning, approach to African employees' health and well-being was also employed in South West Africa, where company agents employed the "Standard of Fitness of Natives for

Mine Works" to assess incoming recruits. The manual recommended that health personnel:

> Line up all the natives entirely stripped (they must not be al-
> lowed merely to drop their trousers and retain them about their
> ankles). Stand them in line about 20 feet away. . . . Make each
> boy walk towards the examiner, observing his gait and whether
> he is lame, etc. When about five feet away, cause him to rise on
> tiptoe then squat, then rise again, then extend both arms above
> his head, extend the arms at right angles to the body laterally,
> then forward, then flex the elbow joints. When in this position,
> cause him to clench and open his hands, and then rotate each
> arm parallel to the long axis of the body. Turn him round and
> look at his spine. These motions, which take less than a minute,
> will enable the examiner to judge whether all the joints resound
> in function. Ask the native a simple question in an ordinary
> voice to ascert in [*sic*] whether he is deaf. Look at his ears, his
> gums and teeth. Cover each eye separately, and ask him to count
> the fingers of your hand to test for blindness. Look at the skin,
> noting the presence of any large scars or varicose veins, or her-
> niae, or flabbiness of muscles or skin.[2]

Based on these cursory, highly suspect evaluations of "natives," it's obvious that the threshold for employment suitability was extremely low. Nor does it appear that these medical agents required much in the way of health training or knowledge to conduct these assessments.

Diamond-Mining Companies and the Recruitment of African Labor

Diamond-mining operations in colonial Africa owed their very existence to the governments that granted them access, often in the form of concessions, to diamond-bearing soils. Colonial states also instituted recruitment schemes to help generate African employees, without which these enterprises would never have gotten off the ground, much less expand. For their part, mining companies also managed to pull Africans to their operations, primarily by providing higher wages and more substantive benefits than other employ-ers. In so doing, these paternalistic enterprises were offering African labor-ers a degree of security in the otherwise unsettling contexts that colonial rule engendered. These companies were often inspired by fellow diamond operators to institute "generous" compensation and remuneration policies.

These corporations adopted these imitative measures not to compete against one another, as most enjoyed monopolies within their respective colonies. Rather, they were implemented to compete against rival industries for prospective employees. In many cases, high-ranking corporate officials encouraged this type of strategic replication across a series of mines over which they enjoyed managerial control. For example, Anglo American held significant stakes in a number of diamond-mining companies scattered throughout West and Central Africa. In this manner, over time the industry experienced a degree of operational homogenization.

In the Belgian Congo, Forminière was able to attract African laborers to its diamond mines using alluring incentives, consistent with those outlined above, but it also relied on coercion, or at least significant pressure, to complement this voluntary workforce. Forminière commenced operations in 1912, five years after the discovery of the first diamond in the south central Kasai region. Granted ample land and exclusive access to the diamond-bearing soils by the colonial state, Forminière was well poised to exploit this bountiful area. Initially unwilling or unable to pay competitive wages, the company instead sold goods, including clothes and shoes, to its employees at subsidized prices, and offered attractive housing. Forminière was consequently able to grow its workforce from several hundred African employees to roughly seven thousand in 1919. The company was also involved, though, if only indirectly, in coercive methods to secure a portion of its African staff. Forminière owned roughly 40 percent of the notorious Bourse du Travail du Kasai, an entity that, following its establishment in 1921, combed the countryside aggressively seeking recruits. In three short years, this agency helped Forminière double its workforce, from ten to twenty thousand, making it the Congo's largest employer. Moreover, in 1928, the colonial state granted Forminière its request for exclusive access to African labor in the Tshikapa area of the Kasai, thereby denying local residents a choice of employers. As this freedom to choose disappeared, corporate incentive and generosity were among the first casualties.

African Traditional Authorities as Industry Brokers

Much as African headmen in South Africa did following the Kimberley discoveries, traditional authorities played important roles elsewhere on the continent in helping mining companies staff their operations. Stripped of much of their authority by the colonial overlords, indigenous chiefs cooperated with the new European masters primarily to attempt to retain a portion of their former social and political privileges. To this end, they often offered up or encouraged young male subjects to fulfill labor contracts on the mines. Only in the Gold Coast and, to a lesser extent, in Sierra Leone did these traditional leaders assume a more authoritative role. In these two settings, British colonial officials permitted indigenous rulers to retain varying degrees of control of the mineral rights associated with the lands that fell within their political domains.

In most other colonial contexts, African traditional rulers simply served as cogs in the various colonial recruiting schemes, attempting to retain what little power they still possessed. In South West Africa, for example, African headmen were essentially on the state's payroll. In exchange for maintaining order and ensuring that male subjects were made available to the various state recruitment agencies, they drew a modest salary. In practice, the South African regime, which oversaw affairs in the neighboring territory, after it had become a League of Nations "mandate" following World War I, strove to "increase the wants" of these headmen. According to this design, these traditional authorities would then pressure their subjects into becoming migrant workers, with the headmen demanding a portion of workers' wages in the form of "presents." Consequently, ethnic Ovambo chiefs, who presided over a large area in northern Namibia from which the mandate's diamond companies derived significant portions of their workforces, were deeply invested in the migrant labor system. In 1929, for example, in order to promote labor migration, the government of South West Africa instituted a five shilling tax on all adult men in Ovamboland, a portion of which went to indigenous leaders to ensure their ongoing collaboration. It's small wonder then, that by 1955, these local headmen had taken it upon themselves to double this tax! The government also introduced the Tribal Trust Funds in Ovamboland in the 1920s to help regional chiefs improve their communities. This pool of money played a major part in these indigenous leaders' enthusiastic involvement in labor recruitment, since it was largely generated by fees levied on migrant mine workers' incomes.

Some chiefs were even more self-serving. For example, during the 1920s, an Ovambo headman named King Ipumbu demanded that each laborer returning from the diamond fields provide him with clothes, knives, or £1 in currency. At one point, he even required that recruits surrender half of their wages to fund his purchase of an automobile. In another case, from 1938, Chief Martin Elifas Kathikua sent a letter to his subjects employed on the diamond mines who were concerned about a newly implemented policy of X-raying workers due to be repatriated to Ovamboland. The missive (below) underscores just how invested in the system of migrant labor African headmen often were, and also their willingness to adopt the pejorative language used by white settlers in Africa: the chief's subjects were "boys" who should not be "cheeky."

> I . . . want to say to you that I hear that you have been very cheeky to the masters who are in charge of the work and that you have also been in gaol. . . . I am tired of all this nonsense of all you people. I am tired of all the bad things I hear about you. You and other boys like you spoil my name. . . . This nonsense that you people speak about the machine is all lies. You know that it is lies. You pretend to be frightened and in this way you frighten one another. . . . You will carry on with this nonsense until there is no more place for you people to earn money. If there is anything to be afraid of I will tell you about it or the Government will tell you about it. . . . Where are you going to find money to buy things for your families when you come back from work. Are you a chief now . . . or how is it that you have become so clever that you know all about the machine. You know nothing about it. You have got to do your work and listen to what you are told. That is all I say to you.[3]

It should come as no surprise that the Ovambo headmen, who benefited so handsomely from the recruitment and migration system, never seriously opposed it. They did, however, attempt to minimize the local disruption it caused by limiting the absence of their subjects to periods when the cycle of subsistence activities required the least amount of manpower and, when possible, to restrict laborers' time on the mines to six months. They also encouraged recruits to depart in groups and to remain together throughout their employment so as to maintain a sense of discipline and ethnic cohesion. So, although these traditional authorities undoubtedly benefited from the migrant labor system, some also took a genuine interest in their subjects' well-being.

In Angola, traditional leaders, or *sobas*, played a similar role in the coercive recruitment scheme in place in that colony. When African police, or *cipaios*, arrived in villages, the headmen were responsible for furnishing the requested number of recruits. In response, many *sobas* implemented a type of rotational system to maximize rest periods for workers who had most recently served, offering up instead subjects who had never served or those who were sufficiently rested from previous stints. However, *sobas* ultimately deferred to the *cipaios'* authority, aware that they risked corporal punishment, arrest, or even servitude on the mines if they didn't follow orders. In order to maintain *sobas'* compliance, Diamang periodically rewarded these headmen with small gifts, including cash, alcohol, seeds, cloth, and surplus Portuguese military uniforms. In 1922, for example, the diamond enterprise was offering small sums of money to *sobas* for each wife who accompanied and remained with her contracted husband on the mines. Diamang also honored cooperative *sobas* with portraits hung in its company museum, though corporate officials could also remove these images as a means of shaming headmen who failed to provide adequate numbers of laborers. In this sense, the museum served as a type of "Headman Hall of Fame," except this shrine featured both inductions *and* removals. Nothing was permanent.

Following the creation of the Bourse du Travail du Kasai in the neighboring Belgian Congo, village chiefs played similar roles to Angola's *sobas* in helping populate Forminière's mines. Headmen who initially refused the demands of the Bourse recruiters were offered a commission in exchange for supplying recruits, or were simply sanctioned. These financial enticements, coupled with the threat of punishment, convinced most regional chiefs to comply. Moreover, because Africans could engage in casual labor, coming and going according to local agricultural cycles, and could also bring family members to Forminière's mines, traditional authorities were reluctant to try to hinder their subjects' pursuit of these attractive employment opportunities.

The Gold Coast constituted the exception to these scenarios. In this setting, mining companies were as beholden to indigenous rulers as they were to the state, because the British colonial authorities permitted African chiefs to retain the mineral rights associated with their traditional lands. In Akwatia, the colony's richest diamondiferous area, this policy enabled headmen to rent access to the highest bidders. In compliance with this practice, African Selection Trust Ltd. (AST), one of the first mining companies to be incorporated in the colony following the discovery of diamonds in 1919, took out its first lease in 1922. The enterprise agreed to pay the local chief, or "stool," £1,300 in "consideration money," a mining rent of £500 per annum and 5 percent of net profits. AST even granted the local chief, Ofori Atta, a seat on its board of directors.

Because the Gold Coast chiefs were well aware of the valuable endowments they controlled, they initially took a measured, patient approach to negotiations with mining companies, knowing that a payoff would eventually come. In many ways, their desire to attract foreign mining capital paralleled the motivations and efforts of the colonial states. Moreover, just as colonial governments displayed little regard for indigenous subjects' welfare, very little of the money that these chiefs, or "stools," received flowed down to local residents, including the mine workers themselves. For example, after a visit to Akwatia in 1929, Governor Alexander Slater commented that it "is one of the most squalid towns in the Gold Coast, there being no sign that one penny of the (mining) rents and royalties has been spent on its improvement."[4] In 1933, the new governor, Shenton Thomas, echoed Slater's statements, declaring that "Akwatia and Asamankese [an adjacent area] are squalid and lacking in improvements and amenities which are to be found in many places of their size enjoying but a fraction of their revenues. Most of the land which is not actually required by the inhabitants themselves has been disposed of, and today the people are left, not only with nothing to show for this huge expenditure [on litigation] of stool funds, but with a debt of several thousand pounds. . . . The division has been brought to the verge of ruin."[5] It is difficult to imagine how these assessments can be reconciled with the claim that appeared at the outset of this chapter that cast Akwatia as "the Bournville of the Gold Coast." Indeed, for the most part, only the lawyers, whom the stools were continuously forced to hire, truly profited from this otherwise ruinous cycle of litigation, debt, and further land alienation.

In nearby Sierra Leone, traditional authorities played a less significant role than they did in the Gold Coast, though they were still more formally involved in the development of the industry in that colony than were headmen elsewhere on the continent. Unlike in the Gold Coast, the British Crown had opted to retain control of mineral rights in Sierra Leone, thereby precluding local ethnic Kono headmen from renting access to foreign mining companies. British officials stereotyped Kono as an "economically backward, remote region infected by sleeping sickness and malaria" and stated that "the Konos had no conception of mining rights." Beyond this unflattering assessment, timing also played an important role in the development of local policy: in the midst of the global Depression, British colonial officials were eager to secure any investment that promised to raise revenue and provide employment.

Traditional authorities in Sierra Leone did, however, manage to receive compensatory funds for the use of lands over which they claimed control—though not from the state. In a gesture of unanticipated goodwill, Sierra Leone Selection Trust (SLST), the company that enjoyed exclusive mining rights in Sierra Leone following its formation in 1934, agreed to pay surface rents to the chiefs. In 1937, for example, these payments amounted to a total of £242 (roughly $20,800 today), a figure that, though somewhat small, was substantially greater than any alternative use value of the land. Corporate compensation was also to be awarded to chiefs for any damage to buildings, trees, crops, or sacred sites that occurred during mining operations. Meanwhile, in 1932, the state had begun to contribute, as well, creating the Protectorate Mining Benefit Trust Fund, into which all mining rents were paid "for the exclusive benefit of the natives." However, these funds were redistributed and applied throughout Sierra Leone, rather than solely within the diamond-bearing regions. Only in the 1950s, in response to ethnic Konos' complaints regarding this practice, did additional funds from the trust start flowing directly to the mining zones "for the benefit of Kono people, with special reference to the local population . . . of the mines."

The Labor Process within the Broader Labor Environment

Over time, the dozens of active diamond-mining companies in operation during the colonial period recruited—forcibly or otherwise—millions of African employees. The labor process and structures that workers on these mines encountered differed depending on whether the diamond deposits were alluvial, underground, embedded in coastal sands, or even offshore. Individual employers also shaped these environments according to the particular working conditions they offered, including the degree of mechanization. Most of the deposits beyond South Africa's great kimberlite pipes were *not* located deep underground, and, therefore, diamond mining was neither as expensive nor as dangerous as other types of mineral excavation, including gold mining. But these settings still featured long, often punishing, workdays. Moreover, for most male laborers, family members quickly became only distant memories, as very few employers permitted women or children onto their mines. Such were the challenges that diamond-mining companies created for their African labor forces during the colonial period.

The Labor Process

Labor conditions were dictated primarily by the depth of the diamond deposits but also by a mining company's commitment—or lack thereof— to mechanization. For the most part, underground mining was limited to

South Africa, with most operations elsewhere excavating alluvial deposits. In South West Africa (Namibia), however, most diamonds were located in coastal desert zones. In order to access the submerged stones, the labor process entailed both removing massive quantities of sand and digging down into the continental shelf, outward from the beaches into the Atlantic Ocean. As you can imagine, the technology and expertise required to render this undertaking profitable were both considerable. Over time, mining operations of all types mechanized to varying degrees, yet they never dispensed with manual laborers. In fact, the employment of Africans on the continent's diamond mines typically grew over the course of the colonial period. Workers generally benefited from the introduction of machinery, which relieved them of some of the most difficult tasks in the mining process. A handful of employees were also trained as machine or heavy equipment operators or technicians. However, these types of professional advancement opportunities were highly limited during the colonial period. Moreover, the wages of blacks, in general, continued to lag far behind the salaries of their white counterparts, who maintained a virtual monopoly on the managerial and engineering ranks.

Mechanization and Alluvial Deposits

Owing to the superficial nature of alluvial deposits, they are the easiest to excavate. These concentrations are typically located in the bottom of stream, creek or river beds, or in adjacent banks and hills. Before accessing these stones, however, three fundamental tasks need to be completed: the diversion of the water flow; the drainage of any remaining water; and, finally, the removal of the newly exposed, non-diamond-bearing layer of earth, unkindly known in the industry as "overburden." During the colonial era, payable deposits typically featured overburden depths of less than 150 feet, but were, at times, as shallow as a single foot. Next, the underlying diamondiferous soil, or "ore," is removed. The excavation of these two layers constituted the most demanding tasks in the alluvial mining process: prior to mechanization, colonial-era companies relied exclusively on shovelers to remove both. Consequently, during the early years of alluvial mining, operators primarily targeted creek valleys, as they typically featured thin layers of overburden. Going forward, companies gradually introduced heavy machinery, which increased the number of diamonds that could be harvested. In every instance, though, the process of mechanization tended to be both fitful and incomplete, with manual laborers continuing to make significant contributions. Although the depth of the diamonds at Kimberley had forced operators to mechanize early on in order to profitably mine those deposits, this form of commercial pressure was absent in alluvial settings.

In Angola, for example, Diamang entered the mechanical excavation age only in 1937 with the introduction of steam shovels. The impact was so negligible, though, that by 1942 this machinery accounted for only 1.8 percent of the overburden removed. Manual laborers continued to remove virtually the entire layer. Moreover, because the (minimal) equipment that the company had introduced was both unreliable and unevenly deployed, many mines continued to be machine-free. Following this initial introduction of machinery, it wasn't until after the Second World War ended and the international demand for diamonds rebounded that Diamang sought to increase the volume of overburden and ore removed mechanically. In the 1950s, the company added scrapers, bulldozers, and draglines to its fleet of excavation machinery. Consequently, the percentage of overburden removed mechanically expanded from 6.5 percent in 1950 to 44.3 percent in 1960. Yet even this increased figure still amounted to less than half the total. In order to excavate the remainder, the company continued to retain thousands of manual laborers. Even into the early 1970s, on the eve of Angolan independence (1975), Diamang continued to utilize droves of inexpensive shovelers. Instead of mechanization lightening workers' loads, Diamang simply redeployed most shovelers to mines on which it had not yet introduced machinery or otherwise ordered them to continue removing what they could, no matter how minuscule the amount.

Diamang's neighbor to the north, Forminière, pursued mechanization on its mines in the Congo at a roughly similar pace, waiting until the late 1930s to introduce machinery into its operations. The divergent labor processes that featured in its two main mining areas reflected the disparate depths and nature of the deposits. In the company's long-standing western zone, along the Kasai River, it initially relied on large numbers of manual laborers to strip away any obstructive vegetation, reroute water flows, and remove the largely alluvial diamonds, using shovels, baskets, wheelbarrows, and, eventually, mine trams. These deposits were relatively small and were typically located near the surface along the Kasai and its tributaries. Conversely, in the Bushimaie valley (near modern-day Mbuji-Mayi), over a hundred miles to the east, where Forminière harvested most of its industrial diamonds, the company aggressively mechanized its operations to access the deeper, less concentrated deposits. The timing of these mechanization initiatives is also germane. In the western zone, Forminière had been mining gem-quality stones for more than twenty-five years prior to mechanizing operations. However, industrial diamonds, and especially the small ones found in the company's eastern zone, became marketable only in the 1930s. Consequently, the introduction of machinery into this area was essential and did not feature the type of delay that occurred in the more established western zone.

Further up Africa's western coast, diamond-mining installations roughly resembled the operations in Angola and the Congo, with two important differences: mechanization occurred even later and a tradition of independent African digging persisted, even if the numbers of these practitioners remained small. These West African mining companies earnestly mechanized operations only in the 1950s. For decades, they had been content to utilize thousands of manual laborers, in great part because shovels largely sufficed to access the area's shallow deposits. A shortage of mining capital in the region also contributed to this delay. Yet, other factors were even more salient, including the availability of large numbers of relatively inexpensive unskilled laborers; the absence of skilled operators and capable managers, both of whom were required in order to profitably utilize machinery; and the geographical unsuitability of many of the deposits.[6] Notwithstanding this range of obstacles, West African mining companies gradually mechanized their operations for a number of reasons, including the desire to mine lower-grade gravels, such as terrace deposits, which required processing greater volumes of soil; the need to replace old and increasingly obsolescent processing plants with more efficient and secure facilities; and the rising costs of African labor, which were partially attributable to trade union activity. As was the case elsewhere, the bottom line dictated exactly when, to what degree, or even if, operations were mechanized.

Regardless of the particular setting or level of mechanization, after laborers stripped away and discarded the overburden, the exposed ore was removed and taken to "washing stations" for refinement. Over time, the equipment used to transport the ore ranged from simple, woven baskets to massive dump trucks—arguably, the most extreme technological evolution on Africa's colonial-era diamond mines. Gradual mechanization in this area of the labor process significantly benefited both mining companies and their African labor forces, as it saved workers from having to transport these soils manually, while also greatly increasing operational efficiency. But, African workers with earth-laden baskets on their heads trudging to washing stations remained a common sight on diamond mines, even after the conclusion of the Second World War. As always, African manual labor was the least expensive option.

Most mining operations implemented an evolving series of haulage systems to transport the diamond-bearing soils before eventually introducing dump trucks. For example, by the mid-1920s, the Angolan company Diamang had introduced wheelbarrows to expedite this process. By the end of the decade, the enterprise had also introduced trams pushed along mobile rails, which could be easily relocated and reused, thereby greatly reducing the amount of physical effort necessary to transport the ore. It wasn't until the 1950s, though, that the first large-capacity dump truck appeared on the company's mines. And even then this heavy equipment would continue to coexist with mine trams until the end of Diamang's operations in the mid-1970s. As with the introduction of trams, the arrival of dump trucks failed to herald an end to manual removal and transport.

Once the ore reached the washing stations, it was refined, producing a diamond-rich concentrate that, remarkably, included less than 1 percent of the original amount of excavated overburden and ore. The fact that so much earth is removed, processed, and eventually discarded is the major reason why mining operations have such a severe environmental impact. But, of course, these sorts of concerns were far from the minds of colonial administrators and mining officials.

Next, workers moved the concentrate from the washing sites to highly secured selection centers, which became regular features on colonial-era mines. At these locations, "pickers" manually selected and removed diamonds from the concentrate, at which point the rough stones were ready to be polished and cut—endeavors that almost exclusively took place in Europe. In the early years of mining, pickers worked outside, near the excavation sites. Even when these workers were moved out of the sun into semipermanent structures (typically prior to the Second World War), the process was hardly more sophisticated or accurate. Over time, technical innovations improved and lightened this portion of the labor process, though it was already composed of the least taxing jobs on the mines. These employees were also the most highly scrutinized, as company officials recognized that exposure to diamonds in increasingly refined forms would entice some workers to try to abscond with the stones. Consequently, diamond companies placed pickers under constant vigilance, typically prohibited them from having long hair or fingernails, and rigorously inspected them, reminiscent of the intrusive searches that African workers on the Kimberley mines had endured. It is worth noting, though, that prior to leaving work these employees were spared the humiliation of the invasive speculum and draconian glove-and-chain apparatus that featured on the South African mines.

Homes Away from Home: Mining Accommodations

Colonial-era diamond enterprises typically housed their African workers in structures ranging from modest grass and mud huts to larger dormitory-like arrangements. Over time, companies steadily improved these facilities, though security concerns rather than comfort remained foremost in their considerations. Think army barracks, not residence halls. Although mining enterprises throughout Africa adopted different elements of the vaunted compound system utilized in South Africa, very few of them embraced that housing arrangement wholesale. There were a number of reasons for this aversion, including less regimented mining processes, (much) smaller workforces and fewer problems with diamond theft. These mining companies typically provided accommodations that were much less severe than compounds and which generally produced little of the acrimony, tension, or hostility that figured so prominently on the South African mines.

Accommodations on Forminière's mines prior to the Second World War were typical of the austere company housing of this period. Arriving recruits were initially allotted time and tools to fashion their own housing or provided with company-constructed accommodations, which had allegedly been fashioned according to Africans' tastes. As in other settings, colonial legislation in the Congo dictated specific standards for employee housing (though these requirements were not always met), including that the sites had to slope to permit water runoff, possess an adequate supply of potable water, and be enclosed. Within Forminière's encampments, straw, clay, dried-brick, and stone houses could be found, with each type required to meet durability, ventilation, and size specifications. The type of construction depended on the nature and size of the diamond deposit that the residents were working, as these features determined the length of time that would be spent at the site. For example, clay houses were to be inhabited for no longer than three years and dried-brick houses for no longer than five years. Forminière was responsible for building latrines, providing incinerators, and periodically disinfecting beds. In general, even these basic accommodations attracted, rather than deterred, prospective recruits to the company's mines.

Forminière also offered enhanced accommodations for select African staff members in its *villages routiers,* to which employees who had worked for at least eight years could "retire." These villages featured brick houses, cassava gardens, mango, banana, and palm trees, kitchens, poultry, and tools for up to nine families—not quite a condominium complex in a contemporary American retirement community but a significant upgrade from standard company housing. Naturally, Forminière was not merely interested in facilitating a relaxing transition into old age for the inhabitants of these settings. Rather, the company wanted these "retirees" to maintain local roads, generate food for the mining operations, and, ultimately, produce children who would someday work for the enterprise. Thus, although Forminière was, indeed, bearing a portion of the social costs of its "retired" workers (in distinct contrast to the other concessionary companies operating in the colony), this outlay was primarily intended to attract individuals who would stabilize, and ultimately reproduce, the workforce.

African employees responsible for sorting diamonds at Forminière also enjoyed upgraded accommodations. Workers at these highly secured "sorting stations" were the only Congolese employees who had access to stones in increasingly refined forms. Because of this accessibility, these workers lived together in the same building, often for months at a time without the possibility of leaving, and the company strictly monitored their every entry and departure from these facilities. As compensation, these employees received higher salaries and enhanced rations, in addition to housing that was superior to the accommodations that workers in "normal" encampments were afforded.

Although theft may have been a continual concern for mine managers in the Belgian Congo, it was foremost in the minds of mining officials in South West Africa as they designed worker accommodations. Given the mandate's political connection to South Africa and De Beers's influential role, its mines featured secure compounds from virtually the onset of operations. These accommodations bore a strong resemblance to their South African counterparts and were, over time, steadily upgraded in much the same way that Kimberley's housing was. Adam Raphael of the London-based *Guardian* newspaper investigated a series of companies operating in South West Africa in 1973 and confirmed these improvements: "Living conditions in the Oranjemund compound bear no resemblance to the squalor of the municipal compound at Katutura [a township associated with the capital city, Windhoek]. Clean, neat, single-story buildings surrounded by trees provided tolerable quarters."[7] So, do Rafael's observations finally confirm the existence of an "African Bournville"? Not quite. Just four years later, a member of a BBC television crew that visited a Consolidated Diamond Mines (CDM) compound noted that, although a very good library and common room existed, the black workers' living quarters were "like seedy barracks" and added that although the company had replaced the notorious concrete sleeping bunks with spring beds covered by inch-thick felt mattresses, as many as ten men and more were confined to a single room. For the time being, at least, the legendary Bournville would remain elusive.

A Healthy Labor Force Is a Productive Labor Force

Over time, the health of African workers became an important consideration for the colonial-era diamond companies. Although alluvial mining was less hazardous for laborers than underground excavation, diamond enterprises of all types increasingly acknowledged the obvious: healthy workforces were generally more productive than unhealthy workforces. These companies correspondingly improved nourishment, sanitation, and health care for their African labor forces, deeming that these measures were fundamental to increasing their profits.

Although the Belgian Congo was, in general, a decidedly noxious place for indigenous residents during the colonial period, Forminière's affirmative approach to its African employees' health was virtually unrivaled in the territory. Primary among the company's concerns was the adequate nourishment of these laborers; as with any operation that utilizes a large number of workers, the enterprise was faced with the challenge of satisfactorily feeding them. Following the commencement of mining operations in 1912, Forminière began purchasing surplus food from local communities. However, it quickly became apparent that this strategy was inadequate. Shortly thereafter, the company allocated a portion of its concessionary lands to raise livestock and cultivate corn, manioc, rice, and groundnuts. At the same time, the Belgian colonial state attempted to ease food shortages on the mines (and in other commercial settings) by enacting an ordinance that forced indigenous residents to utilize land to generate food for local consumption (as well as for export). The government then bought this food at below-market prices and resold it to various companies, including Forminière. F. Peigneus, the governor of the Kasai, subsequently offered the following rationale for this exploitative agricultural policy: "Forminière and the colonial state could feed the mine workers at the lowest possible cost to the company by placing the burden of agricultural production on peasant farmers."[8] In 1922, the colonial government again assisted the mining enterprise, this time by granting the company 185,000 acres of fertile land for the construction of plantations intended to increase the food supply for the mines. Into the 1920s, apparently in emulation of a local ethnic Luba tradition of "agricultural colonization," Forminière also embarked on a large-scale program of (re)settling African "colonists" on new farmlands to produce food for the enterprise. Soon these African communities, whose combined population numbered in the thousands, were dutifully supplying low-cost food to the mines. The success of these settlements and, in particular, their abundant production of cassava, made them magnets for regional residents.

Forminière's medical personnel also contributed to the improvements in the overall health of the African workforce. In fact, the company not only provided health services to its employees but also collaborated with the colonial government to offer medical care to all residents within its concessionary areas, free of charge. The first doctor arrived at Forminière in 1921, and shortly thereafter the company launched a comprehensive medical program. By 1925, in part spurred on by colonial legislation that mandated health care for African employees, but also because Forminière recognized the financial benefits of maintaining a healthy labor force, the enterprise had ten doctors and eleven sanitary agents (health workers responsible for maintaining sanitary conditions in and around the mines) on staff, as well as a training program for male nurses. Furthermore, in conjunction with other companies in the Congo, and complementing Diamang's efforts across the border to the south, Forminière participated in an expansive campaign to eradicate sleeping sickness. Although the mining environment at Forminière exposed workers to diseases such as tuberculosis and pneumonia and featured a higher mortality rate than those found in workers' home villages, the company provided its African employees with health services that were quite good by colonial-era standards.

Health conditions on the Gold Coast colony's commercial mines were also reasonably good, but independent African diggers in that setting suffered because of extremely poor working conditions. A report from the colonial government in 1952 indicated that the sites in which independent diggers were operating were "appallingly primitive. . . . It is common practice for females (and males) to be standing up to the waist in water for long periods daily. . . . It is not uncommon for expectant mothers to be working in such conditions."[9] Moreover, the worked-out pits acted as reservoirs for rainwater and thus offered ideal breeding conditions for mosquitoes; malaria and other insect-borne diseases were rife. Yet colonial officials lamented, genuinely or otherwise, that any attempt to improve the conditions under which these diggers worked and lived would be ineffective, owing to the extensive area covered and the rapid turnover and mobility of these individual operators. Moreover, the diggers themselves apparently did not agitate for improvements. According to a colonial report from the 1950s, "No demand for welfare services among (independent) workers is apparent. Their main object is to make money in order to purchase consumer goods or to send (them) home."[10]

Conversely, conditions on the Gold Coast's commercial mines were far better, though it's hard to imagine how they could have been any worse. From early on, West African diamond companies recognized the benefits of a healthy labor force and acted accordingly, albeit with significant fiscal restraint. Free housing and health care were standard as early as the 1920s, while Consolidated African Selection Trust (CAST) deliberately strove to ensure that overall health conditions on its mines were superior to those on offer from other major employers in the colony. Given that the Gold Coast's gold mines—a major source of competition for African laborers—necessitated that employees work deep underground, CAST also enjoyed an inherent advantage. As early as 1926, Governor Guggisberg commented that the company's "very fine" Akwatia camp was "quite a topic of conversation here in Accra (the capital)."[11] Similarly, an International Labor Organisation (ILO) representative, following a visit to the diamond mines in 1936, declared that "in every respect this is a mine such as I have not seen before. European quarters, roads, machinery, mine villages, a mine hospital and even the sanitation of the ground after exploitation are a whole civilization ahead of anything I have so far seen in West Africa. . . . It is noteworthy that here where conditions appeared the best, I met the least complaints regarding the efficiency, discipline and regularity of the labor force."[12] In 1939, the director of the colony's newly established Labor Department—the very same individual who had originally invoked the "model village" of Bournville—added:

> It is no part of my purpose to dispense encomiums on any particular company, but Akwatia is so outstanding in every way that some account of this mine may prove of value to others. . . . The

mine is adequately equipped with a hospital and dispensary. At the different plants I visited I was interested to see the baths where the boys bathe and change their clothes when leaving work. The most impressive thing of all ... is the way the ground is leveled again after it has been worked ... and there is a repatriation scheme for boys who are sick and whose repatriation is recommended by the Medical Officer.[13]

Although these (self-)congratulatory comments should be read with a certain amount of skepticism, the relatively superior conditions that prevailed on the diamond mines, versus other labor settings and especially the gold exploitations, appear to be beyond dispute. Indeed, observers of all types, including colonial and international officials, were consistently, and seemingly thoroughly, impressed with the health standards on the Gold Coast's commercial diamond mines.

(Un)just Rewards: Workers' Compensation

Colonial-era diamond-mining enterprises typically paid out above-average wages to African employees and also provided a series of other benefits, including health care, access to subsidized items and goods, and, at times, occupational training and/or general educational opportunities. For example, in West Africa, both CAST and SLST offered competitive wages, rewarded long service, provided free housing and medical care for its African staff, and assisted with food supplies. Similarly, in South West Africa, diamond companies offered the highest wages available to Africans and began providing pensions in the early 1970s in response to worker demands. The competition for African labor, often from agricultural employers and other types of mining operations, required that diamond enterprises offer superior wages in order to attract and retain employees. Given the consistently high price of diamonds during much of the colonial era, the companies could easily cover these elevated wage bills.

These mining enterprises could have done much more, though, regarding wages and benefits. For example, although CDM traditionally paid out the highest wages available to indigenous laborers in all of South West Africa, as of the 1970s it was spending only about a tenth of its net profits on workers' salaries. The wages for African employees were even lower than those on offer in South Africa, where 30 to 40 percent of workers' compensation was paid in remuneration; the comparable figure for the mandate was roughly only half that. Even in West Africa, where wages were relatively high, the colonial governments and regional mining companies colluded to manipulate and maintain wage levels. In sum, although wages for African laborers on the diamond mines during the colonial period were, on average, higher than those offered by competing industries, they don't tell the entire story.

Race Relations on Colonial-Era Mines: The South West Africa Case

Racially motivated policies and practices profoundly shaped the interactions between whites and blacks on colonial-era mines. White staff members adhered to the racial boundaries that applied in the broader colonial society, although they also often acted as mediators and were certainly not uniformly hostile. Race relations on diamond mines generally improved over time, although the Cape Colony's racist "Masters and Servants ordinance" continued to echo across the continent throughout the colonial period.

In South West Africa, the mines were deeply affected by the racial attitudes and practices that prevailed in Kimberley, and, for more than four decades, beginning in the 1940s, they operated under the shadow of apartheid that the regime in Pretoria cast across the border. Even before South Africa's assumption of control of the territory, German colonial labor policy was strongly informed by "the methods of the Boers towards the *kaffirs*," that is, the repressive approach to African labor as codified and practiced in the Cape Colony.[14] After World War I, the newly formed League of Nations "mandated" the former German colony to South Africa, and its new mine bosses imported even harsher managerial practices from next door. For example, they regularly highlighted ethnic differences within the African labor force in an effort to preclude racial unity and, on some mines, addressed black workers solely by their employment number in an effort to strip them of their identity. In this atmosphere, it comes as no surprise that in 1924, over fifty black mine workers in South West Africa died of scurvy—an easily preventable disease. Even into the 1970s, mine managers were still being accused of treating their black workers as "inferior children" and denying them key benefits such as sick leave, job advancement opportunities, and spousal accompaniment. During a 1976 interview, an African mining employee of CDM expressed his dissatisfaction as follows: "The working conditions at CDM: I don't say they are good at all and I say this because of the general attitude of the whites who are dominant. The law system is a hiding place for the company. The whites say 'we're just here on business and have no say in the apartheid law.'"[15] Or as another former contract worker put it: "Men in this compound are jailed. They have no right to speak their problems. Men are mourning and sorrowful. Stories outside the compound say 'the people are feeling happy and all is going well!' Never!"[16] Although the situation improved somewhat over time, racial discrimination would only substantially subside following the dismantlement of the apartheid system in South Africa and the creation of the independent state of Namibia in 1990.[17]

Diamond Mining and the Decolonization Process

The conclusion of the colonial era in Africa, a process that stretched from the 1950s to the 1970s over most of the continent, and the ensuing end of apartheid in South Africa and South West Africa (Namibia) prompted significant changes within the African diamond-mining industry. No longer would black workers have to endure formalized and legally sanctioned racism at the hands of white mine managers. Although many mining enterprises, including De Beers and its stable of affiliated mines and companies, survived the political transitions intact, other corporate operations were nationalized or simply disintegrated in the face of civil conflict, as happened in Angola, the DRC, and Sierra Leone (see chapter 7). These volatile and often violent settings rendered formal commercial mining impossible. Consequently, many former employees opted to mine artisanally or, worse, were forced to do so at gunpoint by members of rebel movements or authorities of the newly independent African states.

By again turning our attention to South West Africa, we are afforded an interesting example of how diamond-mining considerations featured in the decolonization process. During the buildup to political independence in the mandate, the prospect of nationalization certainly weighed heavily on the minds of mining company officials, many of whom feared the worst. But because self-rule came only in 1990, the government-to-be and the diamond-mining companies had ample time to engage with each other.

The dominant nationalist organization, the South West Africa People's Organization (SWAPO), rightly identified the mandate's mines as key sites of exploitation and wealth appropriation. The organization regularly articulated sentiments of this nature and also actively courted African mine workers. With its recognition by the United Nations General Assembly in 1972 as the "sole legitimate representative" of the Namibian people,

SWAPO had a reasonably strong hand to play. Regardless, the government and a number of mining corporations continued to deem the organization relatively innocuous. At CDM in the 1970s, for example, the company permitted SWAPO branches to hold public meetings at worker hostels every four months. In 1978, Harry Oppenheimer, then head of Anglo American, CDM's parent company, held talks with SWAPO leaders to better understand what types of mining policies the independence party might institute once in control of the country. Although the nationalist organization indicated that it intended to take a 70 percent stake in the diamond industry, SWAPO's representatives insisted that a decision would be made only after "judicious negotiations" between an independent Namibian government, Anglo American, and the other diamond companies with interests in the country, and that, eventually, "the people would decide." Ultimately, the people didn't really decide. However, SWAPO leaders and the array of mining interests did work to reach an agreement that benefited all parties, including the thousands of African laborers who daily toiled on the country's mines.

AFRICAN DIAMOND mine workers endured extremely difficult conditions during much of the twentieth century, as most of the continent suffered under the grip of European colonialism. Mining companies assigned African laborers the most arduous tasks, paid wages that were incommensurate with workers' contributions, and generally limited professional advancement. Yet these laborers hardly accepted their fate lying down. African employees employed a range of strategies to improve their plight and, via their actions, even prompted some employers to make meaningful improvements. Overall conditions on the continent's diamond mines only began to significantly improve, however, following the conclusion of the colonial period and, in South and South West Africa, the end of the apartheid era. In the next chapter, the focus remains on the diamond mines of colonial Africa, but centers African laborers—rather than colonial states, mining enterprises, and traditional authorities—and, in particular, the strategic and innovative ways that that these workers negotiated the challenging environments in which they toiled.

CHAPTER SIX

The Experiences of African Workers on Colonial-Era Mines

Death does not choose; famine chooses. . . .
I am going to De Beers. . . .
Lad, the day I am going, I mount to ride away,
A woman of witchcraft was already hard at work;
I saw her early going to the graveyard,
She puts on a string skirt fastened with knots,
She takes the arm of the corpse and waves it,
A mouthful of blood, she spits into the air,
She says, "Men gone to De Beers.
They can come home dead from the mines."
To me . . .
I am not dead; even now I still live,
I am a wanderer of the mines.

> —Song that migrant laborers from Lesotho sang en route
> to the South African diamond mines

In the period from 1920 to 1970, conditions were very, very poor. . . . At the world's richest diamond mine, the majority of people who worked there were simply being exploited, and De Beers grew very, very rich as a result.

> —Gordon Brown,[1] former senior manager of the Oranjemund
> diamond mine in South West Africa (Namibia), 1990

IF GORDON BROWN'S statement underscores the exploitation that characterized colonial-era diamond mining, the lyrics that make up the first quotation capture African workers' resiliency: *I am not dead; even now I still live, / I am a wanderer of the mines.* Although most colonial diamond-mining operations were highly organized, reasonably orderly affairs and thus bore little resemblance to the "Wild West" scenario of early Kimberley, they invariably featured exacting conditions for the African laborers, or "wanderers," who toiled for them. Mine workers throughout the continent met these daily challenges—both during their shifts and "after the whistle blew"—by employing a number of efficacious strategies, reminiscent of their South African counterparts. For example, in colonies featuring forced labor schemes, Africans often fled ahead of mining recruiters or, later, once on the job. Conversely, in settings where employment was voluntary, Africans concentrated their efforts on attenuating and overcoming the daily challenges that they faced. Worker strategies could be as simple as singing to propel themselves through taxing days, as furtive as diamond theft, or as confrontational as formal trade union activity.

This chapter continues the examination of colonial-era mines begun in the preceding chapter but shifts the perspective away from colonial administrations, mining companies, and indigenous headmen to focus instead on the experiences of the African workers who engaged with the various diamond operations. Although these "wanderers of the mines" operated in demanding labor environments, they actively shaped their plights by pursuing a range of creative strategies intended to improve their lives. And, as the song lyrics suggest, they may well have cheated death in the process.

The Motivations and Experiences of Migrant Diamond Miners

Faced with the combined pressure that imperial regimes, powerful mining enterprises, and acquiescent headmen exerted, it's no wonder that millions of Africans migrated to diamond-mining locations during the colonial period. Local migratory traditions, population densities, and livelihood possibilities shaped the nature and volume of this constant outflow from rural to industrial areas. Recruits and, in some settings, family members, traveled to these mines over varying distances, in varying numbers, and via various types of transportation. This exodus affected individual communities differently, primarily depending on how long migrant workers remained on the mines and how much in cash or goods they returned with or were able to remit. No one was to return home empty-handed.

African residents of small communities located near diamond deposits typically had the most agreeable engagements with mining operations.

These individuals often became "favored employees" on the mines, as corporate bosses regularly granted them and their local brethren the best jobs available to Africans. Moreover, these residents enjoyed a type of geographic and geological serendipity: the mining enterprises at their doorsteps provided a ready source for cash, and the proximity of the deposits also precluded both long treks and separation from families.

When local communities were sizable, however, residents often needed to be prodded—via coercion, enticement, or both—to work on the mines. Indeed, the very presence of a significant population meant that ample, sustainable livelihood possibilities already existed in the area. Such was the case in the Tshikapa region of the Belgian Congo, the location of Forminière's flagship operations. This area sustained populations of ethnic Penda and Chokwe, who were primarily farmers, but who also traded ivory, rubber, beeswax, hides, and fish. Yet many of these residents also worked for Forminière because they could engage casually with the company and thus maintain their existing livelihoods. Raymond Buell, an American who visited the area during a 1925 tour of Africa, observed that "when one finds a Company which employs casual laborers—that is, natives who sign no contract but may come and go when they like—it may be assumed that such a company had not invoked compulsion to obtain such labor. Apparently the only large company in the Congo which follows the casual labor system is Forminière. . . . [African] labor willingly seeks employment with this company."[2] Although Buell's assessment wasn't entirely accurate, Forminière's casual labor policy did attract large numbers of voluntary employees, even if the enterprise relied on different degrees of coercion to secure others.

When the immediate supply of workers on diamond mines was inadequate, Africans from more distant locations often found themselves the targets of states and mining companies. In South West Africa, for example, ethnic Ovambo residing in the northern zones of the territory would become a primary source of labor for the diamond fields, located hundreds of miles to the south at Lüderitz, which had first opened in 1908. Although German colonial authorities sought to dictate the conduct of these recruits, the Ovambo were able to maintain a certain amount of discretion, in great part due to the colony's sparse population, that is, limited indigenous labor pool. For example, groups of Ovambo recruits often refused to be split up, and invariably rejected work on white settlers' farms, where conditions were considerably worse. By the early 1920s, modest streams of Ovambo laborers were flowing southward to the mines, driven by the possibility of accumulating enough capital to purchase cattle during their contract periods.

In other settings, local labor scarcities similarly worked to the advantage of indigenous residents. In the Gold Coast, for example, the discovery of diamond deposits in 1919 occurred at an inauspicious time in terms of the availability of workers, especially for such a labor-intensive industry. With cocoa farms flourishing and the colonial government also a growing source of employment, indigenous residents had options that were preferable to the fledgling diamond industry. Moreover, many Africans chose to work as independent diggers, a right that residents in most other colonial settings did not enjoy. Finally, a meningitis outbreak in 1919 killed an estimated 60,000 Ghanaians. In this difficult labor market, mining employers could not afford to be picky, but prospective African workers certainly could, and were.

It wasn't until the mid-1920s that the indigenous labor shortage in the Gold Coast eased. Yet throughout this "labor crisis," the diamond industry weathered manpower shortages relatively well, in part because the vast majority of these workers originated from beyond the colony's borders. As word of the opportunities on the diamond mines spread, individuals from the northern savannah regions, such as ethnic Zabrama from Niger, increasingly migrated south to seek employment. Over time, these unskilled migrants, whom southern populations considered "socially inferior," constituted an astounding 80–85 percent of the mines' workforce. In exchange for these migrants' willingness to sell their labor, they were awarded with coveted positions, such as mine overseer. In turn, these workers encouraged, and even paid for, their kinfolk to join them, thereby alleviating some of the financial and psychological deterrents related to traveling so far away. Once there, these migrants typically remained in continuous employment, accumulating leave time over a period of years so that they could return home for extended visits.

Imagining the Mines: Recruits' Strategic Foreknowledge

Prior to departing for diamond mines throughout the continent, recruits gathered as much information as they could about the working environments that these respective settings featured. This foreknowledge served a number of purposes. In colonies with aggressive forced labor schemes in place, it helped residents decide whether or not to flee ahead of the arrival of mining recruiters. Conversely, in less coercive environments, it helped residents determine whether to engage with the diamond industry or an alternative employer. For those Africans who did end up heading to the mines in one form or another, this knowledge helped the recruits mentally prepare for the challenges that lay ahead. In South West Africa, for example, recruiters observed that "even workers who have never been to a mine have extensive 'fore-knowledge' of the mine and its social situation and know which occupations exist . . . what to expect, and what not to do."[3]

Africans obtained this information in a variety of ways. Sometimes, mining companies themselves contributed to recruits' awareness by disseminating information about working conditions and opportunities. Personnel from Consolidated Diamond Mines (CDM), for example, openly discussed with potential Ovambo recruits the prevailing conditions on the company's Oranjemund mines in South West Africa. Even without CDM's disclosures, though, the thousands of Ovambo migrants who made their way south to the diamond mines each year were constantly bringing back accounts of the latest conditions. Prospective recruits processed this continually updated information, often deeming the prevailing working and living conditions associated with a particular operation to be of greater importance than the wages on offer.

In nearby Angola, recruits similarly prepared themselves for mine life by learning as much as they could about the labor environment at Diamang prior to departure. Diamang was unique in that women often accompanied their husbands and worked in a number of different capacities for the company, though not in the mines themselves, and so the many Angolan men and women who had previously worked for the enterprise used their personal knowledge to help themselves (re-)prepare mentally. Even those recruits who possessed no firsthand knowledge had likely observed fellow villagers returning home safely from the mines, which helped allay their concerns. For example, João Muacasso, who first left for Diamang in 1956, explained in an interview: "Many others before me had been selected from my village . . . and those older than me had worked before me so I had a great deal of knowledge about conditions at the company before I left. I did not fear going to the mines because so many people had done it before me and all had survived, so I knew that I could."[4] Other recruits were less sanguine. Mawassa Mwaninga indicated that, after learning that her husband had been selected for work at Diamang, "I was afraid to go because I had heard stories about how the whites beat the blacks on the mines."[5] Similarly, Mateus Nanto explained, "Many from my village had gone (to the mines) before me. So, I already knew about the suffering and the conditions there. I was afraid of going, but it was obligatory, so I had to go."[6] Given the forced labor system in place in Angola, Diamang's African employees had little choice but to make the best of their time on the mines.

African Responses to the Challenges and Opportunities of Mine Life

In order to temper the hardships on the mines, most African workers engaged in a range of low-risk activities, such as sharing tasks and singing songs. These tactics helped them endure the various labor regimens but without undermining or subverting them. A smaller number of employees chose to participate in more precarious undertakings that signaled a reluctance to comply with corporate policies. These more brazen acts included partially or fully withholding their labor, or even participating in diamond theft. Wherever possible, African employees also organized themselves into labor unions (or less formal entities) to express their grievances, with the overall objective of improving working and living conditions; at times, the realization of this goal necessitated formal labor strikes. Although companies generally tolerated collective labor association and expression, they typically dismissed or physically punished individual employees involved in any type of activity that threatened the bottom line. Laborers accused of engaging in work slowdowns or caught stealing diamonds, for example, could expect to experience some form of corporal abuse, as well as possible prison sentences, fines, or worse.

For African men and women on the mines, the challenging nature of the labor process did not end when the whistle blew. On their return to company housing, they typically had to retrieve potable water and prepare meals to satisfy the hunger generated by grueling workdays. Even after colonial-era mining companies achieved food security, foodstuffs available for these evening meals were still periodically scarce owing to shortages or corporate neglect. Some companies also limited the activities in which workers could engage in mine encampments, including drinking. In response to these challenges, residents pursued a number of generally low-risk strategies to make their post-shift lives as bearable as possible. They socialized, danced, and sang, brewed and consumed alcohol, and, when viable, lodged complaints. In some of these residential settings, ethnic, linguistic, occupational, or tenurial divisions were regarded, while in others they were generally ignored. Mining officials typically displayed indifference toward workers' post-whistle activities, deeming that laborers who were allowed to "blow off steam" would be less likely to disrupt the mine environment.

Strategic Engagement with the Labor Process

In many ways, diamond mine workers embraced many of the same strategies that laborers elsewhere in colonial Africa employed, including singing songs while toiling and voicing grievances in response to objectionable working conditions. But the particulars of diamond mining also encouraged actions and generated opportunities that were less commonly encountered in other work environments. One was the formation of unions, which was attributable to both the presence of large numbers of workers with shared grievances and the tradition of labor organization among European mine workers. Another was theft, or IDB (illegal diamond buying). After all, diamonds are as incomparably easy, as they are tempting, to conceal, and eventually sell. African mine workers also withheld their labor for varying lengths of time, which mine managers variously characterized as "substandard effort," "work stoppages," "slowdowns," or "strikes," depending on the nature and extent of the (in)action.

Singing, Articulating Grievances, and Work Slowdowns

African laborers at Diamang, like their diamond-mining counterparts elsewhere on the continent, pursued a wide range of creative tactics to mitigate the daily labor process, including singing. Both male and female employees sang while they toiled, which provided a mental escape from their work but also connected workers to distant homelands. For example, Costa Chicungo, who began with Diamang in the 1950s, indicated that the songs he and his co-workers sang "were . . . to remember family, etc."[7] Other songs, though, had a more pejorative purpose, including one that featured the following morose verse: "The white makes us suffer, punishes us, hits us, offends us and strikes us with . . . the whip."[8] Although laborers employed in a variety of different occupations on mines sang, those who performed tasks that lent themselves to the songs' rhythms, such as shoveling, were the most consistent practitioners. Most Diamang mine bosses tolerated this activity because it appeared to improve morale and productivity. However, African overseers, or *capitas*, occasionally forced laborers to abandon this pursuit when songs denigrated the Portuguese, even though the lyrics were undecipherable to their targets.

Diamang's African employees also issued complaints to company officials, mine inspectors, and colonial administrators about insufficient rations, excessive labor demands, and abusive treatment. This action constituted a calculated gamble, as complainants risked corporal punishment for their perceived audacity. However, the various officials receiving these complaints usually ignored them or, less commonly, addressed them. In the early years of Diamang's operations, complaints about rations were the most prevalent. In 1925, for example, workers conveyed to Angola's governor, who was visiting the mines, that food provisions were insufficient. Later that year, employees passed along a similar complaint to a local colonial administrator during an official visit. In this instance, laborers indicated that mine supervisors frequently hit them and that when they were supposed to receive meat in their rations "it is just bones, while the whites get all the meat." As the legendary Bob Marley's lyrics warned regarding the potentially explosive mix of hunger and outrage: "Them belly full, but we hungry / A hungry mob is a angry mob."[9] Desperate to avoid having an "angry mob" on its hands, and spurred on by "hungry" workers' complaints and its own paternalistic agenda, Diamang achieved food security shortly thereafter.

Over time, complaints about personal mistreatment at Diamang outnumbered rations-related grievances. One example comes from 1956, during the unexpected arrival of a group of headmen, or *sobas,* to whom mine workers protested that "the monthly salary is too small, rations are too small for them and for their families . . . [while] overseers treat them poorly . . . wives should not work . . . and are treated poorly . . . and daily productivity targets are too high and take them, almost always, outside of suitable work hours."[10] Ultimately, these complaints precipitated little change, though the company did spare these workers from corporal punishment. Going forward, employees voiced fewer complaints than in past years, though an incident from 1965 offers an example of workers' ongoing pursuit of this strategy and the enduring risks. In this case, two Portuguese overseers beat and bloodied workers on one of Diamang's mines, prompting the victims to complain to a company engineer, who, in turn, spoke to the perpetrators. Instead of admitting to the hiding or demonstrating any sort of contrition, though, the Portuguese retaliated, meting out further punishment.[11]

African laborers in diamond-mining settings elsewhere similarly articulated their grievances, with similarly mixed results. For example, at Kleinzee, a mine in South Africa's northwest corner, ethnic Ovambo from South West Africa (Namibia) experienced varying degrees of success regarding appeals they made to company officials to address a variety of working and living issues. During the six years that Ovambos were employed at

Kleinzee (1943–49), their complaints resulted in the dismissal of a number of incompetent compound managers, a particularly contemptible pit supervisor, and even a mine manager—quite an impressive tally for such a brief time. As migrant laborers in a foreign country, the Ovambo workers displayed more loyalty to their employer (De Beers) than they did to the state, and even more to the mine bosses they respected.

On diamond mines throughout the continent, African employees also periodically engaged in work slowdowns, took unscheduled or extended breaks, or simply gave less than their all. If mine overseers suspected any of these actions, they typically subjected the accused employees to corporal punishment. More often, though, these actions went undetected. At Diamang, for example, workers began withholding their labor either individually or collectively from the company's inception. Company records from the enterprise's first fifteen years of operations abound with instances of substandard effort. In one example from 1928, a Diamang official compiled a number of flagrant episodes that allegedly highlighted workers' "bad will":

> In mine no. 3 of the N'Zargi mine group, a rate greater than 50m^3 (cubic meters of diamond-bearing soil removed) has not been achieved, although we'd hoped to reach a rate of 70m^3. In this same group, it has been noted that the workers who handle the wheelbarrows abandon them immediately after the European who oversees them turns his back. . . . These workers fill the wheelbarrows only half, or a third, of the way. . . . Those who work in the removal of the overburden layer are satisfied with the removal of 2m^3 per day, when other workers, working beside them, remove 6m^3 in the same amount of time. There are even Africans who, asking permission to excuse themselves with the objective of satisfying certain bodily needs, spend two or even three hours . . . before returning. . . . Already, these types of acts have affected the production for June and July. . . . The current situation is highly prejudicial to the common interests of the company and the state.[12]

Of course, from an African employee's perspective, this "bad will" looks a lot more like "creative solutions to demanding conditions." A subsequent letter to the same official suggests that laborers were employing these tactics intentionally, exploiting less experienced overseers. "Since the Governor's visit, things have gone from bad to worse. Since Agent Calçada left they have been trying out their tricks on Agent Remacle, who does not know what to do. The situation now is that they know they can loaf on the job in defiance of us. We have no control over them whatsoever and are unable to get a day's work out of them."[13] As Diamang's profits escalated and its control over labor increased, the company's tolerance of these tactics diminished, and employees correspondingly engaged in slowdowns less frequently. African workers instead began exhibiting their "bad will" in alternative, though equally creative, ways.

Striking Improvements: Labor Organizing and Work Stoppages

Labor organizing was arguably employees' most effective strategy for improving working and living conditions on colonial-era mines. Unions articulated the grievances of their members, and formal labor strikes constituted the most efficacious, if most extreme, weapon available to African workers during their struggles with mine management.

Although unions were banned in certain settings, such as in Portuguese Angola, they flourished in many others, including South West Africa. Due to the long history of trade union activity in South Africa, mines in its mandate featured strong labor organizations and were also the sites of numerous aggressive work stoppages. As far back as the 1920s, mine workers in the territory had been organizing themselves. During that decade, the Industrial and Commercial Workers Union and several smaller unions had formed at the Lüderitz diamond mine, though these early organizational efforts don't appear to have instigated any widespread or otherwise disruptive work stoppages. The most sensational strike staged in South West Africa would occur only some years later, commencing in 1971 and extending into 1972. Diamond-mine employees participated in this protest against poor working conditions and inadequate wages, as did miners of lithium, zinc, tin, and copper, as well as agricultural laborers. Indeed, it would be easier to identify groups of workers who *didn't* strike during this pervasive unrest. Although CDM officials were convinced that the above-average salaries and living conditions at its Oranjemund mines would preclude labor strife, on January 3, 1972, workers at that facility joined the thousands of protesters from other industries who had already abandoned their jobs. Following the eventual conclusion of the strike, CDM raised wages substantially and adopted a more open, if still cautious, approach to labor organizing. In practice, corporate concessions did not always follow work stoppages on colonial-era mines, but strikes, especially on this scale, did send a strong message to employers that adjustments would have to be made.

Labor organization and the articulation of grievances were also prevalent on diamond mines in the British colonies of Sierra Leone and the Gold Coast, although formal trade unions did not begin to appear until around the time of the Second World War. Before that, significant labor disputes were absent from the industry in West Africa, primarily because mine workers hadn't organized entities through which to channel their concerns. One major factor that impeded the organization of labor unions on these mines was significant regional and ethnic diversity within workforces, which hindered both the development of a common identity and the expression of common grievances. The lack of government legislation granting laborers defined rights or trade unions a definite legal basis also contributed.

Only in the 1940s, following formal approval and recognition from London, did Africans begin to form labor organizations on West African diamond mines. For example, the Yengema Diamond Workers Union (YDWU) formed in Sierra Leone in 1940, and the Gold Coast Mines Employees Union (MEU) organized in 1944. Shortly thereafter, the YDWU amalgamated with DELCO's Mining Employees Union to form the United Mine Workers Union (UMWU), whose first general secretary was Siaka Stevens, the future president and prime minister of Sierra Leone. Following the end of the Second World War, several developments fed both popular dissatisfaction and African labor strife, including spiraling inflation; shortages of consumer goods; growing disillusionment, especially of ex-servicemen; and swollen shoot disease (which affected the cocoa crop).[14] These social and economic factors prompted, for example, diamond mine workers in Sierra Leone to strike for several days in September 1945, which ultimately succeeded in both raising daily wage rates and reducing the work day to eight hours.

For all of the unrest on Sierra Leone's diamond mines, laborers in this setting only periodically resorted to work stoppages. In part, their relative quietude was attributable to the establishment in 1946 of a Wage Board, which was composed of five union, five employer, and three government-appointed representatives. Mine workers were initially encouraged by the creation of this entity, as the board seemed responsive to their demands, and since its decisions on minimum standards had the force of law, labor union confidence was strong. Into the 1950s, however, the board increasingly neglected workers' concerns, which prompted many laborers to (re-)resort to strikes. Other workers simply left the formal industry altogether in order to take up independent digging. Collectively, these developments gutted Sierra Leone's labor unions until they became virtually hollow, powerless shells; by 1954, paid-up membership in the formerly influential UMWU had fallen to only three hundred.

In the Gold Coast, the 1950s also witnessed an increase in labor agitation, but with better results for its participants. From 1952, for example, the MEU Branch at Akwatia began engaging with the corporate management of CAST in an increasingly militant fashion. In June of that year, the union won a substantial wage hike for African employees and pressed the company for further salary increases. After company officials rejected these subsequent demands, the branch struck on December 28, 1953. Although CAST refused to relent, and most employees returned to work by the end of January 1954, the company did offer some minor concessions. Still feeling confident, the MEU was again ready to pick a fight. On November 20, 1955, the union commenced its "100 Day" strike. Participating members paralyzed the colony's productive gold mines, while roughly 900 of CAST's 2,600 diamond mine workers also elected to strike. Shortly after this protest concluded, Gold Coast mining companies increased their wage rates and also improved their conditions of service.

Illicit Diamond Activity and Outright Appropriation

The strategic actions that carried the highest levels of risk for mine workers were diamond theft, illegal diamond mining, and selling. In rationalizing these widespread activities, an African laborer on trial in Kimberley for diamond theft at the end of the nineteenth century had framed his theft as follows: "Of course I stole that diamond. Did you think I was going down in that dangerous mine for a morsel . . . or perhaps *to lose my soul?*"[15] Decades later, African mine workers throughout the continent were still tapping the wealth that illicit diamonds could provide in order to augment their salaries and/or generate revenue outside of formal employment. In both cases, these actions partially addressed inequities within the industry by effectively redistributing a portion of Africa's mineral wealth back to its rightful owners—those individuals who daily risked "losing their souls."

Although Africans engaged in this array of illicit endeavors throughout the continent, these activities were most prevalent on Sierra Leone's diamond mines, which date back to the discovery of deposits in Kono in 1930. In order to (inexpensively) maintain political stability in the colony, Great

Britain had earlier introduced a policy of "indirect rule," which utilized regional paramount chiefs for administrative purposes. The colonial government also instituted a compensatory system whereby miners received a share of any diamonds (or gold) that they discovered in lieu of formal wages. These seemingly pragmatic measures, however, ultimately undermined the state's control by precluding the development of strong governmental institutions that could have curbed escalating corruption and extralegal activity. In their absence, a diamond-fueled "shadow state" steadily gathered.

Ironically, CAST's promise to address security issues in the colony had been a key factor in the government's decision to grant the company exclusive diamond rights in Sierra Leone. In retrospect, both parties had acted naïvely. Indeed, even directly under CAST's nose, on its own mines, theft was rampant, prompting corporate officials to press for legislative action. Simultaneously, thousands of outsiders were streaming into the Kono area, engaging in illegal diamond mining, buying, and selling. In response, in 1935, SLST, the successor to CAST, reached an agreement with the regional Kono chiefs, paying them £50 each to withhold their consent from any outsiders who wished to settle in the mining areas. The following year, the colonial state enacted the Diamond Industry Protection Ordinance, which required outsiders to obtain a state-issued license in order to reside or settle in the newly designated Diamond Protection Areas. The time for licenses, protocols, and formalities, however, had already passed.

Africans continued to participate unabatedly in illicit activities in the region, with the 1950s witnessing a significant spike in illegal mining, selling, and buying. As the parallel, informal mining industry steadily eroded SLST's control over the diamond-bearing regions in the 1950s, even more African diggers were emboldened to converge on the area. In 1955, a group of local miners finally brought the situation to a head by storming a station used by SLST's security and police forces.[16] In an attempt to regain control of the situation, Sierra Leone's government reduced the company's concessionary territory, expelled some 40,000 foreigners from Kono, and granted local miners the right to organize small-scale operations. By licensing these diggers, the state was reactively bestowing legal status on previously illegal activities. However, the train of illicit diamond chaos had long since left the station.

Indeed, by the mid-1950s, the colonial government was virtually powerless to contain the illicit activities of the tens of thousands of individuals— many of whom hailed from beyond Sierra Leone or even Africa—who had descended on the region as part of this West African "Diamond Rush."

Beyond a standard case of "diamond fever," the motivations to join this latest mineral-driven throng included a rise in global diamond prices; available funding for illegal digging and smuggling, particularly from local Lebanese merchants; a growing belief that "Africa's diamonds belonged to Africans"; a series of poor harvests and attendant high levels of rural poverty; and the recognition that local authorities' loss of control meant that fortunes could be made literally overnight.[17] By now, many of these contributing factors should sound familiar. Even the arrival of political independence—a process that started in the early 1950s—failed to calm this new, diamond-fueled "Wild West."

Sierra Leone's mighty struggles with clandestine digging, buying, and selling notwithstanding, perhaps the most blatant example of Africans tapping the continent's diamond wealth in the colonial era comes from Basutoland (Lesotho) during the 1960s. In this case, local diggers had for some time been excavating deposits at Kao, located in the northeast region of this British colony, before these mines attracted the interest of officials from Basutoland Diamonds, a joint venture between De Beers and the General and Mining Finance Corporation. Subsequently forced off the deposits and denied hospitality by the local community on government orders, the diggers took refuge in nearby hills and caves from which they descended at night to steal the company's unprocessed ore.[18] Because of their modus operandi—living in caves and operating stealthily—they called themselves Liphokojoe, a Sesotho word meaning "foxes" or "jackals." Without requiring too much imagination, theses "jackals" could also be considered "Mineral Robin Hoods," as they craftily "stole from the rich" (though it's not clear that they were as interested in "giving to the poor"—beyond themselves, that is). Regardless of what they were called, by the mid-1960s, they had succeeded in chasing out Basutoland Diamonds and taking control of the mine. In the ensuing years, they began to engage in kidnapping, arson, and even murder in an attempt to preserve their hard-fought gains. Only in 1970 was the government finally able to dismantle this troublesome-cum-violent outfit, a group that had brazenly succeeded in capturing a small but symbolically significant portion of the continent's mineral wealth.

After the Whistle Blew: Evening Activities

Following demanding workdays, African diamond mine employees faced additional challenges each evening, including securing food and preparing meals. In order to improve these aspects of their mine lives, workers forged a series of interpersonal relationships with fellow mine encampment residents. Often these social interactions occurred within or were clustered around "brotherhoods," or similar support groups. These and other relationships were both initiated and deepened in the encampments via a wide range of recreational activities in which residents engaged during their time away from the worksites. Unlike the factious personal interaction that characterized the South African compounds, the employee camaraderie that marked most other diamond-mining settings often crossed ethnic and other potential fault lines, even if these social boundaries were, at other times, both acknowledged and respected.

Cultivating Relationships

Workers' relationships with diamond-company officials, African overseers, and fellow employees played significant roles in shaping their post-shift lives. At Diamang, for example, men, women, and children actively cultivated a range of relationships that enhanced their overall mining experiences. In practice, the uncrowded conditions and stabilizing presence of women in the company's encampments were instrumental in fostering a social atmosphere that was highly conducive to this type of camaraderie. Indeed, even when Diamang's encampments featured considerable human diversity, most African employees perceived this miscellany as an opportunity rather than a barrier.

In single-sex encampment settings, such as in South West Africa, male employees turned to each other, rather than spouses or children, for support. In many cases, these men formed "brotherhoods," sometimes but not exclusively delineated by ethnic identity, which emphasized respect, trust, reciprocity, and dignity, and provided a moral framework from which "nonbrothers" could be excluded. In the mining compounds, brotherhoods addressed issues associated with the cramped living conditions, lack of privacy, and threat of theft and assault. Ultimately, whether a particular mine featured brotherhoods, families, wider social networks, or some combination thereof, these relational formations were crucial to workers as they attempted to survive the daily grind of mine life, especially after the whistle blew.

Recreational Activities

Workers and, where permitted, family members developed and expanded their assortment of interpersonal relationships on diamond mines via a range of recreational activities. Because mining companies' extracurricular offerings were often limited, or simply unattractive, employees often engaged in their own pastimes, including drinking, dancing, singing, and drumming—at times, even all at once. In addition to encouraging and deepening social relations, these diversionary pursuits also helped mine workers relieve the tension that built up during intense workweeks. Consequently, mining enterprises largely tolerated these activities.

Encampment residents on mines throughout Africa initiated and cultivated friendships each day after work, but especially on Saturday nights, as this was typically a time specifically reserved for socialization. In addition to drumming, dancing, and drinking, singing was an integral component of these gatherings, providing laborers with opportunities to both reinforce connections to their now-distant home villages and forge new friendships by learning songs from one another. One can only imagine the cacophony produced by the multiplicity of languages and dialects that were present in most diamond-mining encampments. Workers also used evening song sessions to disparage mine managers and their colonial overlords, just as they did during the workday.

In some settings, laborers generated a much wider variety of entertainment. For example, within the male-only compounds on the Kleinzee mine in South Africa, employees boxed, played rugby, and strummed an assortment of stringed instruments. They also danced, with male and female roles variously assigned to participants. Still others played cards, sewed, read books from the company's library, and even organized the Workers' Dramatic Society. These mine workers also sang, but in a much more assertive and organized fashion than on other mines. Employees often sang in a large ensemble, while at other times they arranged themselves into smaller choirs, each with its own repertoire, alternating between hymns learned on mission stations in Ovamboland and work songs. Remarkably, some African singing groups at Kleinzee even asked and received permission to go Christmas caroling within the mining installation. In general, diamond companies in colonial Africa were reluctant to allocate money for workers' recreation, thereby compelling employees, like Kleinzee's courageous crooners, to devise and initiate their own post-shift activities.

IN RESPONSE to the challenging conditions that prevailed on colonial-era diamond mines, African workers engaged in an array of strategic activities, ranging from no-risk to high-risk, in order to improve their lives. Via each undertaking, from migrating in order to secure employment to partaking in a range of recreational endeavors "after the whistle blew," laborers succeeded in generating positive outcomes within their broader mining experiences despite a host of formidable obstacles, demands, and pressures.

As the political "winds of change" began to blow across the continent in the 1950s, these mine workers began to envision the end of the oppressive structures that the colonial powers had engineered and their employers had readily upheld. Political independence ushered in a multitude of professional and personal freedoms that African laborers of all types had never previously enjoyed. Yet security in many mining settings rapidly deteriorated; mine workers, as well as other citizens, were newly exposed to a type of mayhem that the former colonial and apartheid states had kept in check, albeit through institutionalized violence and repression. Rather than providing economic stability for newly independent African states, diamond deposits were instead tapped to facilitate violent power grabs or for rapacious financial ends. It is to these chaotic, post-independence settings that we turn in the next chapter.

CHAPTER SEVEN

A Resource Curse

"Blood Diamonds," State Oppression, and Violence

> Diamonds are a nuisance to the country and I would like nothing
> better than to see every diamond mined out of the ground as soon
> as possible.
>
> —Milton Margai, future prime minister of Sierra Leone, 1958

> It [the conflict in Sierra Leone] is largely a war over control of
> diamonds and a terrible manifestation of man's worst greed.
>
> —Testimony given before a US Congressional Committee on
> September 26, 2000 by Mucta Jalloh, whose forearm and ear
> were amputated by RUF rebels in Sierra Leone on April 19, 1998

JUST ABOUT everyone I meet has seen the film *Blood Diamond*, a reflection of its significant entertainment value and attendant box office success. But for those readers who aren't familiar with the movie, it depicts the chaos generated by blood diamonds in Sierra Leone during the 1990s and the immediate aftermath of this violence in the new millennium. Given the film's action-packed sequencing, there's precious little time to explore the complex origins of the mayhem or to provide much historical context for audiences. Fair enough. But how then did we arrive at this particular form of diamond-related violence that has so fascinated global film audiences and jewelry consumers alike? To begin to answer that question, we must go back to the wave of African political independence that began in Ghana in 1957, which was supposed to herald a new beginning for the continent.

Underwritten by the continent's abundant natural resources, including diamond deposits, the first generation of African leaders was supposed to lead the newly independent states forward. Unfortunately, these resources all too often became targets for both government and dissident leaders, who were keen to use the wealth that these mineral assets generated to either prop up oppressive regimes or, conversely, attempt to topple them. By the 1990s, the term "blood diamonds" had emerged as shorthand to describe the use of these stones by African rebels to wage war against sitting governments. The expression also, however, captured the significant toll that these conflicts were taking on innocent civilians caught in the crossfire or violently pressed into mining service. Although brutal civil conflicts in Angola and Sierra Leone in the 1980s and '90s provided the original impetus for coining the term "blood diamonds," other scenarios in which diamond wealth continues to facilitate violence remain outside the narrow, internationally recognized definition of this expression. Millions of citizens in the Democratic Republic of Congo (DRC) and Zimbabwe, for example, would deem stones currently mined in their countries no less "bloody" than were the diamonds from Angola or Sierra Leone.

This chapter examines the diamond-fueled violence in Sierra Leone, Angola, and Zimbabwe to demonstrate the ways in which African rulers and militants have used this mineral wealth to sow displacement and death. Although the DRC also fits squarely into a discussion of this nature, the ongoing chaos in that beleaguered nation, the remarkably wide, and continually shifting, array of formal and informal entities involved in the looting, and the constant developments render the contemporary situation difficult to accurately assess. In the various settings that the chapter does examine, the important international dimensions of the continent's "conflict diamonds," which the sensational diamond-fueled violence within Africa tends to overshadow, are also highlighted. The remarkable ensemble of global characters and entities involved includes shadowy industry figures, private arms dealers, Cold War superpowers, and even al-Qaeda terrorists. The chapter also considers why "blood diamonds" have been a strictly African phenomenon, and how these stones work their way into legitimate channels and eventually onto the fingers of brides on their "special days." I also incorporate, however, a more optimistic section on the development of new industry regulations known as the Kimberley Process (KP), which was implemented in 2003 by a consortium of NGOs, diamond companies, and major producing, exporting, and importing countries in order to halt the sale of "blood diamonds." Unfortunately, the indifference that prevailed within both the diamond industry and the international community prior to the adoption of the KP meant that Africa's "bloody" diamonds had already affected, often fatally, millions of the continent's residents.

Why Africa? Conducive Conditions

Since independence, Africans' political designs have often been reflected in their divergent approaches to the continent's natural resources. And diamonds have proven no exception to this pattern. Individuals determined to assume and retain power at any cost have used diamond revenues to accomplish this objective, whereas others have applied the wealth in a more equitable manner. Unfortunately, the ease of accessing the continent's numerous alluvial deposits has greatly assisted the personal ambitions of the power-hungry sorts. The violent political upheaval that has destabilized many African countries since independence has further facilitated access; this turmoil has prevented governments from organizing and maintaining orderly admission to their deposits. Finally, buyers of these diamonds seemingly always materialize, irrespective of the seller's repute. In sum, the combination of: alluvial diamonds' accessibility; their utility in seizing and preserving power; and Africa's weak and volatile political institutions, generally engenders domestic chaos for those nations (un)lucky enough to be endowed with these dazzling, deadly stones. In a nutshell, that's "Why Africa?"

Alluvial Diamonds: Easy Access, Complicated Results

If you happen to be the leader—or, for that matter, even a citizen—of an African nation, you, perhaps counterintuitively, may not want your country to have alluvial diamonds. Virtually every African state that has experienced diamond-fueled violence since independence features these types of deposits. Unlike diamonds buried in large, subterranean "holes" that can be easily safeguarded, alluvial deposits are much more expansive and thus not as easy to police. Furthermore, these widely dispersed and more easily accessed diamonds are also often more valuable, as erosion typically leaves behind higher concentrations of gem-quality stones. With these realities in mind, the seemingly sensational words of Milton Margai, the former prime minister of Sierra Leone, that led off this chapter are actually quite reasonable: "Diamonds are a nuisance to the country and I would like nothing better than to see every diamond mined out of the ground as soon as possible."[1] Many Africans would agree, though they might consider "nuisance" not nearly a strong enough word.

The reason why Africans might wish that alluvial diamond deposits were not present in their countries is that the informal, or "artisanal," extraction process associated with these stones is highly rudimentary and extremely affordable and is, therefore, virtually impossible to control. In promising alluvial locations, shovelers dig holes until they reach groundwater. They then pile the diamondiferous soil around the edge of the shallow pits and, processing a pile at a time, shovel the ore into wooden troughs that feature mesh sieves at the bottom. Water is then pumped through in order to separate larger rocks from smaller ones—mimicking the washing stations from yesteryear—while a worker stationed at the bottom of the trough shovels out the refined gravel. Finally, workers dump bucketloads of this gravel into simple sieves and then shake it around, forcing the heavier pebbles, including diamonds, into the center and other materials to the outer edges. Note that the only equipment required is a shovel and a sieve. Indeed, given the unsophisticated and low-risk nature of this type of mining and the negligible capital required to engage in it, virtually anyone—*really, anyone*—can access alluvial deposits. I have, for example, personally witnessed dozens of elementary school-age children, scattering on our approach, illegally mining alluvial deposits in the Angolan bush. Due to this easy accessibility, Africans of all ages have long been encouraged to attempt to pry stones from the continent's alluvial soils, with endless, unscrupulous buyers on hand eager to purchase the resultant bounty. It's not difficult to imagine how in a developing nation in Africa this scenario might effect instability or, worse, complete chaos.

The Culture of the Global Diamond Industry: No Questions Asked

Machete-wielding rebels ominously watching over despondent captives desperately digging for diamonds is the image that most of us have of "blood diamonds." One need only watch *Blood Diamond* to be familiar with the origins of this image. However, it would be misleading to implicate only this type of extralegal mining operation in the escalation of diamond-related violence in postcolonial Africa. For over a century, the formal diamond industry—from De Beers all the way down—has played a key role in facilitating the growth and viability of the informal market for stones, thereby blurring the line between state-sanctioned and unauthorized industries. After all, without purchasers for illicitly mined diamonds, unlicensed operators would have ceased harvesting them long ago—a simple case of supply and demand. Instead, clandestine trading, secretive buying-selling agreements, and the general "no questions asked" culture of the industry have enabled diamonds offered up for sale by violent warlords and subsistence miners alike to find their way into cutting shops and, ultimately, jewelry cases around the globe. The governments of importing countries deeply invested in the industry, such as Belgium, have also been culpable. Belgium? Indeed, as well as many other countries with which we wouldn't normally associate such extreme violence and chaos. These states have historically been wary that stringent regulations—or, really, regulations of any type—could drive the diamond trade elsewhere and, thereby, deprive them of vital revenues. So, yes, Belgium.[2]

Africa's Fragile Political Landscape and Diamond Deposits: A "Bloody" Mixture

It's no coincidence that diamond-related violence has been so prevalent in Africa. It does matter that it's Africa and not somewhere else, and there are specific reasons, beyond easy-to-access alluvial deposits and the industry's "no questions asked" culture, why there has been so much diamond-fueled carnage on the continent. The origins of these myriad factors can be traced back to the colonial era and, in particular, the social, political, and economic distortions of the extended colonial period, which generated a series of highly fragile African states upon decolonization. In turn, their vulnerability offered ideal environments for challengers who sought to seize power. Thrust into the Cold War, newly independent states and their respective dissident groups each sought support from the world's superpowers. Both the USSR and the United States (and their respective allies) duly responded, often in the form of monetary assistance, forgiven debts, military training, and weaponry. These external contributions from highly situational "friends" emboldened both oppressive regimes and rebel movements alike and, beginning in the 1960s, helped generate a dizzying array of coups on the continent. Following the conclusion of the Cold War, training and weapons donations dried up and were largely available only for purchase, rather than as handouts. The era of the free lunch was over. Consequently, belligerents of all types increasingly relied on revenues from commodities such as timber, oil, and a variety of minerals to finance hostilities. Due to their easy portability and consistently high price, diamonds became a logical "conflict commodity."

Even as foreign governments began to reduce military assistance to African states and rebel groups, both overseas and continental governments continued to play important, often nefarious, roles in the blood diamond process by transshipping smuggled stones and/or facilitating the transport of arms to their diamond-rich African allies. For example, in both Sierra Leone and Angola, the rebel movements responsible for destabilizing these countries would have been short-lived or even initially unviable had they not received substantial external support. In fact, in some cases, foreign governments provided assistance *solely* in order to gain access to the diamonds emanating from deposits in conflict-ridden African nations. In the post–Cold War world, cash-poor African regimes and rebel groups rarely had anything other than mineral resources to offer their covetous, external "associates." In this context, greed often trumped ideological affinity, which, for some time, had supposedly been the cornerstone of partnerships between African and non-African nations.

The Shifting Motivations of the Belligerents

Since independence, many African governments and rebel groups have claimed that they were exploiting diamond deposits in the name of "development" or to "invest" in the continent's peoples. But we now know that these combatants engaged (or, in the case of the DRC, continue to engage) in conflict primarily for the massive amounts of wealth available, rather than for any coherent political or social purposes. Even the leaders of contentious groups who were once motivated by competing political visions, such as the leftist MPLA regime and the right-leaning UNITA rebel movement in Angola, over time sacrificed these principles on the altar of avarice. In practice, the easily lootable diamond deposits that financed these "resource wars" have altered the core objective of many African combatants from victory to stalemate. As illogical as it may seem, the deliberate perpetuation of conflict to maintain an impasse has often proven more expeditious in generating wealth than control of the state. Indeed, many of the belligerents involved in Africa's resource wars have come to view disorder not as a disaster, but as a condition that offers more economic opportunities than peace and order.[3] During the Angolan conflict, for example, MPLA and UNITA units coexisted in the country's diamond region, each actively mining. At times, they even cooperated in order to generate wealth for their respective military commanders, and themselves—a scenario that would have been infeasible during peacetime. Ultimately, although profits from blood diamonds have enabled both rebel groups and, to a lesser extent, standing governments to procure significant armaments, these revenues have failed to facilitate any meaningful, broadly beneficial administrative improvements on the continent. One is left to wonder if that was ever the objective.

How to Clean a "Dirty" Diamond

As we know from the preceding chapters, Africa has long generated large numbers of illicitly mined diamonds. Although some of these "dirty" stones have been smuggled out of the continent, many more leave through legitimate export channels, indistinguishable from legally mined or "clean" gems. Whether they are "clean" or "dirty," over 80 percent of all rough stones travel to Antwerp, Belgium, where they are evaluated and sold. From there, over 90 percent of the stones reach Surat, India, where they are cut and polished and then sent on to diamond centers around the world, including New York, London, and Tel Aviv, or, as often happens, back to Antwerp. In these locations, jewelers from around the world purchase these stones, which are then scattered across the globe, coming to rest in glass cases in retail outlets of all types. Both "clean" and "dirty" stones share these well-worn itineraries.

This facile merger of licit and illicit was first accomplished well before the term "blood diamond" emerged. Following civil unrest in an array of newly independent, diamond-producing African nations in the 1960s and 1970s, formal buyers typically remained in-country to purchase stones, but they did so in an increasingly informal fashion. Official production in Sierra Leone, for example, fell from 2,000,000 carats in 1970 to only 48,000 carats in 1988, paralleling a similar decline in the DRC. In these settings, diamond buying and selling steadily shifted from formal, legitimate channels to ones unsanctioned by the states involved. These illicit stones were then mixed with legally mined diamonds while still in the country of origin or, less commonly, later on in the supply chain. "Clean" and "dirty" stones emanating from the same place are, of course, impossible to differentiate, while even an expert is unlikely to be able to identify the origins of individual stones in lots in which diamonds from different deposits are combined. Given the industry's opacity, this type of investigative inquiry rarely occurred, anyway.

This "no questions asked" culture has also facilitated the movement of illicit stones at the international level. Customs officers of importing nations typically concern themselves only with a diamond's "country of provenance"—the last place from which the diamond was shipped, not its "country of origin"—the place where the stone was mined. In this way, throughout the 1990s countries such as Liberia were exporting (smuggled) diamonds to Antwerp in volumes that far exceeded the amount and value of what their mines were capable of producing. Most of the stones actually came from Sierra Leone. Yet no one cared. By looking the other way, the industry was abetting an array of figures, some quite repugnant, to mine and sell diamonds outside of national guidelines and to smuggle them, often across multiple borders. Eventually, the vast majority of these diamonds resurfaced in the world's cutting centers, were resold in gem form, and ultimately ended up in jewelry cases around the world as the foremost symbols of beauty, love, and, ironically, purity.

Sierra Leone: "At the Heart" of the West African Diamond Chaos

Long before *Blood Diamond* was released, Graham Greene's popular novel *The Heart of the Matter* (1948) had highlighted unauthorized diamond mining in midcentury Sierra Leone and the murky trade associated with it. Yet much of the ensuing, even more lurid, history of the informal industry in the country remains widely unknown. Stretching back into the colonial period, unsanctioned diamond mining and trading in Sierra Leone have intermittently caused domestic conflict, destabilized wide areas of West Africa, and been responsible for the death or displacement of millions in the region, while very little of the revenue generated has been reinvested locally in any broadly beneficial manner.

A Long, Troublesome History: Sierra Leone's Illicit Diamonds

Illicit diamond mining and trading in Sierra Leone dates back almost as far as the initial discovery of deposits in the former British colony in 1930. However, it wasn't until the 1950s that the problem became severe enough to threaten domestic stability and tarnish this jewel in Great Britain's colonial crown. By this time, the rampant illicit mining and selling in which the roughly 70,000 African diggers who had descended on the Kono-centered operations of the Sierra Leone Selection Trust (SLST) were engaged was imperiling the company's mining monopoly. Until 1954, the colonial government supported SLST's monopoly by opting to suppress illegal digging, though it also raised taxes on the company to help pay for regional police and monitoring services. Meanwhile, SLST was also actively combating illicit diamond activities in the area, beginning with the establishment in the 1930s of its ever-expanding Diamond Protection Force. Given these security measures, both the state

MAP 3. Sierra Leone. *Map by Brian Edward Balsley, GISP*

and the company felt that this spike in illicit digging would be fleeting. How wrong they were.

By the mid-1950s, the massive "Diamond Rush" to the colony's mines had prompted the state to revoke SLST's mining monopoly and reduce the overall area of the company's mining concessions. The government also strove to achieve a greater degree of control over the diggers by instituting the Alluvial Diamond Mining Scheme (ADMS), which immediately converted all illegal diggings into licensed operations. It also attempted to expel all "native foreigners," that is, Africans hailing from beyond Sierra Leone's borders, in order to ensure that only domestic miners were benefiting. Finally, the colonial regime strategically invited De Beers to install buying stations around the mining areas that SLST had been forced to surrender. As the diamond juggernaut was anxious to maintain its monopoly on rough stones, corporate officials enthusiastically accepted. And because in the 1950s roughly 20 percent of all diamonds that reached the global market had exited Sierra Leone illegally, De Beers paid out high prices in an attempt to reduce the motivation to smuggle stones out.

Although the ADMS was initially successful in providing some much-needed stability during Sierra Leone's transition to political independence in 1961, by the late 1960s it was beginning to show serious signs of strain. A second diamond rush, this time around Koidu, had produced yet another "Wild West" environment, and individual operations now featured hundreds or even thousands of diggers, as opposed to the dozens for which the ADMS had legislated. As part of this latest rush, increasing numbers of rural residents were abandoning farming to seek their fortunes on the mines, reminiscent of the early days of diamond mining in South Africa. Many of these diggers were financed by Lebanese merchants resident in the country, who provided funds to purchase shovels, pumps, and sieves in exchange for the right to purchase stones from the groups they sponsored. In turn, these merchants used the profits to help fund militias operating in Lebanon. Thus Sierra Leone's stones already featured problematic international dimensions, long before the term "blood diamonds" had ever been uttered.

Meanwhile, despite SLST's shrunken concessionary area, its Diamond Protection Force had grown from 85 in 1950, to 662 in 1957, and to over 1,300 in 1971. Government policing kept pace, with expulsions of foreigners featuring code names such as "Operation Parasite" and "Operation Stranger Drive" becoming regular undertakings. From 1957, the state had also been requiring residence permits for anyone in the region who was not an ethnic Kono. However, this attempt to emulate South Africa's pass laws failed, at least in part because corrupt police officers took a greater interest in collecting payments from noncompliers than in enforcing the system. Following Sierra Leone's independence, rival political parties also began competing to tap this wealth in order to generate funds and thereby expand their power. In 1984, SLST finally pulled out of Sierra Leone, further informalizing the country's diamond industry. At that point, things could only get worse, and they did.

By the 1980s, Sierra Leone had become a virtual dictatorship under Siaka Stevens, who had been at the country's helm since 1967, and the nation was quickly unraveling. Stevens and a small circle of trusted allies were unabashedly using diamond revenues to bolster a corrupt regime, indifferent to the societal degradation that saw, for example, life expectancy rates drop to as low as the mid-twenties in some regions. From a peak of over 2,000,000 carats generated in 1970, official diamond exports totaled just 48,000 carats by 1988, though of course informal production and marketing were thriving. With the country in deep disarray, a small group of discontented individuals began to take action, slowly at first, but building to a violent crescendo. Many from this collection of dissidents-turned-marauders had attended Sierra Leone's Fourah Bay College, where they fueled their disgruntlement toward Stevens's government by reading manifestos such as Kim Il-Sung's "Juche Idea" and Muammar Gaddafi's "Green Book"—standard reading for self-proclaimed revolutionaries everywhere. Several of these students eventually traveled to Libya to attend the annual Green Book celebrations, where they linked up with others to plot revolution for Sierra Leone, while also cementing ties with Gaddafi. One of these individuals was somewhat older, characterized by many as both charismatic and ebullient, and had previously spent time in prison for his role in a 1971 coup plot in Sierra Leone. His name was Foday Sankoh. Although most of you have probably never heard of Sankoh, throughout the 1990s and on into the first years of the new millennium his name became synonymous with terror in West Africa.

Hell on Earth: The Revolutionary United Front (RUF)

In 1991, with the vital support of Gaddafi and his good friend, the Liberian president Charles Taylor, Sankoh's Revolutionary United Front (RUF) launched its "revolution." If Gaddafi had been instrumental in the RUF's formation and its initial strikes within Sierra Leone, Taylor would play a much more decisive role going forward. In short, without Taylor, there would not have been an RUF. Unlike Gaddafi, Libya's eccentric, self-proclaimed "King of Kings," Taylor was seemingly much humbler, or at least more rational. The Liberian president had an Americo-Liberian father and had graduated from Bentley College in Massachusetts in 1977 with a bachelor's degree in economics. However, that's about where his apparent innocuousness ends. In 1989, Taylor launched a Gaddafi-backed revolt in Liberia and after years of civil war, was elected president in 1997 in an atmosphere of raw intimidation, (in)famously campaigning on the slogan: "He killed my ma, he killed my pa, but I will vote for him."

Even before assuming the presidency, Taylor had facilitated Sankoh's success by lending him young Sierra Leonean fighters, whom he had been using to help advance his own cause in Liberia, and later, a contingent of his most brutal troops to wage war in the neighboring state. Subsequently, the RUF would "recruit" its own fighters within Sierra Leone, kidnapping children and often forcing them to murder their family members before being force-fed drugs, including a mixture of gunpowder and cocaine (or heroin) known as "brown-brown," which was rubbed into cuts on their foreheads.[4] In this grisly manner, Sankoh assembled a deranged fighting outfit composed of young boys who served as child soldiers, and girls who were used as porters and sex slaves. Many observers wondered if Sankoh was the devil incarnate.

By 1995, the RUF had driven out the population adjacent to the diamond mines via a campaign of terror, sparing only those residents it required to work the deposits. The rebels were now firmly in control of the Kono diamond fields, which bankrolled their violent endeavors. Armed squads of RUF soldiers and captives transported most of the harvested diamonds, that is, the rough stones not sold on the spot to Lebanese or nomadic ethnic Mandingo buyers, to Monrovia, the Liberian capital. In return, Taylor arranged for arms that the RUF purchased to be flown— including on a plane once owned by the NBA's Seattle Supersonics— from Eastern Europe (primarily Bulgaria and Ukraine) to his country and then transported overland into Sierra Leone. In order to arrange this system, Taylor called on old friends, such as Gaddafi and Charles Taylor, as well as international arms dealers, including Viktor "Sanctions Buster" Bout. If you've seen the 2005 film *Lord of War*, starring Nicolas Cage, which is based on Bout's history of illicit activities, you're familiar with how this weapons dealer achieved international notoriety. As a result of this intercontinental collaboration, between 1991 and 1998 over 31 million carats of "Liberian" diamonds were exported to Belgium, with sales between 1994 and 1999 valued at approximately $2.2 billion. Over that same period, more than 75,000 Sierra Leoneans were killed, at least 20,000 mutilated and some 200,000 injured, while roughly 500,000 became refugees, fleeing to neighboring Guinea or Liberia. In total, nearly half of Sierra Leone's population of 4.5 million was forced to leave home in an attempt to escape the terror.

By the mid-1990s, the country had descended into utter chaos. Neglected by the rest of the world, Sierra Leone was hanging on by a thread, if at all. Moreover, two presidential coups during this period had precluded any potential governmental solutions to the violence. Instead, in response to President Ahmad Tejan Kabbah's plea for his countrymen to "join hands for the future of Sierra Leone," the RUF began amputating these potentially unifying hands from their victims, but also, to a lesser extent, limbs, ears, breasts, tongues, and lips. Underscoring this brutality, RUF commanders assumed names such as "General Babykiller" and "Queen Chop Hands" and led gruesome missions such as "Operation Pay Yourself" and "Operation No Living Thing." The RUF had initially entered the country claiming to be fighting on behalf of "the average Sierra Leonean" against the governmental and ruling class corruption that was centered in the country's capital of Freetown. By now, it was abundantly clear that the organization had long since abandoned any social and political objectives, if they had ever existed.

External Assistance? The Internationalization of the Violence in Sierra Leone

Desperate to contain the RUF, in 1995 Sierra Leone's beleaguered president, Valentine Strasser, hired Executive Outcomes (EO), a now-defunct South Africa security, that is, mercenary, company. For those readers who have seen *Blood Diamond*, the private army led by "Colonel Coetzee" is the fictional version of EO. Founded in 1989 by a former South African special forces officer, EO was a formidable outfit, featuring tanks, attack aircraft, fighter planes, advanced communications technology, and hundreds of well-trained fighters. In other words, the exact opposite of the RUF. In exchange for its services, EO was to receive diamond-mining and exploration concessions—basically all the bankrupt government had left to offer. In a matter of weeks, EO's forces drove the RUF back from Freetown, toward which the rebels had been steadily advancing, and recaptured the diamond fields, including the most valuable ones at Kono. Yet despite the positive influence EO was having in Sierra Leone, the international community was outspokenly opposed to this type of intervention and pressured Strasser to end the relationship. The IMF joined this chorus, withholding much-needed financial assistance in protest over EO's involvement.

Following Strasser's eventual capitulation and his cancellation of the contract with EO, chaos predictably returned. The RUF recaptured the diamond areas, a coup removed Strasser from power, and bags of severed hands reportedly began to appear on the steps of the presidential palace following Kabbah's aforementioned imploration to "join hands." A subsequent coup quickly ushered Kabbah from power, as well. Johnny Paul Koroma, the leader of a newly formed rebel group, the Armed Forces Revolutionary Council (AFRC), which was composed of a band of former army soldiers aligned with the RUF, now held the reins of power firmly in his hands. On May 25, 1997, less than a year and a half after the departure of Executive Outcomes, the capital of Freetown fell to a combined AFRC/RUF force, and all hell was unleashed.

Within days, hundreds of bodies were rotting in Freetown's streets, the city completely terrorized. Yet outside of hastily evacuating their expatriates, countries like the United States did little else. The United States was still smarting from the "Black Hawk Down" debacle in Somalia in 1993, and therefore Washington was reluctant to commit, not wanting to bog itself down in another African "tribal conflict." But plenty of other players in the international community were more than happy to get involved. Kabbah, while in exile, had been able to secure weapons with the help of Sandline International, a British private military company that had close ties with Executive Outcomes. Those remnants of the Sierra Leonean army who remained loyal to Kabbah received a portion of these weapons. The arms were also distributed to the Kamajors, a group of ethnic Mende hunters who sought both the eradication of the RUF and a return to stability in Sierra Leone, but who had also developed a strong taste for diamonds. In fact, by this time, just about everyone involved in the conflict shared this "mineral appetite." The Economic Community of West African States Monitoring Group, or ECOMOG, a regional multilateral force mainly controlled by Nigeria, also offered substantial support and firepower. While ECOMOG forces worked to liberate Freetown, the Kamajors, now armed as never before, focused on rural areas, running roughshod over the RUF defenses.[5] In practice, these Kamajor fighters operated more like vigilantes than military forces and ultimately proved to be beyond anyone's control.

By 1999, prospects for the nation had somewhat improved. Foday Sankoh had been captured in Nigeria and sent back to Sierra Leone, where he was sentenced to die for his role in supporting the AFRC. The RUF had been contained, even if it still occupied and continued to exploit the country's most important mines. And, the UN Security Council had passed Resolution 1176, sanctioning diamond sales from Sierra Leone. However, this promising period proved merely to be the calm before yet another storm.

Bolstered by ongoing diamond revenues and the unflinching assistance of Charles Taylor, who had recently taken power in neighboring Liberia, the RUF quickly regrouped and launched "Operation No Living Thing." They stormed Freetown again and left disaster in their wake. A death toll of over 4,000 during a three-week rampage of the capital evinced the madness.

What happened next, though, was almost as unthinkable as the acts of violence themselves. The 1999 Lomé Peace Accords granted RUF fighters amnesty and its leaders top-level government posts, all in exchange for their vow to end hostilities. Under the agreement, the murderous Sankoh was removed from death row and installed as the country's vice president under Kabbah, the man he had helped to oust just two years previously. Furthermore, Sankoh was appointed chairman of the country's Commission for the Management of Strategic Resources, National Reconstruction and Development. In other words, he and the RUF officially retained control of Sierra Leone's lucrative diamond mines. That same year, stones worth an estimated $75 million flowed from the RUF's mines onto the global market, further enriching Sankoh and his supporters. Following the RUF's partial disarmament to the United Nations' peacekeeping force (United Nations Mission in Sierra Leone, or UNAMSIL), it also received legal status as a political party. Remarkably, the agreement had granted the RUF virtually everything for which it had ever fought.

But, why, and *how*? In short, because the Western leaders who helped broker the accord—including the US "Special Envoy," civil rights activist Jesse Jackson—believed it offered the best chance to end the seemingly interminable violence in the country. Susan Rice, the US Assistant Secretary of State at the time, defended the agreement, proclaiming: "There will never be peace and security and an opportunity for development and recovery in Sierra Leone unless there is a solution to the source of the conflict. And that entails, by necessity—whether we like it or not—a peace agreement with the rebels."[6] Pragmatism aside, it's hard to imagine the United States entering into an agreement with an entity such as the RUF, shaking hands with the devil amid a barrage of flashing cameras.

Given the RUF's insatiable greed and unwillingness to fully disarm, Sierra Leone predictably returned to violence shortly after the Lomé Peace Accords had been signed. In response, in May 2000, the United Kingdom launched Operation Palisar, a unilateral military intervention that facilitated the evacuation of foreign citizens and eventually saw British troops successfully turn back RUF advances. Shortly thereafter, UNAMSIL forces arrested

Sankoh in retaliation for the deaths of seven peacekeepers at the hands of RUF troops, thus averting a coup that the RUF leader had been plotting. Leaderless, and facing a UN-imposed ban on all "Liberian" diamonds that promised to choke off the RUF's main conduit for arms, the group agreed to a peace treaty in May 2001. By November of that year, roughly two-thirds of its fighters had turned in their weapons to UNAMSIL, even if others continued to mine and sell diamonds throughout the demobilization period. In January 2002, UNAMSIL announced that the war in Sierra Leone was officially over and that the RUF now existed solely as a political entity. The hell had finally ended.

One Last Gasp: From Regional Havoc to International Terror

Just prior to its dissolution, the RUF had been busy selling diamonds. Included in their buyers were some rather unconventional types. Ahmed Khalfan Ghailani, from Tanzania, and Fazul Abdullah Mohammed of Kenya, two men in their twenties, had been purchasing RUF-mined stones since 1998. Yet, they were not aspiring jewelers or ambitious smugglers. Rather, they were members of the international terrorist organization, al-Qaeda. In fact, Ghailani had played a central role in the destruction of the US embassy in Dar es Salaam in 1998; he would eventually be captured and sentenced in New York to life in prison. In July 2001, as the RUF was in the process of surrendering control of its mines, these two operatives were seeking to convert a significant portion of al-Qaeda's funds into liquid assets, fully aware that the impending 9/11 terrorist strikes would make it harder to move cash. Due to turn over the mines to the government in November of 2001 and promised inflated prices for the rough stones, the RUF had ample reasons to oblige these buyers. In agreeing to this "big payout," the RUF was helping one of the world's most notorious organizations launder millions of dollars worth of assets. In the months and years that followed the fateful events of September 11, 2001, the value and importance of these "bloody" African diamonds to the under-fire terrorist organization became abundantly, tragically clear.

A New Beginning: The Promising Aftermath of the Violence in Sierra Leone

In May 2002, Sierra Leoneans lined up in large numbers to vote, a truly extraordinary development considering that the mayhem in the country had only very recently concluded. Perhaps even more remarkable was the presence of hundreds of amputee victims in the queues. These individuals had lost their limbs to RUF rebels who once bragged that "people without hands couldn't vote for those opposed to the RUF." These victims of RUF terror, however, *did* turn up to vote, waiting in lines for hours before emotionally marking their ballots, often with their toes. After returning Kabbah to power, electors looked on as the Special Court for Sierra Leone, set up jointly by the United Nations and the government of Sierra Leone, determined the fates of the most violent and culpable leaders from the now-concluded conflict, including RUF, AFRC, and Kamajor commanders and, of course, Foday Sankoh. The former RUF leader was indicted on seventeen counts, including murder, rape, pillage, sexual slavery, abductions, forced labor, use of child soldiers, "extermination," and "outrages upon personal dignity." Those who wished to see justice served, however, would be disappointed. While on trial in 2003, Sankoh died from a stroke.

Unfortunately, the positive developments in Sierra Leone failed to spill over into neighboring Liberia. Less than two weeks after the historic elections, thirty tons of rifles and ammunition arrived in Monrovia, largely paid for with, what else? Smuggled Sierra Leonean diamonds, of course. Charles Taylor had been able to rely on old friends to continue to smuggle stones into Liberia, which were now vital to his efforts to maintain power in the face of advancing rebels in his own nation. By 2003, however, Taylor had been forced into exile, fleeing to Nigeria before ultimately being turned over to the United Nations, and, eventually, the Special Court for Sierra Leone, located in The Hague. Following the conclusion of his trial in May 2012, the disgraced former leader was sentenced to fifty years in prison for his central role in Sierra Leone's diamond-fueled pandemonium. While reading the sentencing statement, the Presiding Judge declared: "The accused has been found responsible for aiding and abetting as well as planning some of the most heinous and brutal crimes recorded in human history."[7] One can only imagine the condemnation Sankoh would have received had he lived long enough to hear his sentence announced.

For all of the wealth that West Africa's diamonds have generated over time, they have only minimally benefited the region's inhabitants. These deposits have not always been at the center of the type of violence that devastated Sierra Leone and, indirectly, Liberia, in the 1990s and early 2000s. Yet since the initial discoveries in the colonial era, diamond revenues have rarely been used for constructive purposes in the region. Instead, the stones have been linked to pervasive corruption—either within regional governments or beyond their capacity to control, or both. However, diamonds are now finally playing an important role in helping Sierra Leone recover, while also augmenting development efforts, if only modestly, in Ghana, the Ivory Coast, Guinea, and Liberia. For example, while Sierra Leone officially exported only $1.5 million worth of diamonds in 1999, by 2005 this figure ballooned to $142 million. If these deposits continue to be properly managed and the wealth strategically reinvested locally, West African residents might finally consider diamond fields "assets," as opposed to deadly endowments.

Angola: Sierra Leone's Analogue to the South

Although the violence in Sierra Leone escaped international attention for some time, the roughly contemporaneous hostilities in Angola definitely did not. The conflict in this Southern African nation was a constant topic of discussion in Washington, Moscow, and Pretoria, as well as other continental and international capitals. When the Portuguese left Angola in 1975, the newly independent country immediately plunged into chaos, with three politico-nationalist movements competing for power: the MPLA, FNLA, and UNITA. After the FNLA was defeated militarily, the left-leaning MPLA government, supported by the Soviets and, even more significantly, by Cuba, was pitted against UNITA rebels, who received funding and military assistance from apartheid South Africa and the United States. From 1975 until the end of the Cold War, Angola in effect hosted a "proxy war," with the world's communist and capitalist powers squaring off, though crucially only indirectly. Although the South African regime was staunchly anticommunist, it was primarily engaged in Angola to check the advance of black nationalism that was sweeping south, right up to its own borders and also those of South West Africa (Namibia), its buffer "mandate" (map 4). Amid all of the geopolitical importance of this clash, diamonds also figured prominently—somewhat importantly from 1975 until the fall of the Soviet Union in 1991, and then centrally from the end of the Cold War until the conclusion of hostilities in Angola in 2002. Although the depravity of the Sierra Leone situation was largely absent from this Southern African arena, the term "blood diamonds" owes as much to Angola as it does to its West African counterpart.

The Lengthy Conflict in Angola

Just as the British had left Sierra Leone's diamond fields and industry in disorder on their departure, so too did the Portuguese in Angola. Prior to the country's formal independence in November 1975, hundreds of thousands

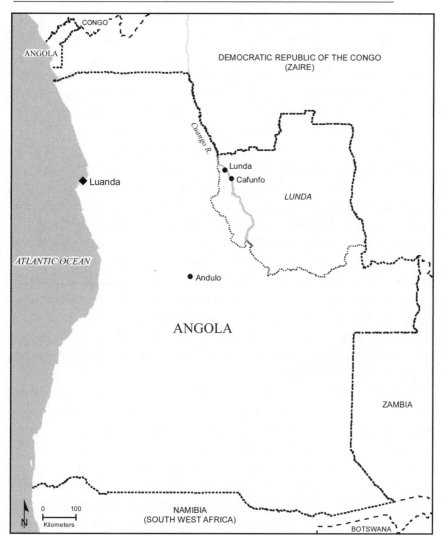

MAP 4. Angola. *Map by Brian Edward Balsley, GISP*

of white settlers had hastily fled, fearful of potential retribution by Angolans who had endured a long period of repressive colonial rule. Included in this exodus was virtually all of the engineering and managerial staff of the monopolistic Diamond Company of Angola (Diamang). The company's operational area, which was situated in the northeastern province of Lunda, did not witness any violence during the war for independence (1961–75). However, as Diamang wound down operations, artisanal miners began to flood into the western area of its concession, along the Cuango River. As this area featured easily accessible alluvial stones, rampant digging quickly drove up illicit output. At the same time, formal production dropped from well over 2,000,000 carats prior to independence to only about 350,000 in 1975–76.

Leaders of the rival UNITA and MPLA organizations had also been eyeing the wealth buried in Lunda's soils and were soon fighting over key towns in the region from which they could launch and oversee proximate mining operations. The MPLA government also nationalized what remained of Diamang, transferring its mineral rights to the diamond parastatal, Endiama. In turn, Endiama contracted De Beers in 1978 to manage production, which the industry giant did successfully before terminating its contract in 1985 in the face of UNITA attacks on its installations and personnel. De Beers concluded that although diamonds were precious, they were not that precious. Formal production declined sharply as a result of this violence, plummeting from $64 million in 1984 to less than $15 million in 1986. In response, the MPLA increased security in the region and, beginning that year, reorganized the mining zone, offering concessions in square parcels, or "blocks," to foreign mining companies. These measures proved extremely profitable, and formal production rose to over one million carats in 1998, valued at roughly $180 million, and to over $234 million the following year.

As the Angolan conflict dragged on through the end of the 1980s and into the ensuing decade, UNITA still periodically attacked formal mining operations, but on the whole the sector was flourishing. Never far from any diamond-related developments, De Beers eagerly returned to Angola, intent on building the infrastructure necessary to tap the kimberlite pipes that were being discovered. Illicit mining and smuggling continued alongside formal operations and totaled roughly $100 million in 1990, $300 million in 1991, and $550 million in 1992. For its part, instead of attempting to suppress this parallel industry, the MPLA opted to participate. To this end, the ruling party purchased the stockpiles that individuals in Lunda had amassed and set up buying centers in the mining region. Meanwhile, as a backdrop to this diamond-related activity, Cuba and South Africa began withdrawing their soldiers from the country in 1989, Namibia gained its independence from South Africa in 1990, and, in 1991, the warring Angolan parties signed a peace accord, with elections set for 1992—quite an extraordinary series of political developments.

Jonas Savimbi, UNITA's charismatic, if maniacal leader, went on to lose the presidential election. But, undeterred, he quickly declared the proceedings fraudulent and led his group back into battle. With the Cold War now over, however, UNITA could no longer count on South African and American support. Conversely, the MPLA was flush with oil revenue from Angola's offshore fields. In short, the rebel group was desperate. Only diamonds could save it now. And they did. Following a series of offensives in Lunda, UNITA captured the most lucrative diamond deposits, which would, over time, generate billions in revenues for the rebel group. In turn, these funds were used to purchase weaponry of all types, including tanks, which originated in an array of Eastern European countries and were eventually flown into UNITA territory. Sure enough, the same Viktor Bout who was active in Sierra Leone was also involved in this diamonds-for-arms scheme, along with many others hungry for UNITA's stones. If the Angolan conflict in the 1980s had reflected Cold War ideologies, the 1990s version could roughly be reduced to "oil versus diamonds." Indeed, although the term "blood oil" never really stuck, both natural resources played equally destructive roles in facilitating and prolonging the violence.

Into the mid-1990s, despite the acute violence in Angola's mining zones, illegal digging and smuggling continued apace. Now a central component of the war, UNITA and MPLA troops regularly battled over the most bountiful diamond deposits. Additionally, tens of thousands of increasingly armed and organized artisanal miners, or *garimpeiros,* and copious private security forces employed by private, formal mining operations were also present. The region was awash with arms. In order to try to stabilize Lunda and, in the process, increase its diamond revenues, in September 1993 the MPLA government contracted Executive Outcomes, just as the Sierra Leone government would do shortly thereafter. As in Sierra Leone, the mercenary/security company was highly effective. In July 1994, EO forces captured the strategic Cuango valley town of Cafunfo in western Lunda, while also scoring military successes elsewhere in the region before leaving at the end of 1995, diamond concessions in hand. Although disdained by the international community, EO was nothing if not extremely good at what it did.

Meanwhile, the MPLA also launched a series of aggressive campaigns to clean up illicit operations in the area. One of these efforts, the 1996 "Cancer II Campaign," resulted in the violent expulsion or death of thousands of *garimpeiros.* Many of these artisanal miners were Congolese, though Malians, Gabonese, and Senegalese were also among the ensnared. Yet for all of the violence administered during its execution, Cancer II failed to dent informal production for any substantial period of time. In many instances, instead of being expelled, illegal miners were actually pressed into service by security officers leading the clean-up operations or were made to pay protection money to continue mining on their own. Thus these campaigns more often compounded, rather than reduced, illicit diamond-related activity in the region.

Throughout the 1990s, Angola's diamond fields grew increasingly militarized and the levels of violence correspondingly escalated. A new development saw smaller foreign firms launch mining operations in partnership with Angolan corporations. These domestic entities were bankrolled by members of the civilian or military elite, while an array of Angolan private security companies provided protection, often in a very aggressive manner. Meanwhile, in mid-1998, having already claimed some 300,000 lives and disabled roughly 200,000 more individuals, largely due to copious land mines, the Angolan conflict returned to full war. This new round of violence mandated air cargo transport and even higher levels of security for mining operators and thus drove many of the smaller outfits out of business. Additionally, UNITA began targeting foreign employees of these companies, further hastening their departure.

The resulting exodus meant that only the "usual suspects" were left standing in Lunda, and what a motley bunch they were. The remaining entities included multinational mining companies, which often featured layers of private security forces and secretive affiliations with Angolan generals; UNITA and, to a lesser extent, MPLA mining operations; and the hordes of *garimpeiro* diggers, who often paid "protection money" to UNITA or government forces in a mafia-style arrangement. Of course, when MPLA generals and other ranking officers were engaged in managing their illicit operations, trying to defeat UNITA receded in importance. At times, uniformed troops participating in these extracurricular operations clashed with private security personnel on corporate concessions that senior military and rebel commanders were also (illegally) mining. Given the array of competing armed parties in the region, Lunda had degenerated into a space in which firepower determined authority, and control was highly splintered and constantly shifting. Once again, individuals who relentlessly sought to access and exploit Africa's diamond deposits had generated a "Wild West" environment.

The year 1998 was a difficult one for US president Bill Clinton, who suffered through the Monica Lewinsky scandal, and also for the global economy, encumbered by the Asian financial crisis, but it was also particularly harsh for UNITA. In June, the UN Security Council passed Resolution 1173, which prohibited the purchase of UNITA-mined diamonds, while the rebels also lost control of a series of premier deposits in Lunda. Even so, buyers of UNITA's newly sanctioned stones were not in short supply. Moreover, the rebel group could still rely on a number of friendly and/or simply corrupt African governments—namely, those in Burkina Faso, Togo, and, for a time, the DRC—to facilitate the flows of arms (in) and diamonds (out). Regardless, the rebel outfit's overall situation was undeniably growing desperate. In 1998, UNITA's revenues from diamond sales fell below $200 million, while the MPLA's oil revenues exceeded $3.3 billion—only roughly $400 million less than UNITA's *total* diamond revenues between 1992 and 1998. Furthermore, in 1999, De Beers announced that it would stop buying Angolan diamonds, prompting UNITA to discontinue the tenders (scheduled sessions for prospective buyers to see what types and quantities of stones UNITA had on offer) it had been holding at its Andulo headquarters. Since enjoying control over approximately 60–70 percent of Angola's diamond production during much of the 1990s, UNITA's fortunes had steadily declined.

In 2000, Angola's diamond scenario was further internationalized via the intervention of Uzbek-Israeli tycoon, Lev Leviev. Extending the long-standing involvement of Israeli diamond traders in Africa, Leviev filled the procurement void that De Beers's departure had generated by negotiating an exclusive contract to market Angola's rough stones through an entity known as Ascorp. Unfazed by the violence in the country and unconcerned with the legal-ethical implications of purchasing Angolan diamonds, Leviev quickly began producing significant revenues for the MPLA government and, of course, for himself. By 2001, for example, tax revenue from diamonds had risen to over $50 million, up from only $10 million in 1998. Leviev had originally sold the Angolan government on the concept of Ascorp by claiming that funneling all diamonds through a single course would reduce smuggling, increase state revenue, and, ultimately, stem the flow of diamonds to UNITA. Unfortunately for the rebel movement, Leviev proved prescient on all accounts.

On February 22, 2002, Savimbi's time finally expired, and with it UNITA's. Savimbi was killed in a hail of bullets by MPLA troops in Angola's eastern Moxico province, and six weeks later a peace treaty was signed, and the civil conflict was abruptly, finally concluded. At the time of Savimbi's death, he apparently had one suitcase stuffed with US dollars and another filled with diamonds. Evidently, he died every bit as dramatically as he had lived. These "blood diamonds," and innumerable stones like them, had enabled UNITA to prolong the Angolan conflict by roughly a decade, resulting in the death or disablement of thousands of additional Angolan combatants and civilians. In fact, the war in Angola had lasted much longer than the conflict in Sierra Leone, in great part because its diamond resources simultaneously supported so many entities—even ostensibly competing ones. And because the individuals most responsible for ending the war were benefiting from its perpetuation, it's not difficult to understand why the conflict was so protracted.

The Kimberley Process: The "Silver Lining" of the "Blood Diamond" Conflicts

As the conflicts in Sierra Leone and Angola were concluding, the United Nations was actively considering ways to try to prevent future "blood diamond" scenarios. The world body had initially been prompted into action following the release of scathing reports in 1998 and 2000 by two nongovernmental organizations (NGOs), Global Witness and Partnership Africa Canada, respectively. Their activist efforts drew attention to the ways that both the formal diamond industry and governments worldwide were abetting the flow of illicit stones. The equally damning Fowler Report, also released in 2000, reconfirmed and updated details concerning the Angolan conflict that had earlier appeared in the Global Witness exposé. Along with roughly a dozen other UN-sponsored studies conducted between 2000 and 2002, these reports highlighted the limited effectiveness of sanctions and the ways that the diamond industry, along with complicit governments, had continued to facilitate the flow of unauthorized stones even after restrictions and penalties had been instituted. In effect, these reports collectively shamed into action both the industry and the culpable states, fearful that gem diamonds might otherwise become a pariah commodity, reminiscent of what had happened to fur some years earlier. After all, it wouldn't have taken much creativity to recycle the popular slogan "I'd rather go naked than wear fur," substituting diamonds for fur. After a series of negotiations with diamond producing, importing, and exporting governments, diamond industry representatives, and civil society organizations, the UN General Assembly created the Kimberley Process Certification Scheme (KPCS). Following the January 1, 2003, implementation of the KPCS, all rough diamonds were required to have a certificate of origin from the exporting country in order to prevent the sale of stones emanating from combat zones.

Although KPCS monitoring continues to be imperfect, the scheme has performed reasonably well. Since its inception, the KP has played a central role in helping to channel diamond mining revenues away from rebel movements, terrorists, and corrupt politicians, while helping elevate the mining sector's tax contributions and boost economic development in producing countries.[8] Currently, the group boasts more than fifty participants, up from the original thirty-five, representing eighty countries (the European Community nations participate as a single entity), with other nations poised to join in the near future. Each year, the KP regulates the sale of hundreds of millions of "clean" carats, while "conflict diamonds" currently constitute less than 0.5 percent of the world's production, down from roughly 10 percent in the late 1990s. The KP has also demonstrated its efficacy by suspending noncomplying members, including Congo-Brazzaville in 2004 (for being unable to verify the origins of all of its exports), Ghana in 2006 (for allegedly certifying stones from neighboring Ivory Coast), and, more recently, in May 2013, the Central African Republic, as a precautionary measure to preclude the "illicit introduction of rough stones into the supply chain" as a result of the political upheaval in that country. Going forward, it appears that the resolve of the nations participating in the KP will remain strong, and therefore the system is poised to continue to help safeguard the integrity of the industry, the economies of Africa's diamond-producing nations, and the livelihoods of the masses of diamond miners operating in them.

For all of the success that the KP has had in rendering it extremely difficult to deal in "conflict diamonds," the system is not designed to stifle the entire range of diamond-related violence. In particular, the KPCS remains hamstrung owing to its narrow definition of "blood diamonds," which requires the presence of rebel forces using sales of these stones to acquire arms in order to overthrow or destabilize incumbent governments. This designation limits the KP's ability to address human rights abuses and an array of other criminal activities associated with diamond mining and trading. For example, beyond the KP's purview lie all of the diamonds linked to money laundering, smuggling, tax evasion, sanction-busting, and state collapse—approximately one in every four rough stones, worth about $2 billion annually.[9] Even more problematically, as the case of Zimbabwe (explored in the next section) so vividly illustrates, the KP's strict definition of "blood diamonds" allows despotic regimes to openly trade stones for weapons and other tools of suppression to terrorize their domestic populations. Despite mounting pressure by NGOs, and some KP members, for the Kimberley Process to broaden its definition of "blood diamonds," the current one and the limitations it imposes are unlikely to change anytime soon.

Also problematizing these efforts are retailers and consumers, who are not insisting on "clean" diamonds as rigorously as the KP had anticipated they would. For example, a study conducted following the implementation of the Kimberley Process found that roughly half of all jewelers were not requiring suppliers to document their stones as "conflict free," even though virtually every industry association requires this assurance.[10] According to one jeweler interviewed as part of the study, "Why open a can of worms? Most people really don't care. . . . It comes up so rarely and only the NGOs care about it. Our customers and potential customers really don't."[11] These jewelers' disturbing sentiments actually point to a major weakness of the KP: its voluntary nature. From government officials in diamond-producing countries to mining companies, customs officials, cutting and polishing houses, jewelers, and, eventually, consumers like you and me, the system works only if all parties are willing to play their designated roles. The good news for supporters of the KP, both within and outside of the industry, is that its general success thus far suggests that compliance, cooperation, and diligence are currently prevailing in a system that is only roughly a decade old, even if considerable room for improvement remains.

Zimbabwean Diamonds: A Dazzlingly Gray Area

Unlike the deposits in Sierra Leone and Angola, Zimbabwe's substantial Marange fields, which lie roughly fifty miles southwest of the eastern city of Mutare, have come online in the Kimberley Process era. As per the KP: when there are no (armed) rebels and, thus, no war, there are no blood diamonds. According to this logic, Zimbabwe's stones are "clean." In fact, in 2010, a monitor for the KPCS did declare these diamonds "conflict-free," enabling the country to sell them on the open market. Yet the diamond situation in this country remains anything but straightforward. So, why the controversy? Since the finds in Zimbabwe in early 2006—the largest in southern Africa since the Kimberley discoveries—the country's security forces have assumed control of the diamond fields, a violent process that has included the rape of women, the conscription of children to perform hard labor, and the beating, maiming, and torturing of members of the local population. Moreover, because President Robert Mugabe's authoritarian regime has so effectively utilized the prodigious profits that it has derived from these deposits to bankroll this thuggery, a diamond-fueled insurrection—a requisite for any KP-confirmed "blood diamond" scenario—remains virtually inconceivable. Even sans machete-wielding rebels and sanctions-busting arms dealers, though, the diamond scenario in Zimbabwe is acutely violent and extremely "bloody."

Zimbabwe and Robert Mugabe: A Once-Promising Past

Not so long ago, Queen Elizabeth II granted knighthood to Sir Robert Mugabe for his "significant contributions" to British-Zimbabwean relations. So how did the Zimbabwean president go from being so admired to losing his knighthood in 2008, fourteen years after receiving it; "earning" *Parade* magazine's ignominious title of "worst dictator of the year" in 2009; and firmly establishing his status as an international pariah by 2012? To answer these questions, we must briefly retreat into history, to the early 1960s, at which time Great Britain was preparing to grant independence to Zimbabwe, known then as Southern Rhodesia. With the imperial power poised to depart, the colony's sizable white settler population rallied behind Ian Smith. In 1965, his administration seized control and signed the Unilateral Declaration of Independence (UDI) from the United Kingdom.

Meanwhile, Mugabe, as secretary-general of the nationalist Zimbabwe African National Union (ZANU) movement, had been advocating the end of white minority rule of any type, which landed him in prison from 1964 to 1974. Upon his release, he rejoined the struggle, actively participating in the nationalist guerrilla campaign to topple the UDI regime. By 1979, the UK had intervened, and the warring parties finally agreed to put down their arms and hold majority elections, which Mugabe won in 1980. Hailed as both a freedom fighter and an adroit politician, Robert Mugabe had rightfully won the respect of peoples around the world.

The 1980s and '90s saw Mugabe retain much of this international esteem, despite his government's ruthless treatment of domestic opposition. However, Mugabe's fortunes soon changed, roughly with the arrival of the new millennium. A tightening grip on power and a poorly run program to return white-controlled farmlands to black Africans (many of whom were Mugabe cronies) as part of an attempt to rectify the inequities of the colonial era prompted Mugabe's fall from international grace. At the same time, the Zimbabwean economy collapsed. In November 1997, for example, the Zimbabwean dollar lost 74 percent of its value during just a four-hour period! Into the early twenty-first century, the country experienced hyper-inflation, rendering its already battered currency useless, before it finally abandoned the Zimbabwean dollar altogether in April 2009. Zimbabwe had become a basket case.

In the midst of this seemingly endless downward spiral, the Marange deposits, centered on Chiadzwa, were discovered, appearing like manna for the embattled leader. In fact, a subsidiary of De Beers had been engaged in limited prospecting for some time in Marange before a British company, African Consolidated Resources (ACR), succeeded it. But unfortunately for ACR, it was on its watch that the major finds were made. Think: Boer farmers almost 150 years earlier futilely trying to keep waves of "rushing" diggers off of their lands. In the far eastern stretches of Zimbabwe, it was Kimberley, all over again.

Zimbabwe's "Wild, Wild East"

As ACR desperately tried to maintain control, profit seekers of all types flooded into the diamond-bearing areas, spurred on by the country's deepening economic crisis. By now, you know the story. Virtually overnight, the region was overrun with informal provisioners of goods and services; a wide range of government and business elites, who were often in competition with one another; and, of course, illicit and artisanal diggers, called *magweja*. And, if the diamond fields weren't already crowded enough, Zimbabwean soldiers and police were also on the scene, charged with "putting a stop to the illegal activities" and "protecting the area." This flurry of activity also extended across the nearby Mozambican border, where eager buyers flush with foreign currency awaited the arrival of stones smuggled out of Zimbabwe. By 2007, influential individuals associated with ZANU or other organs of the state apparatus had become deeply involved in Marange, increasingly utilizing the state's security forces to protect extraction and smuggling operations, as well as to remove local communities, legal title holders, and informal miners, by whatever means necessary. These public officials often competed rather than cooperated, prioritizing personal rather than national interests, and thereby deepened the chaos. As the scholar Richard Saunders has argued, "Unlike other . . . cases of 'blood diamonds' such as Sierra Leone and Angola, where mineral proceeds fueled armed rebellion from outside the central government, Zimbabwe's conflict diamonds posed a threat . . . from within."[12]

The escalating violence in Marange correlated with the passage of Zimbabwe's Precious Stones Act in 2007, which criminalized any mining the central government hadn't formally sanctioned. By the following year, the state had deemed all informal digging to be illegal, including artisanal mining, which had previously been permitted. Consequently, the Marange fields were designated a "no-go zone" and the government began to conduct aggressive operations to remove all unsanctioned diggers from the area. These sweeps included Operation Hakudzokwe kumunda ("You will not return to the field") in late 2008 and Operation Dzokera Kumusha ("Go back home") early the next year. Yet rather than dispersing, many of the estimated 15,000 to 35,000 Africans involved in illicit activities fought back. According to Human Rights Watch and a number of other NGOs, human rights abuses were rife. Owing to the lingering violence, senior government officials decided that the police had been ineffectual in subduing the area and turned to the military. Zimbabwe's Air Force began strafing diggers from helicopter gunships and used teargas, attack dogs, and other extreme measures to terrorize diggers, suspected buyers, and the nearby villagers accused of harboring them. No one was spared. These troops also, however, wanted a piece of the mineral action and began to coerce anyone they could detain, including boys as young as eleven, to mine the deposits on their behalf. By now, Marange's diamonds were, quite literally, soaked in blood.

Not coincidentally, the militarization of the diamond fields coincided with Mugabe's declining domestic political popularity. In 2008, the ascension of the rival Movement for Democratic Change (MDC) and Mugabe's highly suspect reelection prompted regional leaders to intervene. Following formal negotiations, ZANU and the MDC agreed to a power-sharing arrangement, known as the Government of National Unity (GNU). However, there was nothing unified about this government; ZANU elements within the GNU retained exclusive control of the diamond fields, as well as the military and police. These security forces have been instrumental to ZANU's ongoing control in Marange, yet they also regularly permit informal miners to enter the deposits at night in exchange for a share of any stones that these diggers might unearth. Despite the persistence of this type of illegal mining, the Marange deposits continue to be, for all intents and purposes, at the disposal of Mugabe and those elements within the GNU loyal to him.

Predictably, these diamonds have delivered absolutely no benefits to the vast majority of Zimbabweans, while enriching only a select few. Tendai

Biti, Zimbabwe's finance minister and one of the leaders of the MDC opposition, has openly complained that hundreds of millions of dollars from the Marange operations have gone missing. If this accusation is indeed true, it will surprise very few observers. In fact, since the Zimbabwean military took control of the Marange fields, Biti has objected that exactly none of the diamond revenues have found their way into the national treasury. In response, he has called for clearer audit trails, new revenue-sharing arrangements, and greater transparency regarding the sale of diamonds. However, under the existing agreement, the revenues derived from the diamond fields are, conveniently for Mugabe and his supporters, the only streams not subject to oversight by the finance minister. With the wealth flowing directly to Mugabe and his allies, Biti's greatest fear—which he shares with millions of fellow Zimbabweans—is that the aging president (born in February 1924) will continue to utilize these profits to violently retain control of the diamond fields, strengthen his hold on power, and snuff out the nation's nascent political pluralism, at any cost. Indeed, Zimbabwe's prodigious diamond deposits have not only led to the death and dislocation of many citizens but have also virtually crushed its once promising democracy.

Zimbabwe and the Kimberley Process: The Quest for Legitimacy

Following the discoveries at Marange, the stones it yielded were initially sold on the international market, even as global observers began to voice concerns regarding the increasing violence on the diamond fields. In 2007, Zimbabwe's minister of Justice, Legal and Parliamentary Affairs, Patrick Chinamasa, responded by lashing out at critics. The minister declared, not without some bitterness, contempt, and condescension: "Diamonds are not found in many countries in Europe save for Russia. The rest do not have diamonds, but the Kimberley Process committee is based somewhere in Europe so we are forced to comply with their regulations. For us to sell our diamonds, if we have to comply with set procedures, we run the risk of being stuck out."[13] Zimbabwe would, indeed, soon be "stuck out." After visiting the region, an investigative team from the Kimberley Process Certification Scheme delivered an interim report to the Zimbabwean government urging it to suspend the production and exportation of diamonds from the eastern Marange district. In particular, the report denounced "unacceptable and horrific violence against civilians by authorities in and around Chiadzwa. . . . Our team was able to interview and document the stories . . . of victims, observe their wounds, scars from dog bites and batons, tears, and on-going psychological trauma."[14] In 2008, the KP consequently suspended diamond sales from the country, citing rampant human rights abuses. For the growing numbers of critics of the Mugabe regime, the Kimberley Process had delivered an important rebuke.

Undeterred, as dictators so often are, Mugabe remained defiant, striving to rehabilitate the image of his country and its diamonds. As he and his political allies tightened their control over the mines, Mugabe was also busy (re-)presenting Zimbabwe's diamond industry as both "formal" and "legitimate" as part of a successful attempt to secure the certification necessary to openly sell the Marange stones on the international market. Indeed, after considerable delay and controversy, in June 2011 the acting KP chairman, Mathieu Yamba, from the DRC, announced his unilateral decision to lift the Kimberley ban on exports of diamonds from the Marange fields. He made his decision even though independent monitoring, including the KP's own investigation, had confirmed serious human rights abuses at Marange and rampant smuggling from these deposits. So why did Yamba lift the ban? Although lobbying by fellow African diamond-producing nations was partially responsible for his decision, the KP's narrow definition of "blood diamonds" ultimately left the monitoring entity with little choice. There was, after all, no diamond-fueled civil war in Zimbabwe. In November 2011, the Kimberley Process effectively endorsed its chairman's declaration by authorizing limited sales of diamonds from Zimbabwe. Mugabe had finally secured the legitimacy, however tainted, that he so desperately craved.

The KP's endorsement immediately prompted one of its founders, Global Witness, to withdraw from the initiative in dramatic fashion. In order to avert exactly the type of scenario that existed in Zimbabwe, groups like Global Witness had long been campaigning for the KP to broaden its definition of blood diamonds. Although activist organizations like Global Witness have been unable to prevent the authoritarian Mugabe regime from selling diamonds on the open market, the recent tenure of the United States as KP chair has meant that activist organizations' demands are now falling on more receptive ears. For its part, the United States abstained from the 2011 KP vote that authorized the sale of Zimbabwe's diamonds and has also banned the trade of these diamonds domestically, predicated on sanctions that were already in place against the Mugabe regime. Yet the United States acknowledges that, beyond unilateral boycotts and sanctions, much broader participation will be required in order to change the way the Kimberley Process operates. Resistance within the industry and also among certain KP member states, including many from Africa, to any proposed redefinition of "blood diamonds" remains strong. Consequently, no major amendments to the KP's current approach are expected in the near future.

Who's Buying? The Chinese Connection

China's growing influence in sub-Saharan Africa is arguably nowhere more profound than in Zimbabwe. The relationship between the two countries is a long-standing one, dating back to the struggle for black majority rule in what was then (Southern) Rhodesia. Rebuffed by the Soviets during the liberation struggle, Mugabe turned to China, which was eager to assist. Indeed, Mugabe recently reminded international observers that "relations between Zimbabwe and China started when we were fighting colonialism, and after independence we consolidated the relationship. The dimension of co-operation in defense and security is probably the longest and most consolidated of all the other dimensions."[15] The embattled Mugabe has also greatly appreciated China's "no questions asked" policy toward the domestic affairs of its commercial partners. In fact, China has emerged as the nation's only major international supporter. Given Beijing's global quest for both a wide variety of natural resources and new markets for its products, as well as its growing political and economic influence throughout Africa, it's not surprising that China has a major presence in Zimbabwe. Nor should it be surprising that diamonds figure so centrally in this relationship.

Since the early 2000s, coinciding with Zimbabwe's deepening international isolation, Chinese arms, including fighter jets, tanks, and assault rifles, have been streaming into the Southern African nation. The Chinese have also been busy constructing various facilities, including a state-of-the-art military intelligence college, in Zimbabwe. And how is Mugabe expressing his gratitude for this apparent largesse? In diamonds, of course. Under the terms of a deal signed in June 2011, Zimbabwe is borrowing $98 million from the Export-Import Bank of China for the construction of the military college and will pay off the loan with Marange diamonds. These stones will travel east to feed China's expanding appetite for industrial diamonds and to feature in jewelry for consumption by the nation's rapidly expanding middle and upper classes. With the Marange deposits estimated to contain over $200 billion worth of stones, the future looks bright for China's arms, construction, and jewelry industries, as well as for Mugabe's reenergized regime.

Throughout this controversy, it's been the Chinese, rather than the Zimbabweans, who have actually been mining the diamonds. Rather than busy itself with extracting these stones, the Mugabe regime has instead handed Beijing lucrative mining contracts. Even as Zimbabwe waited for KP approval, the Chinese were actively mining and stockpiling roughly two million carats of Marange diamonds. These stones continue to be mined by a joint Chinese-Zimbabwean venture (though the Chinese are entirely responsible for production) called Anjin Investments, which possesses one of only a handful of Marange mining concessions. Anjin is the product of an arrangement between the Zimbabwean state and the Anhui Foreign Economic Construction Group, a public company under China's Ministry of Construction. Anjin maintains a low profile, but it's clear that Chinese military officers, who are stationed at the mines, are involved, as are high-ranking members of the Zimbabwean army. For example, it was recently revealed that one of the Zimbabwean directors of the venture is Brigadier-General Charles Tarumbwa, a serving officer in the country's army, who is, incidentally, barred by sanctions from traveling to or investing in Western countries. Mugabe has also contributed to this venture by exempting the enterprise from complying with a domestic law that requires foreign companies be at least 51 percent Zimbabwean-owned. This self-serving measure has predictably prompted outcry from Mugabe's opponents, including Shepherd Mushonga, a member of the MDC. Speaking about Anjin's preferential treatment, the parliamentarian commented, "In this deal, Chinese have become Zimbabweans."[16] Perhaps this transformation is not as bizarre as it might appear, though. Zimbabwe's diamonds have, after all, seemingly become Chinese.

IT TOOK the actions of depraved RUF soldiers, greed-driven UNITA and MPLA commanders, and two determined, activist NGOs to finally bring to light the unsavory and unregulated conduct of the global diamond industry that had, for so long, remained hidden. Once again, Africa's diamonds were thrust onto the global stage, though certainly not in a positive spotlight. In order to avoid a consumer boycott, the industry energetically, if belatedly, participated in the development of the KPCS. For millions of Africans, however, this initiative came too late. While it would be inaccurate to contend that diamonds were solely responsible for the outbreak of violence in either Angola or Sierra Leone, the protracted nature and high levels of brutality that marked these conflicts are directly attributable to the presence of easily exploitable alluvial deposits. Continued violence perpetrated by an array of murderous groups in the eastern Congo, which is partially fueled by diamond revenues, and the ongoing bolstering of Zimbabwean strongman Robert Mugabe suggest that these precious stones will continue to play roles in the continent's woes.

Although diamonds have contributed to significant distress and destruction in certain places on the continent, Africans have also used these mineral resources to make positive contributions in other settings. While Angola and Sierra Leone are now exploiting their diamond endowments in ways that more equitably benefit their respective citizenries, countries such as Botswana and Namibia have been using their deposits to peacefully develop their nations since political independence. It is to these counterexamples to the violence explored above that we turn in the next chapter.

CHAPTER EIGHT

Mineral Assets

Diamonds and the Development of Democratic States

> Batswana know that diamonds plus development equals democracy.
>
> —Former president of Botswana, Festus Mogae, 2001[1]

> Place of jackals and birds;
> Where Bushmen hardly go;
> Only howling jackals heard,
> Winds and sand do flow.
> Greedy man's lust for wealth,
> Invades the place of solitude.
>
> —Anonymous poem posted at a diamond mine located along
> Namibia's desolate coast in the early 1980s

THE DIAMOND-FUELED violence that consumed Angola and Sierra Leone stands in sharp contrast to the post-independence periods in Botswana and Namibia, the world's first and seventh largest producers of gem-quality stones, respectively. Since assuming control, the governments in these two Southern African countries have utilized diamond profits to build democratic states characterized by pacific foreign and domestic policies. Stable, reasonably transparent nations such as Botswana and Namibia belie notions of African states as "kleptocracies" led by "presidents for life" who heartlessly count their riches while their subject populations starve. Today Botswana is classified by the UN as an "upper-middle-income country," with diamond profits improving the lives of the vast majority of the country's inhabitants.

The assertion by former president Festus Mogae that appears above, alliteratively linking diamonds, development, and democracy, has thus far proven accurate. Africans in both countries are also benefiting from the job opportunities that the industry generates, as diamond mining is the leading employer in both settings. Moreover, although most Namibians and Botswanans continue to work as manual laborers in the industry, others have assumed leadership positions in the mining enterprises active in these countries.

This chapter examines post-independence diamond developments in Botswana and Namibia, including the aggressive renegotiations of production agreements with De Beers and the utilization of the resultant revenues for broad-based national development. Whereas Namibia, which achieved independence from South Africa only in 1990, inherited a long-standing industry, diamonds weren't discovered in Botswana until after the country achieved political independence in 1966. Yet, despite this important chronological difference, the two governments have both utilized their diamond revenues in remarkably similar, socially beneficial ways.

Unfortunately, no simplistic formula exists to explain why some nations, such as Botswana and Namibia, generate "development diamonds" and others "blood diamonds"; there are simply too many variables. Yet the small populations of these two countries allow for greater per capita benefits from diamond revenues, thereby helping limit potential social discontent, while the difficult-to-access deposits in these settings have greatly assisted their governments in managing and controlling their respective diamond endowments. In turn, these factors go some way toward explaining why these two nations have been able to avoid the scourge of "conflict diamonds."

For all of these positive developments in Botswana and Namibia, neither is completely devoid of challenges. Ruling political parties have used diamond wealth to buoy their popularity and easily win election (and reelection), the highly industrial nature of modern mining has limited the overall number of jobs created, and poverty and uneven development remain ongoing concerns. In Botswana, access to deposits has generated tension between indigenous communities and the state, and in Namibia, smuggling remains rampant. These issues notwithstanding, Botswana and Namibia offer an important counternarrative to the "bloody" scenarios explored in the preceding chapter. In order to help amend the negative connotations associated with Africa's diamonds, the industry would do well to highlight the positive developments in these largely peaceful nations—two countries that most diamond consumers have likely never heard of.

Botswana: An "African Miracle"

Botswana's history of diamond production is somewhat unique in Africa. The country's deposits were discovered not during the colonial period but only after it achieved autonomy from Great Britain. The timing could not have been better: Botswana became independent in 1966, and the expansive kimberlite deposits at Orapa were discovered just a year later. Thus, rather than inheriting a diamond industry that had been controlled by foreigners for decades, the mineral discovery was truly an economic bonus for the fledgling nation. The primary advantage of this scenario was that the country could start fresh, rather than reorganizing an existing industry, striving not to interrupt vital revenue streams, and remaining beholden to international capital. Yet the remarkably rapid rate at which Botswana developed economically and socially following the diamond discoveries is not attributable to fortunate timing alone—recall that Zimbabwe's diamonds were also discovered after independence, but with markedly different results. Instead, the series of scrupulous, pragmatic, democratically elected governments that have overseen the country from the capital city of Gaborone from 1966 to the present deserve the lion's share of the credit. Each administration has managed these diamond resources in a cautious, largely equitable manner. Today Botswana's resources consist of four massive, deep, open pit mines, including Orapa, the largest such mine in the world, and Jwaneng, the richest diamond mine by value in the world, each of which is located in a highly remote, easy to police, area. Due to the prudent ways in which Botswana has managed these mineral deposits and developed both peacefully and rapidly—at a rate unmatched even by the so-called Asian Tigers—while situated in the most underdeveloped and conflict-ridden continent in the world, the country is rightfully known as an "African miracle."[2]

The Transformative, "Miraculous," Early Diamond Years

From 1885 to 1966, Botswana was a British protectorate, known as Bechuanaland. In 1964, Great Britain had acceded to Botswanans' call for self-government, with the first elections held the following year and formal independence arriving in September of 1966. Yet beyond the natural excitement associated with the end of the colonial era, Botswanans had little else to celebrate. The new country ranked among the poorest in the world, with an annual per capita income of roughly only $80. Moreover, although Botswana features a relatively small population, at just over two million, the country is landlocked and also features an arid climate, which limits agricultural output. The country was also almost exclusively dependent on just three sources of revenue: the domestic cattle industry; remittances from migrant laborers in South Africa; and aid from the British government—not exactly an ideal economic foundation on which to build and develop the nation.

The 1967 diamond discoveries changed everything. Due to low production costs and the high quality of the stones, virtually overnight the country found itself in a highly enviable fiscal position. Mother Nature had seemingly been kind to Botswana after all. The government immediately nationalized all subsoil mineral resources to ensure complete control over all future revenues. From 1966 to 1990 earnings from diamonds helped propel the country's real GDP growth to a remarkable average annual rate of 10 percent, including 13 percent during the 1980s, while over the same period, real income per capita grew by 6.5 percent. These figures were not just impressive for an African nation; they rendered Botswana the fastest-growing economy *in the world* over these two and a half decades. This economic growth also had a strong social dimension, as the government applied the diamond wealth to advance the nation and its citizenry in a reasonably broad, inclusive fashion. For example, significant investments were made in the country's road, water, and electricity systems, its educational structure, and its national health services. Consequently, according to the United Nations Development Programme's Development Index, which combines both economic and social measures of development, including adult literacy, infant mortality, life expectancy, and access to clean water, by 1992 Botswana featured the highest level of human development on mainland sub-Saharan Africa. Moreover, into the early 2000s, Botswana's per capita GDP of more than $6,000 prompted the World Bank to classify it as an "upper-middle-income country."

The diamond wealth encouraged Gaborone to pursue initiatives that would have been unimaginable during the early post-independence period. Perhaps most important was its decision to renegotiate the country's mining contract with De Beers. In 1975, these efforts resulted in the creation of Debswana, a public-private enterprise owned equally by the Botswanan state and De Beers, hence the somewhat quirky corporate name. The new arrangement constituted a significant improvement on the 15 percent production share that the nation had previously held.

Speaking about these developments, Peter Mmusi, the country's former finance minister and vice president, had the following to say about the government's approach to negotiations: "A purposeful government which acquires the expertise to deal with foreign companies on its own terms need not have a fear of domination by foreign companies, however large they may be. The important word is purposeful—and I believe our government has been able to put together strong negotiation teams, has backed them up with well-worked out negotiating mandates, and has then overseen the implementation of our major mining agreements with detailed care."[3] The nucleus of the "purposeful" government's negotiating team was the highly effective Mineral Policy Committee (MPC). This group consisted of four permanent secretaries representing the key ministries involved and was complemented by representatives from other ministries and also by domestic and international technical experts. The MPC's strategy was to assemble a team of senior local officials, supported by a group of expatriates with technical knowledge, to negotiate with De Beers's experienced representatives. The continuity of the MPC's membership was also a key to its success, as several of its members served for periods of up fifteen years. Although Botswana held the chips—its mines would eventually outpace all others in the world and the output would come to constitute roughly two-thirds of De Beers's overall production—the diamond behemoth had rarely, if ever, been pushed around in this manner, let alone by a recently sovereign African nation.

The year after Debswana's creation, the increased diamond revenues that Botswana was enjoying provided the economic foundation needed to introduce its own currency, the *pula*. Even as early as 1972, Botswana's government had been able to fully finance its recurrent budget, and in 1983, it began running an overall budget surplus. By the mid-1990s, the country's foreign exchange reserves totaled some $4.8 billion, providing it with over two years of import cover and the financial base necessary to ensure the stability of the *pula*. Even though government spending rose by an average of 11 percent a year in real terms between 1970 and 1995, the country was still able to develop its social infrastructure without accumulating any significant foreign debt—a virtually unique accomplishment in sub-Saharan Africa. Moreover, Botswana has been able to avoid borrowing against future mineral earnings, a practice that many resource-rich African governments have too readily embraced. Consequently, the country is able to endure the inevitable fluctuations in commodity prices without having to institute drastic measures while waiting for prices to (re)stabilize.

The 1990s and 2000s: Continued Success, but with Some Cautionary Signs

Throughout the 1990s, the massive profits generated by Botswana's diamond industry continued to facilitate rapid development, while never threatening political stability or an end to multiparty elections. Into the new millennium, Debswana was producing over 30 million carats per year, generating revenues of over $3 billion—approximately one quarter of the world's rough diamonds by value. In the midst of all of this success, though, a series of worrisome, diamond-related structural challenges and issues had begun to emerge. For example, after having replaced beef as the country's leading foreign exchange earner by the early 1980s, by 2001 diamond exports accounted for roughly 87 percent of this type of income, more than doubling the 1981 rate of 40 percent. In other words, as "brilliant" as the diamond revenues had been, the country was growing dangerously dependent on a single resource for its development. Moreover, with the emergence of "blood diamonds," the entire industry—and, thus, Botswana's economy—newly came under attack, its survival seriously threatened. Meanwhile, disadvantaged sectors of the country's population were increasingly and outspokenly criticizing the government for *saving too much,* an exceptional complaint in sub-Saharan Africa. Not everyone, apparently, was benefiting to the fullest extent possible from the country's considerable diamond wealth. Finally, international NGOs had begun to take notice of the government's rather heavy-handed approach to long-established indigenous communities in areas that featured significant tourist potential and promising, though untapped, diamond deposits. Although Botswana has thus far weathered most of these storms, as long as the country continues to rely so heavily on a single commodity, it will remain both economically and socially vulnerable.

The Economic Disadvantages and Dangers of a Single Commodity

Although Botswana has experienced stunning, diamond-fueled growth, the country's economy has not diversified in any meaningful way since the initial discovery of the deposits. By the late 2000s, for example, diamonds were accounting for roughly 30 percent of GDP, 70 percent of export revenues, and 50 percent of government revenue. Even formerly vibrant industries, such as agriculture, continue to wither. For all of the mineral success Botswana has enjoyed, it has failed to spill over into other sectors and has, in some ways, hindered the country as it transforms from a rural, pastoral society into a more industrialized one. For example, the diamond industry employs less than 5 percent of Botswana's working-age population and thus has limited ability to help attenuate the high levels of unemployment in the country—even today, less than a quarter of Botswana's work force is formally employed. For those citizens who are fortunate enough to land a job on the mines, these positions offer reasonably high rates of pay; loyalty bonuses for uninterrupted work; affordable housing for any accompanying family members; and opportunities for children to attend school. Yet because these benefits are so attractive, work seekers are drawn in large numbers to the mines, to the neglect of other industries and sectors, thereby obstructing economic diversification. To try to contain the damage, the government has capped wages on some of its mines, resulting in laborers earning far less than they would in South Africa. Yet even this drastic measure has had little effect on the country's ongoing reliance on a single commodity, leaving the economy uncomfortably vulnerable.

The Threat of "Conflict Diamonds," Even Where There's No Conflict

Although Botswana's diamond mines have never featured drugged children wielding AK-47s or, for that matter, fierce battles involving armed insurgents of any sort, the country was not immune to the uproar surrounding "conflict" or "blood diamonds." NGOs' public awareness campaigns, including World Vision's "*Dying for a diamond? So are thousands of innocent children,*" threatened to cripple the industry worldwide and, therefore, Botswana's economy. Most global consumers of diamonds were unfamiliar with the monumental differences between, for example, Sierra Leone and Botswana, and, instead, simply heard "Africa" and assumed the worst. In response to the international tide that was swelling against African diamonds, Botswana went on the offensive, hoping to protect its industry and ensure its survival.

In order to contrast Botswana's stones with the "dirty" or "bloody" diamonds produced in other African settings, the government strove to inform global consumers that its stones were 100 percent "clean." To this end, in 2001, Botswana launched the "Diamonds for Development" campaign, which showcased the country's progress and illustrated the "good" that mineral assets can facilitate. This initiative was largely a public relations maneuver, but given the importance of the industry to Botswana's economy, the government deemed it critical foreign policy. During the official announcement of the campaign, which deliberately paralleled the unfolding Kimberley Process, President Festus Mogae implored audiences to distinguish between "conflict" and "clean" diamonds: "If this is not done, there is a great danger that mistakes could be made that would result in destroying the trade in diamonds whilst the problem of conflict remains. I truly believe that it would be a tragedy for Africa if the splendid ambition of putting an end to African conflicts were to result in the targeting of diamonds as a symbol of all the complex causes of strife on the African continent. We must use the sharpest surgical instruments and any other methods required to slice out the tiny cancerous growth of conflict diamonds within the world diamond trade."[4] Shortly afterward, Mogae more explicitly defended the importance of the diamond industry for his own country, cautioning that "Botswana supports international efforts to outlaw conflict diamonds, as we believe a single conflict diamond is one too many, but Botswana's diamonds have always been conflict free. . . . The good that diamonds do for countries like Botswana must be recognized and not jeopardized."[5] Not surprisingly, Namibia and South Africa—fellow diamond-producing African nations that were also generating "conflict-free" stones—joined this chorus, as did key elements within the global industry. Thus, even as these entities were playing active roles in the development of the Kimberley Process, they were also embracing Botswana's creative rebuttal to the NGOs' unfavorable campaigns.

At the heart of the "Diamonds for Development" (counter)measure was a litany of social and economic benefits that diamonds supplied for developing nations in Africa. By repeatedly highlighting diamond-facilitated enhancements in health care, housing, education, employment, security, stability, and liberal democracy, Botswana's officials sounded as if they were campaigning for political office as they fought to safeguard the industry. For example, while in Washington, DC, in June 2001 to promote "Diamonds for Democracy," Mogae emphasized that "every time you desist from purchasing diamond jewelry you are probably cutting funding available to provide clean drinking water for a rural village in Botswana or to build schools in the deprived urban centers in South Africa."[6]

In hindsight, it appears that Mogae's dramatic efforts constituted time well spent, as even during this challenging period Botswana's diamond industry continued to flourish, without experiencing any notable interruptions. Moreover, the implementation of the Kimberley Process in 2003 ensured that consumers could easily discern between "clean" and "dirty" stones, formalizing a crucial distinction that Mogae and others had long been stressing. By the late 2000s, the threat seemed but a distant memory. In 2009, US Secretary of State Hillary Clinton could be heard at a press conference virtually echoing Mogae's words from earlier in the decade. "When you buy a diamond from De Beers, part of that money still today goes to help build and maintain roads and clean water systems in Botswana. You can drive anywhere in that country and you can see services that have been paid for by a legal framework, strong regulations, and a national consensus that the money from the Earth and its riches should be spent on the people of Botswana."[7] Instead of passively observing a threat that could have potentially derailed the country's burgeoning economy, the Botswanan government aggressively and successfully confronted it, head on.

Growth without Development?

Although Botswana safely weathered the global "conflict diamond" tempest, gradually mounting domestic criticism concerning economic inequity within the country was proving harder to overcome. Accusations and admissions of corruption associated with Botswana's diamond industry had also begun to plague a government that was otherwise lauded as a model on the continent. Responding to allegations of acute domestic inequality, the government has repeatedly pointed to a range of accomplishments, including the prodigious "rainy-day" reserves it has strategically amassed; the widespread provision of basic services it has overseen, such as greatly improved access to health care, electricity, education, and clean drinking water; and the country's impressive social accomplishments, including literacy rates of 80 percent for adults and 94 percent for youths. However, with poverty levels still uncomfortably elevated, the second highest HIV/AIDS prevalence rate in the world (only Swaziland's is higher), and gross inequality between the country's elites and much of its citizenry, accusations of corruption are particularly damning and have been much harder to dismiss. Clearly, much work remains.

Although Botswana is arguably the world's best example of how diamonds can assist in the rapid, peaceful development of a nation, its deposits can't help it surmount every challenge, nor has the government done enough to address some of the more important ones. While Botswana's diamond revenues have helped reduce poverty levels and have significantly upgraded the standard of living over the past forty years (in 2005, GDP per capita was a respectable $12,387, compared to just $216 in Sierra

Leone), calls persist for the government to spend even more of the mineral profits. Simply put, some Botswanans have benefited from the country's economic success to a much greater degree than others. For example, despite the country's small population, which is only slightly larger than New Mexico's, and the over $3 billion a year it enjoys in diamond revenues, more than half of the population lives on less than $2 per day. At the same time, the wealthiest 10 percent of Botswanan society controls half of the country's overall income—one of the highest levels of income inequality in the world. These deep social inequities remain at the heart of the growing domestic discontent.

To be fair to Botswana's post-independence administrations, these divides existed long before the discovery of diamonds. For centuries, the status of residents was largely dictated by the number of cattle owned, with a small number of chiefs and their relatives dominating the ranks of large-scale cattle holders. These differences remained entrenched following the end of the colonial period, as many of these elites moved into government, thereby forging powerful connections between large cattle holders and the political administration, which, in turn, replicated and perpetuated historical inequalities. In the early years of independence, for example, two-thirds of Botswana's National Assembly was made up of owners of large or medium-sized cattle herds.

In fact, these socioeconomic discrepancies are not just persisting, but deepening, which is squarely at odds with the prevailing public perception that Botswana pursues a broad-based approach to development. In practice, the indifference that the government has often displayed in the face of these social challenges may well be a manifestation of its political overconfidence and complacency: since independence, the Botswana Democratic Party (BDP) has enjoyed exclusive control of the reins of state. The BDP's successes at the ballot box have given it scant reason to revise its governing policies. Yet, until the government addresses a range of serious domestic problems and, in particular, unemployment, accusations regarding its self-serving approach to power will persist.

Even though Botswana's diamond industry serves as the major driving force in the country's economy, this capital-intensive sector employs only roughly 8,000 citizens—about 4 percent of the total labor force. Furthermore, the industry generates few jobs outside of mining, with the exception of public sector positions in the state bureaucracy. As such, diamond mining operates as a type of enclave, both physically and economically. The government of Botswana has been working with De Beers to establish diamond-cutting and -polishing operations in the country, but these initiatives have not generated, and really aren't designed to generate, large numbers of jobs. Additional employment opportunities outside the mining sector are sorely needed.

Botswana's BDP government also troubled the nation by admitting that certain public officials have had unethical links to De Beers as far back as the 1980–88 presidency of Ketumile Masire. In the spring of 2011, for example, an investigation revealed that "De Beers bailed out former President Masire when he was in debt; Masire even acknowledged this. What is now needed is . . . to investigate how such transactions affected the business deals Botswana had been making with De Beers, a company that is profit driven."[8] While Masire did acknowledge that the diamond giant had provided "modest support" to help his farming business in the mid-1980s, he maintained that this financial assistance "did not materially compromise his government's bilateral dealings with the company."[9] These initial revelations naturally came as somewhat of a shock to a country that had prided itself on, and has been lauded by the international community for, governmental transparency and a lack of corruption. Now that the country's halo has been tarnished, foreign investment in Botswana could be adversely affected. It is worth noting, though, that corruption exists everywhere in the world and that this example hardly seems egregious. In fact, in most African diamond-producing nations, a disclosure of this nature would be barely newsworthy, let alone "scandalous." In many respects, the sensationalism surrounding Masire's admission is a testament to the otherwise largely prudent ways that successive Botswanan governments have managed the country's diamond resources.

Gaborone's Heavy-Handedness in "The Last Eden"

Whereas allegations of corruption are relatively new in Botswana, administrations since the 1980s have come under fire for their treatment of the ethnic Basarwa/San populations. This controversy stems from the fact that some of these communities are "inconveniently" located on or near prospective diamond deposits in the country's Central Kalahari Game Reserve (CKGR). The most persistent criticism has been leveled by Survival International (SI), a London-based NGO focused on indigenous rights. SI classifies efforts by De Beers and Botswana's government to remove and, from 2002, to deny water and other basic services to these communities (who may well have resided in the CKGR area for tens of thousands of years), as genocide. The UN Committee on the Elimination of Racial Discrimination has also condemned Botswana for its "ongoing dispossession of Basarwa/San people from their land."[10] Moreover, outcries from international celebrities, including fashion models Iman, Lily Cole, and Erin O'Conner, all of whom had previously advertised for De Beers, helped prompt candlelight vigils outside Botswanan diplomatic offices overseas. Given these allegations, it's somewhat difficult to reconcile Botswana's "Diamonds for Development" campaign with the government's more severe measures in the CKGR. This incongruence naturally raises the question: Just how "clean" are Botswana's diamonds?

Rather than yield in the face of this unwanted attention, Gaborone continued to insist that these indigenous peoples could no longer maintain their lifestyles solely via hunting and gathering, and therefore they jeopardized the country's wildlife resources, that is, valuable tourist assets. Interested in developing tourism, as well as further assisting the diamond industry, in 2002 the government began cutting off water supplies to these CKGR communities. It also, however, allegedly fined, taxed, beat, and tortured members of these populations located in what it promotes as "the last Eden." Although the CKGR had originally been established in 1961 on the ancestral lands of ethnic San groups, the government subsequently relocated members of these communities to "resettlement camps." In their new locations, residents received subsidies, while hunting and gathering was allegedly more feasible—or, at least less intrusive. In 2006, Botswana's High Court finally reached a verdict that ensured the right of return to the CKGR for these relocated populations, highlighting both the country's independent judiciary and its functioning democracy. Smarting from this loss in court and still bitter about the negative international campaign, although Botswana's government complied, it endeavored to make life extremely difficult for those individuals who desired to return to the CKGR.

Upon review, it appears that Botswana's desire to develop its tourist industry, rather than to assist the mining sector, had served as the primary impetus for its initial aggression. Even as it sided with the indigenous communities, the country's High Court had included in its ruling an explicit exoneration of the role of diamonds in the initial relocations. In that sense, it was united with the country's executive in its stance against the accusations that Botswana's stones were tainted or should somehow be characterized as "blood diamonds." As further confirmation, De Beers eventually discontinued prospecting in the contested region due to the absence of any commercially viable deposits, though it was also mindful of the potential global backlash against "corporate bullying."

Unfortunately for Botswana's government and its diamond industry, the release of the film *Blood Diamond* shortly after the High Court's verdict seemed to revive the issue, especially in light of the administration's heavy-handed actions following the court decision. Audiences worldwide were flocking to the film, thereby reigniting the "blood diamond" flame. As part of this resuscitation of the issue, activists launched a new campaign intended to cast Botswana's stones as "conflict diamonds" and, concomitantly, scuttle the country's blossoming tourist industry. However, these campaigners' fanciful attempts to analogize the governmental indiscretion in Botswana to the mayhem in Angola and Sierra Leone only trivialized the "blood diamond" conflicts. For example, during the boycott of the first De Beers store in the United States in the mid-2000s, the US American activist Gloria Steinem, who had recently returned from the Kalahari, declared: "The fact is . . . De Beers is supporting the genocide of this culture. . . . And I certainly feel completely clear in calling for a boycott of every diamond."[11]

In response, the government of Botswana hired a prominent public relations firm, while its senior officials, including President Festus Mogae, defended the country's human rights record and its "clean" diamonds in front of a series of high-profile audiences around the world. These efforts were bolstered by no less a person than Leonardo DiCaprio himself, the star of *Blood Diamond*, who publicly lauded Botswana for utilizing its diamond revenues for socially productive ends. After all of the bad publicity that *Blood Diamond* had indirectly generated, the film was finally poised to make a positive contribution to the country's economic development. Ultimately, Botswana's impressive administrative track record enabled it to counter and quickly dispel what were largely a series of hyperbolic attacks and accusations; consequently, Survival International's calls were largely ignored both within Botswana, and far beyond its borders.

Despite the problems outlined above, the majority of the population and the international community continue to perceive Botswana as a largely benevolent state. Massive investments in education, transport, social welfare, and health, including the free distribution of antiretrovirals to HIV-positive individuals, are largely responsible for these widely favorable views. In light of these socially beneficial measures and the history of responsible resource management, the campaign against Botswana's stones seems ultimately to have been, at best, misguided, and, at worst, uninformed and wasteful.

Namibia: Two Decades of Diamond-Fueled Progress

Although Namibia and Botswana have managed their diamond deposits in similar ways in recent decades, their historical trajectories are very different. Most notably, diamonds have profoundly affected Namibians since the initial discoveries in this former German colony of South West Africa, all the way back in 1908, almost sixty years before the Orapa finds in Botswana. Following these finds, African laborers in South West Africa who had been working on railroad projects were quickly transferred to the diamond-rich beaches. Once there, they were made to crawl on their hands and knees, sifting through the burning sands for valuable stones with tin cans around their necks into which they placed any finds, and often gagged so as to prevent them from concealing diamonds in their mouths. The end of the German occupation at the conclusion of World War I came not a moment too soon for these and other Namibians. Yet the seventy-one years of hostile South African overrule that ensued were barely preferable; the plight of most indigenous Namibians closely resembled the challenging experiences of black South Africans under white minority rule in that country.

In contrast to the peaceful decolonization process in Botswana, Namibians, like their South African neighbors, were forced to fight for independence, led in this endeavor by SWAPO, the South West Africa People's Organization. In fact, the violence associated with SWAPO's nationalist struggle was, for a time, closely linked to the conflict in neighboring Angola, one of the epicenters of blood diamonds. Only following independence in 1990 were Namibians finally able to assume control over the country's rich diamond deposits and allocate the revenues for the overall betterment of the population.

Since independence, Namibia has traveled a largely pacific path, with SWAPO transitioning from a liberation movement to the country's ruling political party. Determined to overcome the nation's heavy heritage, a series of SWAPO administrations have committed to using Namibia's mineral wealth for national development in a transparent, peaceful manner. It is during this post-independence period that the parallels with Botswana begin to materialize. Like Botswana, Namibia also features a small population—at just over two million people—and diamond deposits that are difficult to access and, thus, reasonably easy to safeguard. These demographic and geological features have played key roles in the country's avoidance of domestic, diamond-related turmoil.

The Seeds of Post-Independence Diamond Success

Unlike Botswana, Namibia inherited a well-established, highly profitable diamond industry at independence. Following the Second World War, the mandate experienced a mining boom which, going forward, accounted for between one-half and three-quarters of its total exports. At the time, Namibia's diamond industry was controlled by the monopolistic Consolidated Diamond Mines (CDM), a subsidiary of Anglo American. The alluvial stones that the enterprise was mining were primarily washed down to the sea near Oranjemund by the Orange River and lay buried in coastal sands or embedded in the gravels of marine terraces on the floor of the Atlantic Ocean, stretching out from the mainland. The nature of these formations rendered over 90 percent of Namibia's diamonds gem quality. Consequently, in the early 1970s, CDM was the world's largest producer of gem diamonds and, given the high value of these stones, was generating almost half of Anglo American's total (net) profits.

As SWAPO launched its struggle for independence from South Africa, the movement's leaders naturally eyed these valuable deposits, but any attempt to access them would have been suicidal. The open terrain of the coast and adjacent restricted entry zone that stretches back into the interior failed to offer sufficient cover for the guerrilla outfit, which was most active and successful in the tropical areas of northern Namibia. As one former SWAPO fighter, who later became the country's director of mines, declared: "We could not have operated there. The South Africans would have simply bombed us."[12] In many respects, post-independence Namibian governments have benefited from the absence of fighting in these diamondiferous coastal regions. With little trouble, CDM engineers could have breached the retaining walls that the company had constructed and simply watched as the ocean rushed back in and re-covered the exposed deposits. In this sense, SWAPO's most important military operation was, arguably, one that it never conducted.

In addition to the coastal mines that SWAPO coveted, Namibia also features more deeply submerged underwater deposits, which workers first began accessing in the 1950s. In fact, the history of seabed mining owes more to a pioneering Texan named Sam Collins than to De Beers or any other multinational mining company. Motivated by tales of individuals retrieving diamonds from the sea floor using pumps, and also by occasional diamond finds in the shallows off of the coasts of Namibia, Angola, and South Africa,

Collins's Marine Diamond Corporation began mining in 1961. Success was instantaneous: in the first five days of mining, 1,018 high-quality carats were "sucked up" and over 550,000 would follow. However, the maverick Texan's operation soon succumbed to the unpredictability, high risks, and even higher costs associated with this type of mining. Faced with mounting expenses, Collins gave way to De Beers in 1965. The behemoth moved in aggressively, buying control and picking up where Collins had left off.

Namibia's Diamonds for Namibia—Finally!

Soon after Namibia's independence, its SWAPO-led administration and De Beers validated an agreement regarding the country's diamond deposits. Inspired by the Botswanan scenario, this accord also produced a joint mining enterprise (with a similarly generated title): the Namdeb Diamond Corporation. Equally owned by the state and De Beers, Namdeb was responsible for production for the next twenty-five years. For the diamond giant, this arrangement was preferable to a potential nationalization of the industry and, quite simply, De Beers needed to secure this vital output in order to continue to manipulate global carat prices. The agreement also helped the recently formed Namibian state establish an economic foundation: diamonds quickly constituted roughly 40 percent of its annual foreign exchange earnings, while Namdeb remains the country's largest employer. However, unlike in Botswana, the Namibian government denied De Beers mining exclusivity and, even today, a number of smaller operators continue to mine in the country, especially offshore—reminiscent of the plucky Texan, Collins.

Today Namdeb's "Diamond Area 1," an expansive, 32,000 square-kilometer tract of sea, beach, and desert, is the intensely guarded home of Namibia's most profitable deposits. The area's borders mirror those of the original *Sperrgebeit*, or "forbidden territory," first demarcated by Namibia's German colonial overlords. In order to harvest diamonds from this zone, Ovambo "cleaners" sweep the crevices of the exposed bedrock with whisks or use vacuum machines that prevent them from touching the valuable targets— all the while operating behind massive, ten-story-high "retaining mounds," at times hundreds of feet out into the ocean (fig. 6). Over time, Namdeb has moved even further out, mining, for example, in waters over four hundred feet deep. In these settings, massive drills mounted on specially designed ships break up the sea floor while pumps suck up the resultant diamond-rich debris into recovery plants (fig. 7). Unlike simple alluvial installations elsewhere in Africa, these operations require significant amounts

FIGURE 6. Namibian stamp: *J. van Niekerk, ORANJEMUND Alluvial Diamonds, 1991. Courtesy of Odino Grubessi*

FIGURE 7. Namibian stamp: *Namibian Marine Technology*, 2002. *Courtesy of Odino Grubessi*

of capital and technical knowledge. Thus, while De Beers certainly needed Namibia, the newly independent country also very much needed the mining enterprise—a perfect, diamond-sealed marriage.

Lustrous Challenges: Domestic Diamond-Related Problems and Concerns

Constituting less than 10 percent of Namibia's GDP, diamonds are not nearly as important to the country as they are to Botswana. But they have provided a valuable source of income and helped the country remain debt-free. At the same time, these stones have also generated numerous problems for Namibian governments, seated in Windhoek, the country's capital city. As in Botswana, Namibia's rapid development has been uneven. Although broad strides have been made in the provision of education and health care, roughly half the population still lives below the international poverty line of $1.25 a day, and unemployment lies somewhere between 20 and 33 percent. Moreover, although the country features a multiparty democracy, a single party (SWAPO) has dominated post-independence politics, just as in Botswana. Meanwhile, smuggling has long confounded Namibia's diamond industry, which has otherwise been able to avoid many of the problems typically associated with mining operations in Africa. Although Windhoek is duly concerned, this assortment of challenges does not pose a lethal threat to the Namibian economy. Indeed, the country also has a lucrative uranium-mining industry and a strong tourism sector. Readers may recall that Brad Pitt and Angelina Jolie, regular visitors to Namibia (though admittedly not average tourists), chose the country as the location for the 2006 birth of their daughter Shiloh.

Given the difficulty in accessing Namibia's diamond deposits and the expansive restricted entry zone that surrounds them, it is somewhat surprising that smuggling has been such a major challenge for the industry. Yet just as mine workers in every setting throughout history have attempted to spirit diamonds away from extraction sites, the same has held true in Namibia. Although the country's deposits certainly don't lend themselves to rebel activity or diamond-fueled insurrection, losses attributable to smuggling have blighted an otherwise largely issue-free industry. Nor are the (suspected) sums of this contraband insignificant. At the commencement of the new millennium, Namdeb was reporting production of approximately 1.5 million carats annually, worth more than $400 million, yet estimates of the value of smuggled stones reached upward of $180 million, or roughly 30 percent of total output.

Over the years, employees based in the highly secured mining center of Oranjemund have been especially creative in devising different smuggling techniques. Beyond "simple ingestion" (the stuff of amateurs), miners in the late 1990s were ingeniously using homing pigeons to carry off the stones from their mining hostels, over armed guards and perimeter fences.[13] The expression "the birds are flying" meant just that: a stream of diamonds was literally being flown out of Diamond Area 1. In fact, this system was exposed only after an overloaded pigeon attracted the attention of security guards. In response, Namdeb immediately banned the birds, and they are now shot on sight. No matter—at least for the miners, anyway. Workers replaced the birds with arrows and smuggled in crossbows, piece by piece, eventually launching hollowed, diamond-filled projectiles out, careful to avoid helicopter patrols. This otherwise crafty scheme ended only after an arrow hit a patrolling security jeep.

Of course, raiding the workers' hostels would have been the most expedient countermeasure to these smuggling ploys. Yet this option wasn't politically palatable, as veterans of SWAPO's heroic struggle for independence are well represented in the smuggling circles and half of Namdeb is owned by the SWAPO-led state. In other words, government officials' former comrades-in-arms have been appropriating a portion of the state's main asset, but for reasons of political delicacy, and corruption, no one has the appetite or will to halt it. As the stones continue to "fly out," Windhoek just winks and nods. In fact, the smuggling organizations are so powerful that they effectively intimidate workers from turning in randomly found diamonds, even though employees are entitled to receive 70 percent of a stone's value in reward money for this act. According to John Ward, a Namdeb geologist, speaking just prior to the millennium, no employee had voluntarily turned in a stone for decades: "The smuggling syndicates have crueler incentives, like breaking legs, to get people to not turn them in."[14] Given this type of physical deterrent, it's no wonder that the compensatory funds in Namdeb's voluntary turn-in program have grown dusty over the years.

Destructive Engagement: Namibia and the Regional Diamond Landscape

Regardless of the smuggling problem within Namibia's diamond industry, the country continues to be perceived as a prudent steward of its domestic mineral assets, responsibly and transparently developing the nation. Beyond its borders, though, Namibia's record is not so sterling. In its diamond-related interactions with the DRC and Zimbabwe, for example, the government in Windhoek has made decisions that are inconsistent with its domestic policies and actions. Indeed, although a great number of African countries have been sucked into the seemingly endless civil conflict in the Congo, not all of them actively looted that troubled country's natural resources. In addition to supporting rebel leader-cum-DRC president Laurent Kabila (now deceased), the Namibian military's "official" duties in the DRC included diamond exploration and mining in Forminière's former concessionary area, only in part to offset the costs of its intervention. After denying allegations regarding this activity for over two years, in 2001 Windhoek finally admitted that a Namibian firm, curiously named "August 26 Holding Cargo," was involved in this exploitation and, moreover, was a subsidiary of a parastatal entity formed by the country's Ministry of Defense. This admission provides the missing logic necessary to understand why Windhoek became involved in the DRC in the first place, a nation in which it has no clear strategic interests and which is situated some five hundred miles from its closest border. As is so often the case, it was all about the money.

Namibia's record in Zimbabwe is little better. Windhoek rushed to Robert Mugabe's defense as he came under increasing international criticism for the violent manner in which his regime was exploiting the Marange deposits. Pursuant to the dispatch of a Kimberley Process (KP) team of investigators, Namibia, along with the governments of India, Russia, and China, warned against calling attention to human rights abuses in Zimbabwe. As rotating chair of the KP at the time (2009), Windhoek openly absolved the Zimbabwean government before the team even began its investigation. Namibia's deputy minister of mines even went so far as to vow that Zimbabwe would *never* be suspended from the KP "family" and that the outside world should give the embattled country "the benefit of the doubt."[15] By then, however, the time for giving Robert Mugabe the benefit of the doubt had tragically long since passed. Southern African governments have long defended Mugabe, in great part because of their shared histories battling oppressive white regimes in the region, but Namibia's advocacy while serving in such a pivotal position exceeded the traditional, knee-jerk expressions of support. Shortly thereafter, Namibia drafted the annual KP resolution to submit to the UN General Assembly, but made no mention of either Zimbabwe or human rights. This action undermined the Kimberley Process, making it appear toothless. Thus although Namibia has engaged with its own diamond resources both responsibly and peacefully, the same cannot always be said regarding deposits located elsewhere in the region.

IN CONTRAST to the protracted violence that plagued Sierra Leone and Angola, Botswana and Namibia serve as largely refreshing "blood diamond-less" counterexamples. Although not devoid of either internal or regional challenges and controversies, these two major diamond-producing countries have acted as reasonable stewards of their significant deposits, allocating sizable sums for domestic investment and development in a transparent manner. Remarkable accomplishments, for sure, but not the sort that are likely to attract attention from either the global media or, certainly, Hollywood. But, that may well be exactly how the two countries like it, even if Namibia has benefited from the significant attention it has derived from repeated visits to the country by the celebrity supercouple, "Brangelina." Both Botswana and Namibia have benefited from small populations and the absence of sprawling, land-based alluvial deposits that rebels in Sierra Leone, Angola, and elsewhere have so easily accessed and exploited. The post-independence governments in Gaborone and Windhoek have also carefully secured their diamond assets and aggressively negotiated and renegotiated deals with their natural production partner, De Beers. The success of both Debswana and Namdeb offers hope that public-private mining endeavors elsewhere in Africa will similarly be able to transform diamond deposits from domestic liabilities into national treasures.

CHAPTER NINE

Africa's Diamonds

A Rough Past with a Brighter Future

> Yes, diamonds every time. I think people buy diamonds out of vanity and they buy gold because they're too stupid to think of any other monetary system which will work—and I think vanity is a more attractive motive than stupidity.
>
> —Harry Oppenheimer's response when asked if he had a preference for diamonds or gold, 1957

DESPITE ALL the mineral wealth that has been removed from Africa's soils over the centuries, the continent still has much more "vanity" to offer. In fact, the extraction from Africa of a range of natural resources, including mineral ores, is poised to increase dramatically in the coming years, with legions of covetous outsiders as eager as ever to access and haul them away. As Paul Collier has reminded us, "Africa is the last frontier for resource discovery, having long been relatively neglected by mining and other resource-extraction companies, owing to difficult political conditions. But rising commodity prices are overcoming reluctance, and prospecting is generating a multitude of new discoveries."[1] Diamonds fit squarely into this latest African mineral revolution, and it will be up to the continent's leaders to ensure that the wealth is properly managed and equitably divided. But will they? After reading the preceding chapters, it's easy to see how greed and the quest for power will strongly influence these proceedings. Yet there is also reason to be optimistic, as it appears that African countries striving to imitate Botswana's restrained model of resource management will far outnumber those nations mimicking Zimbabwe's more aggressive, repressive approach.

This chapter reflects on what we've learned about Africa's diamond past, introduces some promising recent developments that have failed to make headlines, and, with these lessons and insights in mind, considers what the continent's diamond future might look like. As should be clear by now, Africa's mineral resources must be considered in a global, not just a continental, context. From the original "rushers" to Kimberley, to the colonial-era mining enterprises, to the contemporary international consumers of Africa's diamonds, the continent's stones have always had global dimensions. And even more so now, given our increasingly integrated, globalized world. So although much of the burden to administer the revenues from this impending mineral windfall lies with Africa's leaders, the international community of states, mining corporations, and, ultimately, consumers also has a key role to play. The Kimberley Process provides an excellent example of how different entities within this diamond-linked community can work together to enhance, or even just protect, the lives of Africans in diamond-producing nations. Yet much more needs to be done if the corruption, looting, and squandering of Africa's mineral resources is to be relegated to the past.

Lessons from the Histories of Africa's Diamonds

By now you know a great deal about what's transpired in Africa's dynamic "diamond past." As should be obvious, the film *Blood Diamond* dramatized only a small, albeit disturbing, part of this history. Many of the movie's themes, however, including acute violence, greed, and exploitation, are regrettably consistent with the continent's roughly 150-year engagement with these "stones of contention." As we move forward in time from Africa's diamond origins at Kimberley, these themes continue to hold, even if mining in the colonial era was significantly less chaotic. In fact, in many cases, the monopolistic companies that dominated the diamond landscape during the colonial period were more broadly beneficial to African societies than what succeeded them. In addition to an absence of wide-scale violence and the above-average wages and benefits that these companies provided, they also offered Africans a sense of stability in an otherwise rapidly changing world. During my own research in Angola, for example, former employees of Diamang openly shared with me their fondness for the Portuguese colonial period given the chaos that beset the country's diamond-yielding areas following independence in 1975.

During the period when colonial capital was exploiting African labor, the system was easier to comprehend, or was at least more straightforward: mining companies provided wages, housing, and, at times, even educational opportunities and pensions, in exchange for workers' compliance and performance. The racial configuration of these scenarios was also clear: white-run companies operating in white-ruled colonies oversaw black manual labor forces. Fast-forward into the independence era, and the racial dynamics have become much more muddled. From "blood diamonds" to the current situation in Zimbabwe, Africans have been at the forefront of the exploitation and oppression of fellow Africans: greed and the quest for power are apparently color-blind.

At the very least, it appears that the era of "blood diamonds" is over (even if "blood coltan"—a highly contentious mineral mined in the DRC—and other African "conflict minerals" continue to emerge). Although there will always be buyers unconcerned with a diamond's provenance or how it arrived on the market, the Kimberley Process has eliminated the large-scale sale of stones to finance revolution or destabilize a sovereign state. As we have learned, though, the KP as it currently stands is only a half-measure. It addresses "traditional" blood diamonds, as they were originally, narrowly defined, but none of the other forms of violence associated with contemporary diamond mining and trading. And even if the definition is revised, and there is little to suggest that it will be, what can we realistically expect from the KP? Don't authoritarian regimes always find markets for coveted exports? Don't, for example, Saudi Arabia, Venezuela, and Iran have regular, eager buyers of their crude? Meanwhile, for their part, global consumers seem to consider diamonds to be more like "essential" oil than "shunned" fur, so it's highly unlikely that retail sales will sag due to any popular concern over the KP's current limitations. These realities notwithstanding, shouldn't attempts be made to at least try to sanction sales of diamonds by hostile regimes? It seems that certain governments, organizations, and elements within the diamond industry think that the answer is "yes," though any changes to the current system will certainly be gradual, if they happen at all. In the meantime, although the KP's detractors are both numerous and understandably dissatisfied, given what the system has already accomplished during its brief existence, these critics have probably been a bit harsh.

Promising Developments: A Brighter Future?

With each passing day, Africa's diamond industry is further removed from the "blood diamond" era, and, in many respects, its future looks rather promising. The series of "diamond wars" have mercifully concluded, the KP is firmly in place, and prospecting and excavation continue apace. Moreover, African employees, including women, are assuming ever-higher positions within the diamond industry—a far cry from the colonial days when indigenous workers were almost exclusively found shoveling earth under the relentless sun. For this transformation to be complete, though, the industry will have to assist the one group that continues to operate on the margins: artisanal miners. Many Africans continue to engage in informal, or artisanal, mining—an often unjustly illegalized and thus highly vulnerable undertaking—often as a last resort. In an attempt to improve the plight of these miners, the Diamond Development Initiative, an international collaborative effort reminiscent of, and linked to, the KP, has been formed, but much more on this front will be required going forward. For all the success that increasing numbers of Africans are enjoying within the industry, mining for diamonds must benefit all those involved if the entire continent is to develop.

Under the Radar: Individual Advancement and Societal Progress

Although far removed from international headlines, increasing numbers of Africans are succeeding at the very highest levels of the industry. The examples of Tokyo Sexwale and Nompumelelo "Mpumi" Zikalala of South Africa illustrate this ascension and suggest that the Africanization of the industry on the continent is well under way.

Tokyo Sexwale is a veteran of the ANC's struggle against South Africa's apartheid regime, having spent time in prison on Robben Island. In 1994, he swept into political office as a member of the widely victorious ANC, elected to serve as the premier of Guateng Province. In 1998, he resigned this post and purchased a series of alluvial mines along the Orange River from a company whose origins could be traced back to one of the founding fathers of diamond mining in Africa: Barney Barnato. Surely, the symbolic nature of this transaction was not lost on this upstart mining executive. Two years later, Sexwale exchanged these mines for shares in Trans Hex, a major mining enterprise based in Cape Town, acquiring an 8 percent share in the company and assuming the role of deputy chairman. Since then, Sexwale has enjoyed further commercial success within the diamond sector and beyond, including his current role as South Africa's Minister of Human Settlements. His accomplishments show that Africans can, and will, play important roles in shaping the industry.

Nompumelelo "Mpumi" Zikalala's ascension has flown even further under the global media's radar, but it is, if anything, even more newsworthy. Her involvement in the mining industry dates back to 1996, when she commenced her De Beers–funded studies in chemical engineering. Roughly a decade later, she became the first female general manager of De Beers's Kimberley Mines. Yet Zikalala seems to be unfazed by her rather unlikely success at the world's most storied diamond enterprise. As she once explained, "[Because] I've grown within the company . . . it is easy for me as De Beers has a high percentage of women. Internally it's a normal thing, but some external people still find it different."[2] She confirmed these persisting industry attitudes, recalling, "In Kimberley I had people coming through saying, 'Hi, could we please speak to Mr Zikalala,' and I would say, 'There is no Mr Zikalala, only Ms Zikalala.'" In 2008, she became the general manager of Voorspoed, the De Beers mine that produces coveted pink diamonds—the first woman, and also the youngest, to serve in this capacity for the mining giant. In fact, although the percentage of women in mining in South Africa remains at less than 10 percent overall, at Voorspoed it is closer to 35 percent. Zikalala also proudly reminds us that these female employees are not restricted to office positions. "They're not all secretaries, accountants and human resources employees[;] the women that we have do the technical side of things as well." Although diamond mining has long been dominated by men, Zikalala and her colleagues may well be the future face(s) of the industry on the continent, not just the recipients and wearers of the lustrous stones.

Hope for the Industry's Forgotten Participants

At the bottom of the diamond hierarchy are the most vulnerable members in this multibillion-dollar industry: artisanal miners. More than a million Africans are currently engaged in artisanal mining on the continent's alluvial deposits, supplying most of the 20 percent of global output that is produced in this manner. These individuals operate under extremely challenging conditions, and they and their families are almost always mired in poverty. Residing on the social and economic margins, these "absolute poor," as the UN defines them, are also regular victims of violence at the hands of aggressive police, private security forces and criminal gangs. And, when diamond sanctions hit producing countries, these subsistence miners are inordinately—often devastatingly—affected.

One positive development on this otherwise discouraging front has been the Diamond Development Initiative (DDI), which grew out of the KP. First proposed by De Beers, the company teamed up with a group of NGOs, including Global Witness and Partnership Africa Canada (PAC), to form the DDI and turn the industry's attention to the all-but-forgotten artisanal miner. The list of funding entities also includes renowned jewelers, such as Tiffany & Co., as well as the governments of Sweden, England, and Belgium. Dorothée Gizenga, a Congolese Canadian with experience in both the government in Ottawa and PAC, has served as the executive director of the organization since 2008. Under her leadership, the DDI has been engaged in a wide variety of projects, including removing children from artisanal mining in the DRC and setting minimum, industry-wide standards regarding social, economic, environmental, labor, trading, and governance issues for mining operations in developing countries. Although it is still too early to assess the efficacy of the DDI, the initiative has already substantially improved the lives of many of Africa's artisanal miners.

Concluding Remarks

Almost a century and a half has passed since Erasmus Jacobs picked up a glimmering stone in the South African veld and forever altered the world's diamond landscape. Since that time, Africa has remained at the heart of the industry. Yet, the continent's once lofty position has slipped somewhat: as of last year, Africa could claim only six of the world's top ten producers. As consumers have an increasing number of choices regarding the provenance of their diamonds, it is more important than ever that Africa generate "clean" gems and further distance itself from the "blood diamond" era. Thankfully for African producers, the pieces are in place to continue this ongoing process, and the most recent signs have been encouraging. The Kimberley Process, the Diamond Development Initiative, and the personal examples of Sexwale and Zikalala suggest that Africa has turned an important corner in its complex relationship with its diamond resources. However, major diamond-related issues, including the extreme violence in Zimbabwe and the DRC, remain unresolved, and the 2012 guilty verdict in the trial of Liberia's former president Charles Taylor offered a painful reminder of diamond-fueled greed and brutality in Africa's recent past. If, as De Beers's famous advertising has suggested, "A Diamond Is Forever," government and industry leaders on the continent will need to continue to take measures to ensure that "vain" consumers, like those cited by Harry Oppenheimer at the outset of this chapter, will regard their purchases of Africa's stones with pride, rather than shame. With that in mind, thinking back to the first pages of this book and knowing what you now know, would *you* purchase an African diamond?

STUDY GUIDE AND SELECTED READINGS

Digging Deeper

THIS SECTION is intended for readers and instructors who wish to delve more deeply into the book's contents via further discussion and/or reading. For each chapter, questions are posed that are intended to generate conversation about the various topics examined in the book, followed in each case by an ensuing list of relevant source materials, referred to as "selected readings," which include films, websites, articles, and books. The secondary sources identified typically elaborate on the particular themes explored in the book, while the reports and documents found on the websites listed constitute ideal primary source materials on/around which to build course assignments or simply assist with more focused research.

Chapter 1—An Introduction to Africa's Diamonds

Chapter 1 introduces readers to the global history of diamonds, with a focus on the importance of these stones to Africa's past and present. It frames the narrative and engages with the core themes that are considered in the ensuing chapters.

Discussion Questions

1. Owing to a range of media reports and popular culture expression, global citizens are becoming increasingly aware of the African origins of much of the world's diamond supply. How had you been exposed to Africa's diamonds before reading this book? How did these sources typically portray these diamonds? After reading this book, have your impressions changed? If so, in what ways?

2. Mineral deposits have greatly influenced the human experience in every region of the world. How has the mineral wealth of the United States shaped its history? In what ways do these historical influences in America compare and contrast with the African scenario?

3. Global societies have long placed considerable value on diamonds. Why have these stones historically been so coveted? Does this allure explain the extremely limited success that industrial diamonds have had in the jewelry market?

4. There has been extensive debate about whether natural resource deposits constitute a "blessing" or a "curse" for their respective host countries, especially in sub-Saharan Africa. After reading the book, do you think Africa's diamonds have been a "blessing," a "curse," both, or neither? How would you characterize America's mineral deposits?

Selected Readings

Epstein, Edward Jay. "Have You Ever Tried to Sell a Diamond?" *Atlantic*, February 1, 1982.
———. *The Rise and Fall of Diamonds: The Shattering of a Brilliant Illusion*. New York: Simon and Schuster, 1982.
Green, Timothy. *The World of Diamonds*. New York: William Morrow, 1981.
Greene, Graham. *The Heart of the Matter*. London: Heinemann, 1948.
Hart, Matthew. *Diamond: The History of a Cold-Blooded Love Affair*. New York: Plume, 2002.
Kendall, Leo P. *Diamonds: Famous and Fatal, The History, Mystery and Lore of the World's Most Precious Gem*. Fort Lee, NJ: Barricade Books, 2001.
Zoellner, Tom. *The Heartless Stone: A Journey through the World of Diamonds, Deceit, and Desire*. New York: St. Martin's, 2006.

Chapter 2—Africa's Mineral Wealth: Material and Mythical

Chapter 2 examines external notions of Africa as a treasure trove of mineral wealth in the pre-Kimberley period, as well as some of the mining endeavors in which Africans were engaged that helped fuel these impressions. The chapter explores the often divergent ways that Africans and outsiders regarded these resources and how, over time, these valuations shaped Africans' encounters with those Europeans and Asians who reached the continent's shores.

Discussion Questions

1. Outsiders have long been attracted to Africa's mineral wealth—both real and imagined—notions of which in many instances reached mythical proportions. What role(s) did Christianity play in this process? And, for their part, how did Africans pique these "outsiders'" initial interest in these mineral endowments and subsequently fuel external images of the continent as a "treasure trove"?

2. Despite this long-standing external interest, Africans were able to safeguard their mineral deposits for centuries. How was this possible, and why did their ability to do so begin to erode?

3. Although Europeans had relatively limited success in locating Africa's legendary mineral deposits, notions of the continent's mineral riches persisted. Why was it so important for Africa to be a land of immense mineral wealth in the European imagination?

4. Much time has passed since the early impressions of Africa as a "treasure trove" developed and considerably more is now known about its geology, yet greatly exaggerated notions of Africa's mineral wealth continue to persist. What connects these original, grandiose impressions with those that circulate today, centuries later?

Selected Readings

Birmingham, David. *Portugal and Africa*. Athens: Ohio University Press, 1999.

Bovill, E. W. *The Golden Trade of the Moors*. London: Oxford University Press, 1968.

Brooks, Michael E. "Prester John: A Reexamination and Compendium of the Mythical Figure Who Helped Spark European Expansion." PhD dissertation, University of Toledo, 2009.

Curtin, Philip D. "The Lure of Bambuk Gold." *Journal of African History* 14, no. 4 (1973): 623–31.

Elkiss, Terry H. *The Quest for An African Eldorado: Sofala, Southern Zambezia, and the Portuguese, 1500–1865*. Waltham, MA: Crossroads Press, 1981.

Garrard, Timothy F. "Myth and Metrology: The Early Trans-Saharan Gold Trade." *Journal of African History* 23, no. 4 (1982): 443–61.

McIntosh, Susan Keech. "A Reconsideration of Wangara/Palolus, Island of Gold." *Journal of African History* 22, no. 2 (1981): 145–58.

Newitt, Malyn. *Portugal in European and World History*. London: Reaktion Books, 2009.

Thornton, John. *Africa and Africans in the Making of the Atlantic World, 1400–1800*. 2nd ed. New York: Cambridge University Press, 1998.

Wilks, Ivor. "Wangara, Akan, and Portuguese in the Fifteenth and Sixteenth Centuries." In *Mines of Silver and Gold in the Americas*, edited by Peter Bakewell, 1–39. Aldershot, UK: Variorum, 1997.

Chapter 3—From Illusion to Reality: The Kimberley Discoveries, the Diamond "Rush," and the "Wild West" in Africa

Chapter 3 considers the explosion of mining in South Africa following the discovery of the Eureka Diamond and the identification of significant diamond concentrations in the late 1860s in and around what became the commercial center of Kimberley. Although African diggers held their own for some time following the discoveries, they were eventually pushed to the margins to make way for foreign capital and local white mining interests.

Discussion Questions

1. Despite Africans' strategic participation in the initial diggings in South Africa, their access was steadily eroded. How did this happen? Can you think of analogous situations in America? Elsewhere in the world?

2. The early decades of mining caused significant environmental destruction. Should this devastation be understood as a "necessary evil" of diamond mining operations of all types? Are contemporary states and mining companies more attentive to the environment than governments and (both corporate and small-scale) miners were during the early Kimberley period? Why or why not?

3. De Beers grew from a promising firm into the industry behemoth. Given the social, economic, and political realities on the ground in South Africa, was this type of emergence, and eventual dominance, inevitable? How much of De Beers's exponential growth is personally attributable to Cecil Rhodes? The Oppenheimers?

Selected Readings

Lewsen, Phyllis, ed. *Selections from the Correspondence of J. X. Merriman.* Vol. 1, *1870–1890.* Cape Town: Van Riebeeck Society, 1960.

Matthews, Z. K. *Freedom for My People: The Autobiography of Z. K. Matthews: Southern Africa, 1901 to 1968.* London: Rex Collings, 1981.

Morton, William J. "The South African Diamond Fields, and a Journey to the Mines." *Journal of the American Geographical Society of New York* 9 (1877): 66–83.

Newbury, Colin. *The Diamond Ring: Business, Politics, and Precious Stones in South Africa, 1867–1947.* Oxford: Clarendon Press, 1989.

Robertson, Marian. *Diamond Fever: South African Diamond History 1866–9 from Primary Sources.* Cape Town: Oxford University Press, 1974.

Shillington, Kevin. "The Impact of the Diamond Discoveries on the Kimberley Hinterland: Class Formation, Colonialism, and Resistance among the Tlhaping of Griqualand West in the 1870s." In *Industrialisation and Social Change in South Africa: African Class Formation, Culture, and Consciousness, 1870–1930,* edited by Shula Marks and Richard Rathbone, 99–118. New York: Longman, 1982.

Turrell, Rob. "The 1875 Black Flag Revolt on the Kimberley Diamond Mines." *Journal of Southern African Studies* 7, no. 2 (1981): 194–235.

Turrell, Robert Vicat. *Capital and Labour on the Kimberley Diamond Fields, 1871–1890.* Cambridge: Cambridge University Press, 1987.

Williams, Gardner F. *The Diamond Mines of South Africa: Some Account of Their Rise and Development.* London: Macmillan, 1902.

Worger, William H. *South Africa's City of Diamonds: Mine Workers and Monopoly Capitalism in Kimberley, 1867–1895.* New Haven: Yale University Press, 1987.

Chapter 4—Consolidation and Control: The Birth and Growth of the Cartel

Chapter 4 explores the means by which De Beers revolutionized the diamond industry and over time became internationally synonymous with these stones. Although the pioneering company remarkably achieved a near monopoly on the supply of rough stones and was able to powerfully manipulate consumer demand, it faced significant challenges throughout the course of its meteoric commercial ascension.

Discussion Questions

1. Although Kimberley society was sharply divided along racial lines, the emerging mining companies quickly and effectively subjugated and harnessed both white and black workers. Can you think of parallels in other contexts? Other industries?

2. In many respects, regional Africans had few survival options other than to work on the diamond mines. What political, social, and economic developments served to "push" Africans to the mining companies?

3. The transition to underground mining ushered in a new era of operations that was extremely lucrative for the companies that facilitated and oversaw it. But how did the African work force fare, and what new challenges did they face?

4. The introduction of compounds drastically altered the experiences of the African labor force. What were some of the reasons that mining companies were motivated to adopt compounds and to subsequently upgrade them? Were they operationally necessary, or would a less severe housing regime have sufficed? How did Africans strategically respond to the implementation of the compound system?

5. Although De Beers eventually came to dominate the diamond industry, it was neither inevitable nor without challenges. What types of challenges did the enterprise encounter during its ascension to the top of the industry and once it established itself there? Could some of these have been avoided? If so, how?

6. De Beers's durable and efficacious advertisements have undoubtedly contributed to the popularity of diamonds. How might the diamond industry have fared in the absence of this sustained advertising campaign? Why?

7. De Beers has maintained operations throughout dramatically shifting geo-political contexts for well over a century. How have these changing environments affected DeBeers's operations and how has the company strategically responded to them?

Selected Readings

Kanfer, Stefan. *The Last Empire: De Beers, Diamonds, and the World.* New York: Farrar, Straus and Giroux, 1993.

Knight, John, and Heather Stevenson. "The Williamson Diamond Mine, De Beers, and the Colonial Office: A Case-Study of the Quest for Control." *Journal of Modern African Studies* 24, no. 3 (1986): 423–45.

Roberts, Janine. *Glitter and Greed: The Secret World of the Diamond Empire.* New York: Disinformation, 2003.

Smalberger, John M. "I.D.B. and the Mining Compound System in the 1880s." *South African Journal of Economics* 42, no. 4 (December 1974): 398–414.

———. "The Role of the Diamond-Mining Industry in the Development of the Pass-Law System in South Africa." *International Journal of African Historical Studies* 9, no. 3 (1976): 419–34.

Turrell, Rob. "Diamonds and Migrant Labor in South Africa, 1869–1910." *History Today* 36, no. 5 (May 1986): 45–49.

———. "Kimberley: Labour and Compounds, 1871–1888." In *Industrialisation and Social Change in South Africa: African Class Formation, Culture, and Consciousness, 1870–1930,* edited by Shula Marks and Richard Rathbone, 45–76. New York: Longman, 1982.

———. "Kimberley's Model Compounds." *Journal of African History* 25, no. 1 (1984): 59–75.

Chapter 5—Creating "New Kimberleys" Elsewhere in Africa

Chapter 5 traces the establishment of diamond mining operations through-out Africa as it came under European colonial rule. The chapter explores the diverse diamond mining environments that colonial states, extractive companies, and African headmen collaboratively created in a range of different settings across the continent.

Discussion Questions

1. Colonial states were vital partners in the expansion of the diamond industry in Africa. In what key ways did these governments assist mining companies during the colonial era? Why were some colonial regimes more zealous than others in providing assistance?

2. Indigenous leaders often found themselves in precarious positions following the commencement of diamond mining operations in or near the areas over which they held sway. In what different ways did these traditional authorities engage with the emerging industry during the colonial period?

3. African laborers had a wide range of experiences on colonial-era diamond mines. What were the most important structural and operational factors that shaped African workers' experiences?

4. Although colonial states often assisted with the procurement of African labor for diamond mining operations, the companies also recruited on their own, often in parallel. In what ways did these various mining enterprises attempt to attract African labor? Were they successful? Why or why not?

5. The process of decolonization varied from place to place in Africa, influenced by a number of factors. How did the presence of a vibrant diamond industry in a colony shape this process?

Selected Readings

Clarence-Smith, W. G., and R. Moorsom. "Underdevelopment and Class Formation in Ovamboland, 1845–1915." *Journal of African History* 16, no. 3 (1975): 365–81.

Cooper, Allan D. "The Institutionalization of Contract Labour in Namibia." *Journal of Southern African Studies* 25, no. 1 (1999): 121–38.

Cronje, Gillian, and Suzanne Cronje. *The Workers of Namibia.* London: International Defence and Aid Fund for Southern Africa, 1979.

Derksen, Richard. "Forminière in the Kasai, 1906–1939." *African Economic History,* no. 12 (1983): 49–65.

Gordon, Robert J. *Mines, Masters and Migrants: Life in a Namibian Compound.* Johannesburg: Ravan, 1977.

Greenhalgh, Peter. *West African Diamonds, 1919–1983: An Economic History.* Manchester: Manchester University Press, 1985.

Vellut, Jean-Luc. "Mining in the Belgian Congo." In *History of Central Africa,* vol. 2, edited by David Birmingham and Phyllis M. Martin. London and New York: Longman, 1983.

Chapter 6—The Experiences of African Workers on Colonial-Era Mines

Chapter 6 continues the examination of colonial-era diamond mines but adjusts the angle of approach away from states, corporations, and indigenous authorities in order to consider the motivations, strategies, and experiences of African laborers. In response to a host of social and occupational challenges, laborers creatively shaped their plights by employing an array of strategies.

Discussion Questions

1. Colonial-era diamond companies typically offered reasonably attractive labor conditions for African employees vis-à-vis other industries, but often struggled to sufficiently staff their operations. Why were some Africans motivated to seek work on diamond mines and others to avoid the mines?

2. Although working and living conditions on colonial-era mines were often extremely challenging, African laborers did not accept these circumstances

passively. How did these mine workers, both individually and collectively, improve their lives, or at least alleviate some of the most severe challenges on the mines?

3. In certain settings, African diamond mine workers organized labor unions or comparable entities. Were these effective? Why or why not?

Selected Readings

Carstens, Peter. *In the Company of Diamonds: De Beers, Kleinzee, and the Control of a Town.* Athens: Ohio University Press, 2001.
Cleveland, Todd. "Rock Solid: African Laborers on the Diamond Mines of the Companhia de Diamantes de Angola (Diamang), 1917–1975." PhD dissertation, University of Minnesota, 2008.
Forminière. *Forminière, 1906–1956.* Brussels: Editions L. Cuypers, 1956.
Gottschalk, Keith. "South African Labour Policy in Namibia 1915–1975." *South African Labour Bulletin* 4, no. 1–2 (1978): 75–106.
Kamil, Fred. *The Diamond Underworld.* London: Allen Lane, 1979.
Thabane, Motlatsi. "Liphokojoe of Kao: A Study of a Diamond Digger Rebel Group in the Lesotho Highlands." *Journal of Southern African Studies* 26, no. 1 (March 2000): 105.
Uyind-a-Kanga, Mafulu. "Mobilisation de la main-d'oeuvre agricole: La dépendance de la zone rurale de Luiza des centres miniers du Kasai et du Haut-Katanga industriel (1928–1945)." *African Economic History*, no. 16 (1987): 39–60.

Chapter 7—A Resource Curse: "Blood Diamonds," State Oppression, and Violence

Chapter 7 explores the ways that Africans have used diamond revenues to prop up oppressive governments, to destabilize others, and, in both of these scenarios, to precipitate widespread displacement and death. The most notorious development of this nature was the emergence of "blood diamonds," or "conflict diamonds," which helped fuel a range of civil conflicts on the continent; even though this era has arguably ended, diamond-fueled violence persists.

Discussion Questions

1. Were Africa's diamonds severely tainted as a result of the "blood diamond" phenomenon? What made Africa more vulnerable to this particular type of violence? Is the continent uniquely susceptible?

2. Although "blood diamonds" became internationally notorious, attempts to label other violence-fueling commodities haven't been nearly as effective. Why is there no public outrage over "blood oil" or other "bloody/conflict-fueling" natural resources?

3. Although often (mis)understood as a broadly African phenomenon, "blood diamonds" emerged only in specific places on the continent. What factors led to the development of blood diamonds in Sierra Leone and Angola but not elsewhere?

4. Despite the controversy that continues to swirl around it, the Kimberley Process has been at least somewhat successful in curbing the violence to which African diamonds contributed. Do you think this type of approach could be reemployed to curtail other violent practices in Africa, or elsewhere, such as poaching?

5. Although the deployment of Executive Outcomes was highly controversial, the outfit was undeniably successful in halting, at least temporarily, the "blood diamond" violence in both Sierra Leone and Angola. Should the international community condone interventions by private security companies such as Executive Outcomes, to quell violence when more formal militaries are hesitant to intervene? Why or why not?

6. Although "blood diamonds" are understandably associated with Africa, a number of international entities and individuals played key roles in the generation of this deadly phenomenon. Should "blood diamonds" be understood as "African," "international," or both?

7. Zimbabwe's recent diamond discoveries and the government's handling of the resultant output have divided the international community. What does the debate over Zimbabwe's diamonds reveal about global politics, economics, priorities, and morality?

Selected Readings

Blood Diamond. Film. Warner Bros., 2006.

Campbell, Greg. *Blood Diamonds: Tracing the Deadly Path of the World's Most Precious Stones.* New York: Basic Books, 2004.

Cilliers, Jakkie, and Christian Dietrich, eds. *Angola's War Economy: The Role of Oil and Diamonds.* Pretoria: Institute for Security Studies, 2000.

Diamonds of War: Africa's Blood Diamonds. Film. National Geographic, 2003.

Global Witness. NGO. www.globalwitness.org/library/rough-trade.

Hirsch, John L. *Sierra Leone: Diamonds and the Struggle for Democracy.* Boulder, CO: Lynne Rienner, 2001.

Kimberley Process. www.kimberleyprocess.com/.

Le Billon, Philippe. "Fatal Transactions: Conflict Diamonds and the (Anti)Terrorist Consumer." *Antipode* 38, no. 4 (2006): 778–801.

Malaquias, Assis. "Diamonds Are a Guerrilla's Best Friend: The Impact of Illicit Wealth on Insurgency Strategy." *Third World Quarterly* 22, no. 3 (2001): 311–25.

Partnership Africa Canada. NGO. www.pacweb.org/en/.

Saunders, Richard. "Conflict Diamonds from Zimbabwe." Briefing note, September 2009. www.bicc.de/fataltransactions/pdf/briefing_note_conflict_diamonds_from _Zimbabwe.pdf.

Smillie, Ian. *Blood on the Stone: Greed, Corruption and War in the Global Diamond Trade.* London: Anthem, 2010.

UN Peacekeeping Mission in Sierra Leone. www.un.org/en/peacekeeping/missions/past/unamsil/.

Chapter 8—Mineral Assets: Diamonds and the Development of Democratic States

Chapter 8 offers counterexamples to the violent scenarios that were considered in chapter 7 via an examination of the ways that the leaders of independent African governments, namely Botswana and Namibia, have used diamond profits to build democratic states characterized by pacific foreign and domestic policies. Although these nations' diamond industries are not completely trouble-free, they offer hope for African countries still struggling to effectively manage their diamond resources.

Discussion Questions

1. Although "blood diamonds" contributed to the violent destabilization of certain African states, other diamond-producing nations remained conflict-free, including Namibia and Botswana. How would you explain the absence of "blood diamonds," or "conflict diamonds," in these settings?

2. Although neither Namibia nor Botswana featured open, diamond-fueled rebellions, their industries are not entirely free of other forms of violence. Because of this, should the stones from these countries be considered "clean"? Why or why not?

3. Although Botswana was devoid of "blood diamonds," its leaders were acutely concerned about the damage that these "tainted stones" could inflict on its diamond industry. Was this anxiety reasonable, or did its government overreact in a counterproductive manner?

4. In recent decades, NGOs have played an increasingly important role in monitoring the actions of companies and individuals involved in the extraction of African diamonds. How would you characterize the NGO concern over Botswana's industry?

5. Namibia features bountiful diamond deposits in areas that are somewhat exceptional in the African context. How have the locations of Namibia's diamonds influenced its industry, past and present?

6. Namibia's diamond industry has long been influenced by the country's unique political history. How have domestic, regional, and international political developments influenced Namibia's diamond industry over time?

7. Based on a shared history of racial oppression and struggles for eventual liberation, Robert Mugabe continues to enjoy a significant degree of regional

political support. Considering this connection, should Namibia continue to support Mugabe's right to retain exclusive access to Zimbabwe's diamond deposits and use the profits as he sees fit?

Selected Readings

Good, Kenneth. "Interpreting the Exceptionality of Botswana." *Journal of Modern African Studies* 30, no. 1 (1992): 69–95.

Hillbom, Ellen. "Diamonds or Development? A Structural Assessment of Botswana's Forty Years of Success." *Journal of Modern African Studies* 46, no. 2 (2008): 191–214.

Jefferis, Keith. "Botswana and Diamond-Dependent Development." In *Botswana: Politics and Society*, edited by Wayne Edge and Mogopodi Lekorwe, 300–318. Pretoria: Van Schaik, 1998.

Jefferis, Keith R., and T. F. Kelly. "Botswana: Poverty amid Plenty." *Oxford Development Studies* 27, no. 2 (1999): 211–31.

Koskoff, David E. *The Diamond World.* New York: Harper and Row, 1981.

Samatar, Abdi. *An African Miracle: State and Class Leadership and Colonial Legacy in Botswana Development.* Portsmouth, NH: Heinemann, 1999.

Solway, Jacqueline. "Human Rights and NGO 'Wrongs': Conflict Diamonds, Culture Wars and the 'Bushman Question.'" *Africa* 79, no. 3 (2009): 321–46.

Taylor, Ian, and Gladys Mokhawa. "Not Forever: Botswana, Conflict Diamonds and the Bushmen." *African Affairs* 102, no. 407 (2003): 261–83.

Chapter 9—Africa's Diamonds: A Rough Past with a Brighter Future

Chapter 9 reflects on the material introduced over the preceding chapters in order to consider what the continent's diamond future might look like. Although many Africans are still operating on the vulnerable fringes of the industry, there have been a number of promising developments that suggest that diamonds are well-poised to play a positive role in shaping Africa's short- and long-term future.

Discussion Questions

1. Africa's diamonds have always featured global dimensions. In this age of heightened globalization, are these even more pronounced now than in the past? Why or why not?

2. Africa's diamond deposits possess enormous development potential for the continent. How confident are you that the diamonds will help Africa develop in an equitable manner going forward?

3. There is considerable controversy surrounding the Kimberley Process's definition of "blood diamonds." Should this body revise its definition to

include scenarios that feature diamond-related violence even in the absence of open rebellion? What role should the United Nations play, if any?

4. Ultimately, the industry is dependent on consumers for its survival. What can, or should, consumers do to help end diamond-related violence in Africa and elsewhere?

5. Some Africans have enjoyed success within the contemporary diamond industry in Africa, including Tokyo Sexwale and Nompumelelo "Mpumi" Zikalala. Are these two individuals representative of a new, empowered African segment of the industry? Or are they exceptions that draw much-needed attention away from the ongoing suffering of countless Africans in both the formal and informal industries?

6. Despite improvements in working conditions for African employees in the formal diamond industry, artisanal miners remain highly vulnerable, regular victims of violence, and often mired in poverty. How could the plight of artisanal miners be improved?

7. The Kimberley Process has been lauded by some for helping end the flow of "conflict stones." Is the era of "blood diamonds" really over? Why or why not?

Selected Readings

Comprehensive source of Charles Taylor's trial. www.charlestaylortrial.org/.
Diamond Development Initiative. www.ddiglobal.org/.
Rapaport Group Diamond Information Services. www.diamonds.net.
Human Rights Watch. NGO. www.hrg.org.

NOTES

Chapter 1: An Introduction to Africa's Diamonds

1. This popular media output also includes Lupe Fiasco's "Conflict Diamonds" (2006), which is a remix of Kanye's West's "Diamonds from Sierra Leone"; Nas' "Shine on 'em," also from 2006, which appeared on the *Blood Diamond* soundtrack; and the 2007 VH1 documentary *Bling'd: Blood, Diamonds, and Hip Hop*.

2. Arab writers and geographers of the thirteenth century make occasional mention of Ethiopia's involvement in the diamond trade, though little more is known of the role(s) it played. Godehard Lenzen, *The History of Diamond Production and the Diamond Trade* (New York: Praeger, 1966), 82.

3. The indicator minerals are ilmenite, pyrope garnet, and chrome diopside.

4. Additional sources included Borneo (controlled by Japan); smuggled supplies from both Venezuela and Brazil; and diamonds confiscated from German citizens, European Jews, and other victims of the Second World War.

5. The term "Dutch Disease" describes a phenomenon in which a country's natural resource(s) industry distorts other segments of the economy owing to large influxes of foreign currency. The term was coined following the Netherlands' economic experience after the discovery of sizable natural gas deposits in the North Sea in the 1960s.

Chapter 2: Africa's Mineral Wealth

1. Patricia McKissack and Fredrick McKissack, *The Royal Kingdoms of Ghana, Mali, and Songhay: Life in Medieval Africa* (New York: Henry Holt, 1994), 25.

2. The emergence of these polities was a product of the influx of Shirazi Arabs from the Persian Gulf, local residents of Africa's eastern coastal regions, and, to a lesser extent, Indians. Via the introduction of Islam and the creation of (Ki) Swahili, a Bantu language with Arabic elements that originally served as a lingua franca, a novel, hybrid culture that shared its name with the language arose in this region of Africa.

3. Kevin Shillington, *History of Africa* (New York: St. Martin's, 1995), 100.

4. Susan Keech McIntosh, "A Reconsideration of Wangara/Palolus, Island of Gold," *Journal of African History* 22, no. 2 (1981): 145.

5. McKissack and McKissack, *Royal Kingdoms*, 19.

6. Michael E. Brooks, *Prester John: A Reexamination and Compendium of the Mythical Figure Who Helped Spark European Expansion* (PhD diss., University of Toledo, 2009), 134.

7. David Birmingham, *Portugal and Africa* (Athens: Ohio University Press, 1999), 14.

8. Ibid., 16.

9. Innocent Pikirayi, *The Zimbabwe Culture: Origins and Decline in Southern Zambezian States* (Walnut Creek, CA: AltaMira, 2001), 174.

10. Terry H. Elkiss, *The Quest for an African Eldorado: Sofala, Southern Zambezia, and the Portuguese, 1500–1865* (Waltham, MA: Crossroads Press, 1981), 72.

Chapter 3: From Illusion to Reality

1. Stefan Kanfer, *The Last Empire: De Beers, Diamonds, and the World* (New York: Farrar, Straus and Giroux, 1995), 34.

2. Marian Robertson, *Diamond Fever: South African Diamond History, 1866–9 from Primary Sources* (Cape Town: Oxford University Press, 1974), 221.

3. Matthew Hart, *Diamond: The History of a Cold-Blooded Love Affair* (New York: Plume, 2002), 36.

4. Gardner F. Williams, *The Diamond Mines of South Africa: Some Account of Their Rise and Development* (London: Macmillan, 1902), 196.

5. Tom Zoellner, *The Heartless Stone: A Journey through the World of Diamonds, Deceit, and Desire* (New York: St. Martin's, 2006), 122.

6. Alan Cohen, "Mary Elizabeth Barber, Some Early South African Geologists, and the Discoveries of Diamonds," *Earth Sciences History* 22, no. 2 (2003): 162.

7. Phyllis Lewsen, ed., *Selections from the Correspondence of J. X. Merriman*, vol. 1, *1870–1890* (Cape Town: Van Riebeeck Society, 1960), 5.

8. Rob Turrell, "The 1875 Black Flag Revolt on the Kimberley Diamond Mines," *Journal of Southern African Studies* 7, no. 2 (1981): 200.

9. Peter Kallaway, "Labour on the Kimberley Diamond Fields," *South African Labour Bulletin* 1, no. 7 (1974): 54.

10. Robert Vicat Turrell, *Capital and Labour on the Kimberley Diamond Fields, 1871–1890* (Cambridge: Cambridge University Press, 1987), 102.

11. William H. Worger, *South Africa's City of Diamonds: Mine Workers and Monopoly Capitalism in Kimberley, 1867–1895* (New Haven: Yale University Press, 1987), 73.

12. Judy Kimble, "Labour Migration in Basutoland c. 1870–1885," in *Industrialisation and Social Change in South Africa: African Class Formation, Culture, and Consciousness, 1870–1930*, ed. Shula Marks and Richard Rathbone (New York: Longman, 1982), 123.

13. Williams, *Diamond Mines*, 188.

14. Z. K. Matthews, *Freedom for My People: The Autobiography of Z. K. Matthews: Southern Africa, 1901 to 1968* (London: R. Collings, 1981), 3.

15. Williams, *Diamond Mines*, 325.

16. Worger, *South Africa's City of Diamonds*, 87.

17. Turrell, "1875 Black Flag Revolt," 195.

18. Robertson, *Diamond Fever*, 149.

19. Turrell, *Capital and Labour*, 29.

20. Brian Roberts, *The Diamond Magnates* (New York: Charles Scribner's Sons, 1972), 121.

21. Colin Newbury, *The Diamond Ring: Business, Politics, and Precious Stones in South Africa, 1867–1947* (Oxford: Clarendon, 1989), 59.

22. Turrell, *Capital and Labour,* 204.

23. Rob Turrell, "Kimberley: Labour and Compounds, 1871–1888," in *Industrialisation and Social Change in South Africa: African Class Formation, Culture, and Consciousness, 1870–1930,* ed. Shula Marks and Richard Rathbone (New York: Longman, 1982), 63.

24. Turrell, *Capital and Labour,* 99.

25. Matthews, *Freedom for My People,* 1–2, 9.

26. Worger, *South Africa's City of Diamonds,* 95.

Chapter 4: Consolidation and Control

1. Tom Zoellner, *The Heartless Stone: A Journey through the World of Diamonds, Deceit, and Desire* (New York: St. Martin's, 2006), 126.

2. Gardner F. Williams, *The Diamond Mines of South Africa: Some Account of Their Rise and Development* (London: Macmillan, 1902), 322.

3. William J. Morton, "The South African Diamond Fields, and a Journey to the Mines," *Journal of the American Geographical Society of New York* 9 (1877): 76.

4. Phyllis Lewsen, ed., *Selections from the Correspondence of J. X. Merriman,* vol. 1, *1870–1890* (Cape Town: Van Riebeeck Society, 1960), 194.

5. William Crookes, "The Romance of the Diamond," *North American Review* 187, no. 628 (March 1908): 374.

6. John M. Smalberger, "The Role of the Diamond-Mining Industry in the Development of the Pass-Law System in South Africa," *International Journal of African Historical Studies* 9, no. 3 (1976): 422. The reference is to the January 25, 1872, edition of the *Diamond Field.*

7. Williams, *Diamond Mines,* 402.

8. Rob Turrell, "Kimberley: Labour and Compounds, 1871–1888," in *Industrialisation and Social Change in South Africa: African Class Formation, Culture, and Consciousness, 1870–1930,* ed. Shula Marks and Richard Rathbone (New York: Longman, 1982), 65.

9. William H. Worger, *South Africa's City of Diamonds: Mine Workers and Monopoly Capitalism in Kimberley, 1867–1895* (New Haven: Yale University Press, 1987), 266.

10. Rob Turrell, "Kimberley's Model Compounds," *Journal of African History* 25, no. 1 (1984): 64.

11. Lewsen, *Correspondence of J. X. Merriman,* 203. Merriman wrote the letter on January 10, 1886.

12. Crookes, *Romance of the Diamond,* 376.

13. Turrell, "Kimberley's Model Compounds," 59.

14. Colin Newbury, *The Diamond Ring: Business, Politics, and Precious Stones in South Africa, 1867–1947* (Oxford: Clarendon, 1989), 75.

15. Z. K. Matthews, *Freedom for My People: The Autobiography of Z. K. Matthews: Southern Africa, 1901 to 1968* (London: R. Collings, 1981), 7.

16. Turrell, "Kimberley's Model Compounds," 73.

17. Newbury, *Diamond Ring*, 125.

18. *The Diamond Empire* (film), Janine Roberts, 1994.

19. Newbury, *Diamond Ring*, 124.

20. Ibid., 113.

21. Lilian Charlotte Anne Knowles, *The Economic Development of the British Overseas Empire* (London: Routledge, 2005), 73.

22. For all the trouble that the war caused De Beers, the siege was particularly hard on the African community of mine workers, who were forced to remain in Kimberley well after their contracts had concluded, leading to at least 1,500 deaths, primarily as a result of typhoid and dysentery outbreaks.

23. For an account of how De Beers has been able to manipulate global diamond consumption trends, see Edward Jay Epstein, "Have You Ever Tried to Sell a Diamond?" *Atlantic* (February 1982): 371–82.

24. Ian Smillie, *Blood on the Stone: Greed, Corruption and War in the Global Diamond Trade* (London: Anthem, 2010), 44.

25. Debora L. Spar, "Markets: Continuity and Change in the International Diamond Market," *Journal of Economic Perspectives* 20, no. 3 (Summer 2006): 202.

26. The Government of Botswana, home to De Beers's largest mines, owns the remaining 15 percent.

27. Matthew Hart, *Diamond: The History of a Cold-Blooded Love Affair* (New York: Plume, 2002), 37.

Chapter 5: Creating "New Kimberleys" Elsewhere in Africa

1. The index translates the anthropometric relationships of height, weight, and thoracic perimeter into a single number. The Pignet index was invented in 1900 by Maurice-Joseph, a French army doctor, in order to help determine recruits' fitness levels.

2. Allan D. Cooper, "The Institutionalization of Contract Labour in Namibia," *Journal of Southern African Studies* 25, no. 1 (March 1999): 124.

3. Ibid., 133.

4. Peter Greenhalgh, *West African Diamonds, 1919–1983: An Economic History* (Manchester: Manchester University Press, 1985), 106.

5. Ibid., 107.

6. Ibid., 185.

7. Gillian Cronje and Suzanne Cronje, *The Workers of Namibia* (London: International Defence and Aid Fund for Southern Africa, 1979), 55.

8. Richard Derksen, "Forminiere in the Kasai, 1906–1939," *African Economic History*, no. 12 (1983): 54.

9. Greenhalgh, *West African Diamonds*, 182.

10. Ibid., 183.

11. Ibid., 128.

12. Ibid.

13. Ibid., 129.

14. Keith Gottschalk, "South African Labour Policy in Namibia, 1915–1975," *South African Labour Bulletin* 4, no. 1–2 (1978): 75.

15. Cronje and Cronje, *Workers of Namibia*, 56.

16. Ibid.

17. I will examine the situation in Namibia more extensively in a later chapter.

Chapter 6: The Experiences of African Workers on Colonial-Era Mines

1. Former mine manager Gordon Brown is not the former British prime minister of the same name.

2. Richard Derksen, "Forminière in the Kasai, 1906–1939," *African Economic History*, no. 12 (1983): 53.

3. Robert J. Gordon, *Mines, Masters and Migrants: Life in a Namibian Compound* (Johannesburg: Ravan, 1977), 86.

4. Interview by the author, João Muacasso, August 11, 2005, Cafunfo, Angola.

5. Interview by the author, Mawassa Mwaninga, November 22, 2005, Cafunfo, Angola.

6. Interview by the author, Mateus Nanto, August 12, 2005, Cafunfo, Angola.

7. Interview by the author, Costa Chicungo, May 13, 2005, Dundo, Angola.

8. Interview by the author, Paulo Leão Vega and António Sulessa, May 17, 2005, Dundo, Angola.

9. Bob Marley, "Them Belly Full (But We Hungry)," *Natty Dread*, 1975.

10. Museum of Anthropology at the University of Coimbra (MAUC), Portugal, Diamang archive, folder 86D,2 8°, Diamang, *Spamoi Relatório de Dezembro 1955* (January 12, 1956): 12.

11. MAUC, folder 86B,6a 5°, letter from A. Mendes to the Rep. da Diamang, January 28, 1965, 1.

12. MAUC, folder 86 13°, letter from E. S. Lane, Representante na Lunda, to Snr. Chefe de Fronteira do Chitato, "Ocorrencias com trabalhadores nas explorações," September 12, 1928, 1–3.

13. MAUC, folder 86 14°, letter from Lute J. Parkinson to E. S. Lane, December 21, 1928, 1.

14. Peter Greenhalgh, *West African Diamonds, 1919–1983: An Economic History* (Manchester: Manchester University Press, 1985), 134.

15. Rob Turrell, "Kimberley's Model Compounds," *Journal of African History* 25, no. 1 (1984): 176.

16. John L. Hirsch, *Sierra Leone: Diamonds and the Struggle for Democracy* (Boulder, CO: Lynne Rienner, 2001), 27.

17. Greenhalgh, *West African Diamonds*, 153.

18. Motlatsi Thabane, "Liphokojoe of Kao: A Study of a Diamond Digger Rebel Group in the Lesotho Highlands," *Journal of Southern African Studies* 26, no. 1 (March 2000): 105.

Chapter 7: A Resource Curse

1. Peter Greenhalgh, *West African Diamonds, 1919–1983: An Economic History* (Manchester: Manchester University Press, 1985), 199.

2. See, for example: Greg Campbell, *Blood Diamonds: Tracing the Deadly Path of the World's Most Precious Stones* (New York: Basic Books, 2004), 41–42, 124–25; Ian Smillie, *Blood on the Stone: Greed, Corruption and War in the Global Diamond Trade* (London: Anthem, 2010), 4, 13, 21–24, 56, 69, 85–86, 93, 122, 126–27, 149, 155, 170.

3. Jakkie Cilliers and Christian Dietrich, eds., *Angola's War Economy: The Role of Oil and Diamonds* (Pretoria: Institute for Security Studies, 2000), 5.

4. Smillie, *Blood on the Stone*, 103.

5. Campbell, *Blood Diamonds*, 85.

6. Ibid., 91.

7. http://www.cnn.com/2012/05/30/world/africa/netherlands-taylor-sentencing/.

8. Gavin Hilson and Martin J. Clifford, "A 'Kimberley Protest': Diamond Mining, Export Sanctions, and Poverty in Akwatia, Ghana," *African Affairs* 109, no. 436 (2010): 435.

9. Smillie, *Blood on the Stone*, 17.

10. Rob Bates, "Kimberley Confusion," *JCK* 175, no. 8 (2004): 74.

11. Ibid., 75.

12. Richard Saunders, "Geographies of Power: Blood Diamonds, Security Politics and Zimbabwe's Troubled Transition," in *Legacies of Liberation: Postcolonial Struggles for a Democratic Southern Africa*, ed. M. Clarke and C. Bassett (Toronto: Fernwood, forthcoming 2014).

13. Tinashe Nyamunda and Patience Mukwambo, "The State and the Bloody Diamond Rush in Chiadzwa: Unpacking the Contesting Interests in the Development of Illicit Mining and Trading, c. 2006–2009," *Journal of Southern African Studies* 38, no. 1 (March 2012): 159.

14. Celia W. Dugger, "Team Monitoring Diamond Trade Rebukes Zimbabwe, Citing Abuses of Miners," *New York Times*, July 8, 2009, 4.

15. Leslie Wayne, "The Chinese Solution," *100 Reporters*, October 31, 2011, http://100r.org/2011/10/the-chinese-solution/.

16. Columbus S. Mavhunga, "Zimbabwe's Parliament Approves $98 Million Loan from China," *CNN World*, June 1, 2011, http://www.cnn.com/2011/WORLD/africa/06/01/zimbabwe.china.loan/.

Chapter 8: Mineral Assets

1. *Batswana* is the plural form of Tswana, the dominant ethnic group in Botswana. However, since not all residents of the country are ethnic Tswana, I use *Botswanans* in this chapter when referring to multiple citizens of Botswana.

2. The "Asian Tigers" are Hong Kong, Singapore, South Korea, and Taiwan, each of which has a highly developed economy, having experienced rapid growth between the early 1960s and 1990s. Abdi Samatar features the expression "An African Miracle" in the title of his 1999 book about Botswana, *An African Miracle: State*

and Class Leadership and Colonial Legacy in Botswana Development (Portsmouth, NH: Heinemann, 1999).

3. Samatar, *African Miracle*, 81.

4. Ian Taylor and Gladys Mokhawa, "Not Forever: Botswana, Conflict Diamonds and the Bushmen," *African Affairs* 102, no. 407 (2003): 272.

5. Ibid., 271.

6. Ibid., 273.

7. Quoted on the De Beers website, at http://www.debeersgroup.com/operations/mining/mining-operations/debswana/.

8. Thero Galeitse, "BCPYL wants De Beers, BDP relations probed," *Botswana Gazette*, April 27, 2011, 1.

9. Ibid.

10. Taylor and Mokhawa, "Not Forever," 274.

11. Jacqueline Solway, "Human Rights and NGO 'Wrongs': Conflict Diamonds, Culture Wars and the 'Bushman Question,'" *Africa* 79, no. 3 (2009): 340.

12. Philippe Le Billon, "Diamond Wars? Conflict Diamonds and Geographies of Resource Wars," *Annals of the Association of American Geographers* 98, no. 2 (2008): 360.

13. Unfortunately, both the immediate destination and subsequent trails of these pigeon-smuggled stones remain somewhat murky.

14. Donald G. McNeil, "Oranjemund Journal; Find a Diamond in the Sand? Just Don't Pick It Up," *New York Times*, April 27, 1998.

15. Celia W. Dugger, "Group Won't Suspend Zimbabwe on Mining Abuses," *New York Times*, November 6, 2009, http://www.nytimes.com/2009/11/07/world/africa/07zimbabwe.html?_r=0.

Chapter 9: Africa's Diamonds

1. Paul Collier, "The Last Resource Frontier," *Project Syndicate*, February 25, 2011, http://www.project-syndicate.org/commentary/the-last-resource-frontier.

2. "De Beers Voorspoed Mine: The New Face of Mining in South Africa," *International Resource Journal* (May 2010), http://www.internationalresourcejournal.com/resource_in_action/may_10/de_beers_voorspoed_mine.html.

INDEX